Reading and Writing
American History

Volume II

Reading and Writing American History

An Introduction to the Historian's Craft
Second Edition

Peter Charles Hoffer
University of Georgia

William W. Stueck
University of Georgia

VOLUME
2

Houghton Mifflin Company
Boston   New York

Editor-in-Chief: Jean Woy
Associate Editor: Keith Mahoney
Associate Project Editor: Rebecca Bennett
Associate Production/Design Coordinator: Deborah Frydman
Manufacturing Manager: Florence Cadran

Cover Design: MinkoImages
Cover Image: The City of New York, Currier and Ives, 1884. Courtesy Library of Congress.

Illustration Credits
p. 7: The Metropolitan Museum of Art, Catharine Lorillard Wolfe Collection, Wolfe Fund, 1906; p. 81: Copyright the Dorothea Lange Collection, the Oakland Museum of California, The City of Oakland. Gift of Paul S. Taylor; pp. 85, 86: Library of Congress; p. 87: Chicago Historical Society; p. 106: The Trustees of the Imperial War Museum, London; p. 118: AP/Wide World Photos; p. 120: Corbis-Bettman; p. 125: Dan Weiner, courtesy of Sandra Weiner; p. 127: AP/Wide World Photos; p. 128: Corbis-Bettman; pp. 135, 136, 139, 140: Photofest NY.

Printed in the U.S.A.

Library of Congress Catalog Card Number: 97-72988

ISBN: 0-395-88630-9

123456789–B–01 00 99 98 97

Contents

Preface

If your institution has a history requirement, as ours does, most students in your survey course will be conscripts. The course is part of their core curriculum. The reason they *should* take history — the reason that it is required for a liberal-arts education — is obvious to us, but students may find that reason distant and abstract. At the outset, we face the obstacle of persuading students of the relevance of the past.

Today's students are very present minded. This perspective may result from the general widening of opportunities for undergradute education, or from the increasing pressure on young people to find a niche in the business or professional world before they leave college. Some universities have catered to those demands, allowing their professional schools to infiltrate undergraduate education and impose a dizzying load of pre-professional courses on students in the second and third years of undergraduate study. The ideal of a liberal-arts education, like the ideal of college as a sanctuary from the blooming, buzzing confusion of the workplace, has receded in the face of anxious careerism. Even if history courses offer a humanistic perspective on modern values, we cannot blind ourselves to the realities of college life. Students will leave our classrooms and step into a world whose distractions are so numerous and enticing that the past may not seem relevant.

History courses compete for students' time and attention not only with extracurricular demands often hostile to scholarly inquiry but with many other courses in the undergraduate curriculum. In a sense, we sell history in a buyer's market. Our effectiveness as teachers can be measured by the extent to which we can persuade our students to give their history course at least the same time and effort they devote to other courses. One way to do this is to load the class with extra reading and outside assignments. If every instructor in every other course — all sellers in this market — adopted this stratagem, our increased demands would be effectively neutralized by the across-the-board escalation of the workload, in the manner of the "prisoner's dilemma."

There is another, better way to convince students that history is relevant: offer them the chance to become an apprentice historian — a *doer* rather than a consumer. If history is the vital connection between past and present, then training in the skills and methods of thinking about history is more than a legitimate way to attract students' attention; it is an integral part of the introductory course. Students who begin to *do* history will appreciate the study of history as no passive reader of textbooks can, no matter how hard he or she studies.

We know from experience that, because there is so much to cover in American history surveys, little time remains to deal with basic questions of historical methods and skills. Mindful of this fact, in *Reading and Writing American History*, Second Edition, we combine a manual on historical methods, a set of exercises that help students to hone their skill in using those methods, and a reader in primary and secondary sources that runs parallel to the chronological progression of topics in the survey course. *Reading and Writing American History*, Second Edition, is also suitable for methods courses for the history major.

A Manual

The old proverb "The teacher opens the door, the student must walk through it" has guided our plan for the book. We bring students face to face with the basic questions that every history teacher and scholar confronts. We begin by explaining why history is such a vital field of study and how every culture's conception of history gives its members a sense of identity. We treat basic problems in the philosophy of history, including the difference between fact and opinion and the ways in which historians use historical evidence. We introduce primary and secondary sources, source criticism and classification, and explain how to find historical sources and specific facts.

Subsequent chapters cover a wide range of reading and writing skills, from how to use the library to how to construct an essay. We introduce varieties of historical analysis, including causation, change and continuity, reasoning by analogy, the role of the individual in history, and the use of numbers.

A Workbook

Every point we make is reinforced by exercises. Some can be performed on the spot. Others require a trip to the library. Some exercises are textual, and we provide the text. Others require students to *find* the text. We have included nontextual materials — maps, pictures, and graphs — so that students can *see* the past as well as read about it. The materials cover a wide range of subfields in American history.

The methods treated in each chapter build on lessons in previous chapters. Within chapters, each exercise rests on those that come before it. The first exercise is often a "think piece," requiring students to ponder a historical question; subsequent exercises entail more writing. Because we understand that grading so many written exercises would be no mean task, many exercises are designed for "self-grading" or for class discussion. Space is provided for out-of-class assignments. The pages are perforated so that you can require students to turn in their work, and they are three-hole-punched so that students can retain their work in one place. We encourage you to pick and choose among the exercises and assignments, personalizing the course.

A Reader

Most exercises include readings, which allow you to link training in methods and skills to the substance of your course. These selections include primary and secondary sources and mix traditional and current historical concerns. Students are thus exposed to both the classics of historical writing and the most recent contributions. Many selections serve as springboards for discussion as well as skills practice.

The reading selections in each chapter are keyed to the chronological progression of events in American history. This chronological progression not only allows you to couple instruction in skills and methods to your lectures and discussions but also make this book a supplement to your textbook or to other required readings. We have found in our own teaching that the best way to ensure learning is through repetition. The selections in *Reading and Writing American History*, Second Edition, afford you the opportunity to repeat lessons using a variety of relevant materials.

New to this Edition

When the first edition of *Reading and Writing American History* was published in 1994, we were confident that college and university administrators and teachers regarded American history as the centerpiece of a college education. In the scant five years since then, the college survey course in American history has faced two stiff intellectual tests. The second edition of *Reading and Writing American History* is designed to respond to these challenges.

The first challenge grows out of an invitation college and university instructors have issued to themselves to incorporate the many different voices of Americans in the basic undergraduate curriculum. Most independent colleges and state university systems still require the study of history as part of the liberal arts core, but the survey course in American history is no longer an automatic choice for students or their teachers to fulfill this obligation. Multicultural programs and diversity requirements have moved surveys of American history off center stage, or supplanted them with special courses.

The authors of *Reading and Writing American History*, Second Edition, are committed to the idea that the survey in American history is *the* multicultural course, for there is no nation that compares with ours in its ethnic diversity. We are truly one people made up of many peoples. This second edition attempts to capture and explore fully that diversity by adding additional readings, exercises, and discussion materials on Native Americans, African Americans, and women. We have broadened the geographical scope of the volumes to include the peoples of the Southwest and the Caribbean.

The second trial that the American history survey course faces arises from the technology and information revolutions of our time. Many schools have introduced a computer literacy component to their basic undergraduate requirements. History may seem incompatible with such futuristic courses, but the fact is that historians have long used and valued the computer. Quantitative historians have relied on computer driven software to calculate statistical associations and researchers have built computer databases from historical sources to study elections, population, and economic changes over time. More recently, many historical collections, archives, and libraries have gone online to make information available to users of the Internet and the World Wide Web. To meet the challenge of computer aided instruction, we have added to this edition up-to-date facts on word processing software and Web sites for historians, along with rigorous exercises on computer assisted library searches and Internet research in historical sources. The result, we hope, is a second edition that combines the training in skills and ways of thinking that have long made history the "mother of all intellectual disciplines," with the most modern techniques and information sources for students of history.

Acknowledgments

The final version of *Reading and Writing American History*, Second Edition, was a collaborative endeavor. The authors have worked together at every stage of the project; Volume 1 is the work of Peter Hoffer, and Volume 2 is the work of William Stueck. Many of our colleagues in the teaching profession also provided incisive and helpful comments. We are grateful to the following: Steven R. Boyd, University of Texas, San Antonio; Dr. A. G. Dunston, Eastern Kentucky University; Beverly Garrison, Oral Roberts University; Theresa Kaminski, University of Wisconsin, Stevens Point; Chester Pach, Ohio University; Robert Schulzinger, University of Colorado, Boulder; Peter Shattuck, California State University, Sacramento.

P. C. H.
W. W. S.

To the Student

Think of a few of the monumental events of the last decade: the rise of Solidarity and the eventual overthrow of communism in Poland; the destruction of the Berlin Wall and the reunification of Germany; the growth of student unrest in China and its brutal suppression at Tianamen Square by the communist government; and the demise of the Soviet Communist party and subsequent breakup of the U.S.S.R.

What do all these events have in common? Several things, you might say. They all occurred outside the United States. They all involved a general crisis of communism. They all took place during your lifetime. They all had important implications for the American people. They all are part of history.

Perhaps the last fact did not occur to you. You may tend to think of history as the distant past rather than events of the last generation or even the last decade. In part, this may be because your previous history classes stopped long before the present. Although it is difficult to attain the perspective on recent events that we possess on more distant times, the fact remains that the former are very much a part of history. Thus when you enter a course entitled "The United States Since 1865," you have every right to expect it to extend all the way to the present. A major purpose of this volume is to demonstrate the connections between the distant past, the recent past, and the present, through frequent movements back and forth among them. It also will show you that many skills used to analyze the past apply to your present and future as well.

History often can appear to be a series of dry facts about the past. It is true that dates, names, and events are essential components of history, but they alone do not constitute the discipline. Facts must be constructed through the accumulation of evidence. They also must be interpreted. Facts about the past, along with the methods used to construct and to understand them, make up the study of history.

These ten chapters examine many facts of American history since 1865, but, just as important, they introduce you to the methods that historians use to study the past. The exercises will require you to examine the works of historians and help you to grasp the discipline by exposing you to its products. In addition, because nothing facilitates the learning process better than practice, this book provides numerous opportunities to actually *do* history. Whether evaluating others' efforts or creating your own history, you will develop skills that should serve you well in a variety of endeavors outside the classroom. In the end, what you will take from this course will not be most of the facts. Instead, you should have a new perspective on the past and its relation to the present and the future. You also will have mastered a series of skills applicable to the workplace and beyond. These include basic abilities, such as comprehending a reading assignment and using the library-card or online catalog, as well as more complicated challenges, such as evaluating primary and secondary sources, writing essays, and interpreting numerical data. We hope that these skills will help you to derive greater satisfaction and a deeper knowledge of American history from your course.

This second edition of *Reading and Writing American History* is not intended to replace your textbook but to be used in conjunction with it or with the primary and secondary source anthologies your instructor has assigned for your course. The explanations, reading, and exercises in this worktext treat history as a way of knowing, a set of skills for making sense of the past. You may not be able to travel back in time or bring the dead to life, but you can use your intelligence and imagination to recreate those lost worlds in your own mind. *Reading and Writing American History*, Second Edition, was devised to give you the skill to navigate that journey into the past.

Reading and Writing
American History

VOLUME II

1 WHAT IS HISTORY, AND WHY DO WE STUDY IT?

Reconstruction

History is the "universal discipline" because it deals with every aspect of human endeavor. Jonas Salk's discovery of a vaccine for polio, the election of John F. Kennedy as president, the child-rearing practices of the Quakers, and the introduction of the miniskirt all qualify as part of the human past and therefore as history.

If, in one sense, history is "everything that has happened in the past," in another sense it is far less than that (see Figure 1.1). Human beings have recorded only a tiny portion of what has happened to them. And only a small part of what was recorded has survived. Of the surviving materials, a significant amount is either inaccurate or misleading. In short, the past that we can know is far from complete. Partly to distinguish between the actual past and what we know of it, we sometimes define history as "the study of the past."

However incomplete our knowledge of it may be, the past is an important guide in understanding the present and anticipating the future. Stop for a moment and think about what you expected of this course when you first walked into class. Chances are, you based your judgment on one of two sources, and both were historical: your own experiences with history courses and accounts from fellow students who have already taken this course. You used the past — or testimony about it — to understand the present.

There are limitations to predicting the future from knowledge of the past. Perhaps your previous history teachers emphasized mastery of facts. To score well on examinations, you merely had to provide specific information, such as names of important figures and dates of key events. As a result, you may assume that memorization, the learning of one fact after another, is the primary task in studying history. This assumption will lead you astray in this course. Remembering facts is important, but if you devote all your attention to memorizing names and dates, you will have difficulty. This book emphasizes understanding processes and trends and developing a variety of skills in addition to memorizing facts.

History does *not* always repeat itself. Each event of the human past is unique. No two individuals teach a history course in exactly the same way. Sometimes instructors change their approach to a course from year to year. In short, using the past as a guide to the present and future can be tricky.

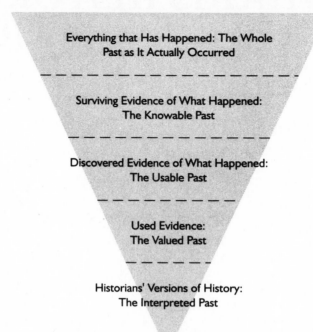

Everything that Has Happened: The Whole
Past as It Actually Occurred

Surviving Evidence of What Happened:
The Knowable Past

Discovered Evidence of What Happened:
The Usable Past

Used Evidence:
The Valued Past

Historians' Versions of History:
The Interpreted Past

FIGURE 1.1 *History as It Is; History as We Know It*

There is another way in which we use the past to guide us in the present: the past tells us who we are and gives us our identity. Without a sense of history, we would have difficulty understanding ourselves in relation to others. We could not grasp how and why our ethnic, racial, national, or religious groups distinguish themselves from others, or how and why particular generations — our own, our parents', our children's — perceive the world in different ways.

Just as personal histories are basic to individuals' identities, certain events and ideas from the past are fundamental to the way groups define themselves. Imagine our self-image as Americans without any awareness of the idea that human beings possess "certain inalienable rights," among them "life, liberty, and the pursuit of happiness." To be sure, our thoughts may not turn very often to our country's Declaration of Independence from Great Britain in 1776. Indeed, some of us may not have associated the idea mentioned above with that document. Yet many of the ideas stated in our Declaration of Independence have become so deeply ingrained in the identity of Americans as a group that, without the Declaration, we would have a wholly different conception of ourselves. This book seeks to refine your sense of identity as part of a pluralistic, vibrant society.

Reading and Writing American History also asks you to "do" history rather than just study it. This book encourages you to become an active, rather than a passive, learner. It aims both to familiarize you with the way historians think and to help you use that knowledge to enrich your own life. You should emerge from this course with a fuller grasp of how the past relates to your present and future, and with a capacity to apply this understanding to the world at large.

Chapter 1 introduces many of the skills you will be developing as you use this book. The chapter covers the Reconstruction era immediately following the Civil War. You will have the opportunity to compare Reconstruction to life in contemporary America and uncover patterns of change in the late nineteenth century. You also will learn to distinguish fact from opinion and to identify the various purposes of historical writing. Finally, you will be introduced to the history textbook, its nature and purposes, and how to use it. The exercises in this chapter open the gate to the study of history. By the end of this course, you will have gained a broad array of skills, from analyzing films and television programs to constructing essays based on historical sources.

Past and Present

By taking us out of the present, the study of history alerts us to conditions other than those we encounter in our own lives. Studying a contemporary society other than our own might also serve this purpose. One advantage of going back in time, however, is that we can see how our society has changed, how what we face here and now in some ways differs from what our ancestors confronted in a bygone era. We tend to assume that current conditions — air pollution and inflation, for instance — are changeless phenomena, that they always have been with us and will be forever. Yet the study of the American past reveals that many of the conditions we live with today simply did not exist in earlier times. This fact suggests that our future, in turn, may not resemble the present. The study of the United States since 1865 can provide us with new perspectives on the present and new visions of the future. This section tests your skill in comparing past and present.

EXERCISE 1: *Comparing Past and Present*

The outcome of the Civil War ensured the Union's survival and slavery's destruction, but it left a host of other issues unresolved. In particular, the question of what the end of slavery would mean for African-Americans remained. Would they move rapidly toward equality with European-Americans, or would they remain relegated to a position of inferiority? Because the vast majority of African-Americans lived in the eleven states of the former southern Confederacy, the process of reintegrating them into the Union would go far in settling this question. This transition period saw an intense struggle, the outcome of which set the pattern of race relations in the United States well into the twentieth century. The following selections reflect some of the prevalent attitudes of the time and provide focal points for comparing a critical period of the past with our own times.

A The following excerpt is from a speech by Congressman Ignatius Donnelly (R, Minn.) in February 1866. Donnelly is speaking in support of a measure providing federal government funds for public schools for African-Americans in the South. Read the selection and answer the questions that follow it.

> . . . Having voted to give the negro liberty, I shall vote to give him all things essential to liberty.
>
> If degradation and oppression have, as it is alleged, unfitted him for freedom, surely continued degradation and oppression will not prepare him for it. If he is not to remain a brute you must give him that which will make him a man — opportunity. . . .
> If he is, as you say, not fit to vote, give him a chance; let him make himself an independent laborer like yourself; let him own his homestead; let the courts of justice be opened to him; and let his intellect, darkened by centuries of neglect, be illuminated by all the glorious lights of education. If after all this he proves himself an unworthy savage and brutal wretch, condemn him, but not till then.[1]

1. What argument is Donnelly rebutting? _____

_____

2. What is the key point in his argument? _____

_____

3. What specific measures does Donnelly suggest the government should take to assist

   African-Americans? _____

_____

4. What noun does he use to refer to African-Americans? _____

_____

5. Why do you suppose that noun is no longer used to refer to African-Americans? _____

_____

_____

6. Today, some members of Congress argue in favor of "affirmative action" for African-
   Americans in the form of quotas in certain job categories and in the student bodies of

   institutions of higher learning. Does Donnelly advocate such action? Explain. _____

_____

_____

B The next excerpt is from a speech in December 1866 by Senator George Henry
Williams (R, Ore.). The issue addressed is woman suffrage, which was bound to arise in
Congress during a period of intense debate on the rights of African-Americans. (Any-
time politicians devote extensive attention to the rights of one group, other groups that
feel aggrieved are likely to see an opportunity to air their discontents.) During the years
immediately following the Civil War, a group of feminists petitioned Congress for an
amendment to guarantee women the right to vote. Unlike African-American men, however, they did not enjoy early success. The arguments of Senator Williams prevailed.
Read the passage and answer the questions that follow.

> . . . it has been said that "the hand that rocks the cradle rules the world"; and there is
> truth as well as beauty in that expression. Women in this country by their elevated so-
> cial position can exercise more influence upon public affairs than they could coerce by
> the use of the ballot. When God married our first parents in the garden . . . they were
> made "bone of one bone and flesh of one flesh"; and the whole theory of government
> and society proceeds upon the assumption that their interests are one, that their rela-
> tions are so intimate and tender that whatever is for the benefit of the one is for the
> benefit of the other; whatever works to the injury of the one works to the injury of the
> other. I say . . . that the more identical and inseparable these interests and relations can
> be made, the better for all concerned; and the woman who undertakes to put her sex in
> an adversary position to man, who undertakes by the use of some independent politi-
> cal power to contend and fight against man, displays a spirit which would, if able, con-
> vert all the now harmonious elements of society into a state of war, and make every
> home a hell upon earth.[2]

1. What are Williams's two main points?

   a. _____

   _____

b. _____

_____

2. Why is woman suffrage no longer an issue in the United States? _____

_____

3. With what issues do feminists preoccupy themselves today? _____

_____

4. What differences between the 1860s and the present does the change in issues

   confronted suggest? _____

_____

C The Civil War and Reconstruction left bitter memories in the South. The majority of European-Americans there accepted union only grudgingly, and they fought effectively in the aftermath of war to prevent African-Americans from achieving anything remotely resembling equality. In the following account, a European-American from Virginia, who had fought in General Robert E. Lee's Confederate army, expresses his attitude toward northerners and Reconstruction thirty years after its end. Read the passage and answer the questions that follow.

> As a fit climax to, and exhibitory of, Yankee hatred, malice, revenge, and cruelty practiced during the war, the North bound the prostrate South on the rock of negro domination, while the vultures, "carpet-baggers" and "scalawags," preyed upon its vitals. . . . The South . . . rose in its own might . . . and drove away the birds of prey, and her people are now free and independent, controlling their own state affairs without let or hindrance. . . . The South has always been the most chivalrous, conservative and Americanlike, holding more closely to the traditions, customs, and manners of the old days, where the high and unselfish principles of right, justice and honor, which go to make up the true gentleman and patriotic citizen, have always prevailed. The pure Anglo-Saxon blood still predominates in the South, as well as the spirit of the cavalier. Blood will tell.
>
> The average Yankee has a very poor conception of what is right and honorable in his . . . intercourse with his fellow-man. . . . To drive a sharp bargain, to get money no matter how, . . . and diffuse and enforce his own ideas and notions, seem to be the *summa summorum* [highest of the highest] of all his ends. . . .
>
> . . . the South is coming to its own again. . . . The days of retribution will come when the evil deeds the North perpetrated in the South during and since the war, will be avenged, not in kind perhaps, but in some way.[3]

1. To this writer, how do northerners and southerners differ? _____

_____

2. This writer's views were common to European-Americans in the South from the generation that fought in the Civil War. How do you think these views compare with those of European-Americans who reside in the South today? _____

_____

3. Are there any differences today between your generation and your grandparents' generation? _____

_____

4. How do you explain the differences? _____

_____

D The next two documents combine visual and written material. The first was drawn by Thomas Nast, the most famous political cartoonist of that era. Nast's cartoons in the magazine *Harper's Weekly* received widespread attention and often were credited with helping to bring to justice the notorious New York City boss William Marcy Tweed. Nast also used cartoons to express his views on Reconstruction. Initially, he showed great sympathy for the freed slaves, but by March 14, 1874, when the cartoon shown in Figure 1.2 appeared, his attitude had changed. The second document, a copy of a painting called *The Gulf Stream*, shown in Figure 1.3, is by Winslow Homer. Homer used watercolor and oils to depict Americans in natural settings. Many of his works made a social statement. Homer painted *The Gulf Stream* twice, first as a watercolor in 1884, seven years after Union troops left the South. He redid the work in oil in 1899 following a decade in which African-Americans in the South increasingly suffered from lynching and from segregationist laws passed by state legislatures. Examine these illustrations carefully, and then answer the questions that follow.

FIGURE 1.2 *Thomas Nast Comments on Black Reconstruction Legislators*

FIGURE 1.3 *Winslow Homer's* **The Gulf Stream**

1. Compare the physical and behavioral depiction of African-Americans in Nast's cartoon with that of the African-American in Homer's painting. _____
   _____
   _____

2. What messages are the two artists trying to convey? _____
   _____
   _____
   _____

3. Which depiction would be more likely to appear in a popular journal in the United States today? Why? _____
   _____
   _____

Many Different Pasts

Unlike the history of some other nations, our history is not the story of a single group, its members all speaking the same language, living in close proximity to each other, and practicing the same religion. Americans have hailed from many places and have represented many cultures. We are a pluralistic society, even more so today than we were in 1865.

Pluralism, of course, offers many advantages. The wide range of popular pastimes we enjoy, for example, results in part from the many cultures housed in our nation. (Think of the various games available to us and their origins: bocce from Italy, soccer from England, lacrosse from the Native Americans, Parcheesi from India, jai alai from Spain, and many more.) Yet pluralism also can lead to disagreement, misunderstanding, and conflict. The study of pluralism in our past can help you to exploit its virtues and survive its pitfalls in your own time and place.

Understanding pluralism in American history requires that you take an imaginative leap outside yourself. The world in which you have lived and the values you have derived from it have conditioned your vision of the past. Your immediate environment — your family, your friends, your church or temple, your community — has provided a network of impressions and beliefs. Because this network, or frame of reference, differs from that of members of past generations, a barrier separates you from them. Differing frames of reference have produced barriers between you and members of other cultures as well. By coaxing you to move outside your frame of reference, your American history survey course may persuade you to abandon some of your long-standing prejudices, or at least help you to understand people who do not behave the same as you do.

A first step in moving beyond your own frame of reference is to grasp the distinction between fact and opinion. Take a moment to reflect on selection C in Exercise 1. Think about whether most of the statements there are fact or opinion. A historical fact is a sound statement about what happened in the past, reached through the assembling of reliable pieces of historical evidence. Historical facts do not lie around ready-made like pebbles on a beach. They result from a laborious sifting through and piecing together of evidence, a process much like reassembling an ancient Greek vase from a mound of fragments.

But even documents that seem to be factual cannot speak to us. We assign meaning to their words, pictures, or images. To do so, we must use *historical consciousness* — that is, we must try to comprehend how people in the past thought and acted, and to imagine the conditions they faced. Every historical fact has behind it an exercise in historical consciousness, an effort by someone to move backward into another time and place.

Often opinion is not based on fact. At other times opinion goes well beyond fact in rendering a judgment. In either case, the writer's or speaker's own impressions and beliefs play a prominent role. Many of the views you hear expressed about the past represent opinion rather than fact simply because they do *not* rest solely on an attempt to relive the past. Opinion, in other words, may lack historical consciousness. It is sometimes difficult to distinguish fact from opinion, but you do it every day outside the classroom. Recall, for instance, the last time you heard a friend describe a mutual acquaintance. Chances are, the description contained a combination of fact and opinion, with an emphasis on the latter. Either in your own mind or out loud, you probably disagreed with or qualified parts of that description.

EXERCISE 2: *Distinguishing Between Fact and Opinion*

Separating fact from opinion is not always easy, as you will see in this exercise. Yet developing this skill is essential. Much of the historian's training and much of your coursework demand the ability to make this distinction. Because historians try to do more than merely assemble facts, distinguishing them from opinions is essential to both reading and writing history.

Try your skill with the following passages on Reconstruction. To get you started, we have circled a statement of opinion and underlined a statement of fact in selection A. We also provide an explanation of our choices. Do selection B on your own; use the same methods of identifying one statement of fact and one of opinion as we do in A.

A. What is perhaps most puzzling in the legend of reconstruction is the notion that the white people of the South were treated with unprecedented brutality, that their conquerors . . . literally put them to the torture. . . . In fact, . . . the great mass of ordinary Southerners . . . were required simply to take an oath of allegiance to obtain pardon and to regain their right to vote and hold public office. But what of the Confederate leaders. . . . Were there mass arrests, indictments for treason or conspiracy, trials and convictions, executions or imprisonments? Nothing of the sort.[4]

Explanation: The author disagrees with the view that white southerners were "literally put . . . to the torture." In subsequent sentences he presents facts to make his case. However, one dictionary meaning of the word *torture* is "great mental suffering; agony."[5] Certainly the effort of Radical Republicans to move southern society in the direction of racial equality produced such suffering in many whites. Thus the author's judgment, though backed up by factual data, is hardly beyond dispute, because the data says nothing about mental suffering. Therefore, we have circled the first sentence as a statement of opinion. By contrast, the underlined sentence is readily documented as fact. The average white male southerner had only to take an oath of allegiance to the United States to regain his voting rights and the right to hold public office.

Try your hand at selection B; circle a statement of opinion and underline a statement of fact.

B. Politically, the Republicans had failed in their attempt to remake the South, but an effort is no less worthy for being in vain. They had hoped to make the race issue secondary to the economic one in the white voter's mind. They had no choice. Concentration on the race or wartime loyalty question would have doomed the Reconstruction coalition to minority status from the start. The strategy failed; . . . [but] for one brief moment, the Republicans shattered political patterns and opened up possibilities for men of all races and economic conditions. The moment passed, but the reconstructed states would not be the same again. The South transformed, though not in the way Republicans would have liked.[6]

Historians' Purposes

Historians pursue a variety of goals in practicing their craft. One objective, suggested at the outset of this chapter, is to teach lessons about the past that can be used in the present and future. Such lessons may have explicit moral content, as when an early biographer of George Washington concocted the story of young Washington and the cherry tree to demonstrate to American youth the importance of honesty. Historians sometimes direct their lessons toward influencing opinion on public policy issues. For example, many historians early in the twentieth century tried to dissuade readers from believing that the federal government should promote equality between the races. They claimed that people who held this belief during Reconstruction possessed questionable motives, such as the desire to advance the Republican party's fortunes by permitting African-Americans to vote. At other times, the historian simply attempts to entertain, to tell a story about the past that will capture and hold people's attention. Even in this day of television, VCRs, and movie theaters, many people continue to spend some of their leisure time reading historical articles and books.

EXERCISE 3: *Identifying Historians' Purposes*

Read the following selections and identify the historians' primary purpose. Alongside each passage, write *teaching lessons* or *telling a story.* Be prepared to explain your choice.

A The following selection is by a famous African-American, W. E. B. Du Bois, who was the first person of his race to earn a Ph.D. from Harvard University. Du Bois engaged in a variety of reform activities involving African-Americans. He also wrote some history. This selection is from his book on Reconstruction, which was published in 1935.

> One is astonished in the study of history at the recurrence of the idea that evil must be forgotten, distorted, skimmed over. We must not remember that Daniel Webster got drunk but only remember that he was a splendid constitutional lawyer. We must forget that George Washington was a slave owner, or that Thomas Jefferson had mulatto children, or that Alexander Hamilton had Negro blood, and simply remember the things we regard as credible and inspiring. The difficulty, of course, with this philosophy is that history loses its value as an incentive and example; it paints perfect men and noble nations, but it does not tell the truth.[7]

B The following selection is from a biography of Andrew Johnson, who succeeded to the presidency after Abraham Lincoln's death on April 15, 1865.

> Johnson had gone to bed early that night. Shortly after 10:15 he was awakened by a loud knock at the door. When he did not respond immediately, his fellow boarder at the Kirkwood House, former governor Leonard J. Farwell of Wisconsin, called in a loud voice, "Governor Johnson, if you are in this room I must see you." The vice president sprang out of bed. "Farwell, is that you?" he replied. "Yes, let me in," was the answer. The door opened, and Farwell, who had just come from Ford's Theater, excitedly told Johnson the news. The president had been shot. The vice president, stunned, grasped Farwell's hands, and the two men fell upon each other, holding on for mutual support. Soon there were guards outside to prevent any attempt to murder Johnson. Secretary of State Seward already lay seriously wounded in his home, and no one knew how widespread the assassination plot was.[8]

C The following excerpt is by David Donald, the Pulitzer Prize–winning biographer of Charles Sumner. Sumner was a U.S. senator from Massachusetts who, both before and after the Civil War, worked diligently to advance the cause of African-Americans. In 1856 his attacks on slave owners in the South led Congressman Preston Brooks of South Carolina to assault Sumner with a cane, nearly beating him to death. The act outraged many northerners, including the essayist and poet Ralph Waldo Emerson. Emerson is referred to at the end of the passage, which deals with Sumner's death in 1874.

> Through the morning Sumner lingered in semi-conscious condition, while close friends like . . . [Judge George F.] Hoar visited his bedroom and many others paid their respects in the study. In constant attendance at his bedside were his secretary and . . . representatives of the [African-American community] . . . he had tried to befriend. "I am so tired," Sumner would complain from time to time. "I can't last much longer." Though his mind wandered, he fixed on two subjects. "My book," he kept muttering, referring to his *Works,* "my book is not finished. . . ." Turning to his secretary, he said: "I should not regret this if my book were finished."
>
> Even more insistent was the dying man's concern for his "bill.". . . When Hoar came to the bedside about ten o'clock in the morning, Sumner recognized him and managed

to say: "You must take care of the civil-rights bill, — my bill, the civil-rights bill, don't let it fail.". . .

At about 2:00 P.M. on March 11, in great pain, Sumner begged for another injection of morphine, but when the doctors convinced him that it might be harmful, he appeared to grow more quiet and comfortable. . . . Half an hour later, however, he was seized by a violent spasm, followed by vomiting. Suddenly throwing himself back on the bed and gasping for air, he died.

Just before his death Sumner turned with complete lucidity to Hoar and said: "Judge, tell Emerson how much I love and revere him." Remembering Emerson's tribute to Sumner at the time of the Brooks assault, Hoar replied: "He said of you once, that he never knew so *white* a soul."[9]

Essential History: Your Textbook

We now turn from the nature of history to one of the most common instruments of a survey course: the textbook. A textbook is a synthesis — that is, it pulls together in compact form a huge amount of information covering a broad field of study. Textbooks encompassing large fields often have more than one author. Each author takes on the primary responsibility for the portion of the book that fits his or her area of specialization most closely.

Whereas American history textbooks may possess certain things in common—for example, they all address a wide range of topics in American history—they can vary a good deal in style, coverage, and interpretation. Some textbooks have numerous pictures, many of them in color, while others have only a few black-and-white images. Some are written for advanced students, others for beginners. Some emphasize political history; others favor social history — the everyday lives of ordinary people. Some textbooks offer a liberal interpretation of the American past, viewing change as necessary and good; others present a conservative interpretation, celebrating stability and continuity. If your instructor's key objective is to expose you to a wide range of opinions about the American past, his or her choice of textbook may present a variety of interpretations. If your instructor prefers to emphasize a particular subfield in American history — such as social history — in class, he or she may have chosen a book with a different emphasis, perhaps political history. Or your instructor may have chosen a book that reflects his or her own interpretative and topical preferences. Regardless of your instructor's choice, your textbook offers a blend of fact and opinion, and you should read it with that in mind. In other words, you should approach your textbook thoughtfully and critically, just as you would your daily newspaper or weekly news magazine.

EXERCISE 4: *Reading Your Textbook*

Whatever the particular characteristics of your textbook, it is likely to play an important role in your preparation for classes and tests. This exercise should help you to learn to use your text effectively.

The first step is to make use of chapter headings and introductions. Textbook authors use these devices to prepare readers for what lies ahead. On the line below, write the chapter title of the first chapter your instructor has assigned.

_____

With that title clearly in mind, read the chapter introduction. In the space provided, summarize in your own words what you expect the chapter to cover. What is the main topic? If it is Reconstruction, describe in a few words what you think Reconstruction means without using the word itself. What are the chronological boundaries of the chapter?

_____

_____

_____

_____

_____

Now read through the body of the chapter, writing down each subheading on a separate sheet of paper as you go along. Under each subheading, add the basic points made in that section. These points should be *not* simple facts alone (such as "Andrew Johnson succeeded Abraham Lincoln as president in April 1865") but rather conclusions that help give facts some meaning, plus a fact or two to illustrate each conclusion. (For example, you might note that Johnson differed from most Republicans in Congress during 1866. You could include the point that Johnson wanted the federal government to do less to assist the freed slaves than the Republicans wanted it to do. You also could list an illustration of the point, perhaps Johnson's opposition to funding for the Freedman's Bureau.) If you need a list of basic facts in chronological order, look through the chapter to see if it provides any chronologies or time lines. If it does not, then compile one of your own on a separate sheet of paper, but include only facts that seem essential for understanding the chapter title and subheadings.

When you finish reading the chapter, write in the space provided the key points made in its conclusion — for example, "Today Reconstruction generally is considered a failure, just as it was in the late nineteenth century, but in a different way." Do these concluding points follow logically from the material you wrote down from the chapter? If not, work through the chapter again to see whether you have missed something.

_____

_____

_____

_____

_____

If you follow this procedure for every textbook chapter, you will be taking a giant step forward in preparing for classes and examinations. Although your supplementary readings may not have all of the same learning aids as your textbook, they will have chapter titles, introductions, and conclusions. Even if the introductions and conclusions are not clearly designated, the first paragraphs and last paragraphs usually summarize where the chapter is going and where it has been, respectively. Try to do two things as you read each assignment: (1) take notes, using titles and subheadings as guidelines, and (2) focus on key generalizations and the basic facts behind them, rather than on every detail. You may find these suggestions useful in understanding classroom lectures as well.

Tables, Charts, and Graphs

Most textbooks contain a variety of illustrations. In addition to breaking the monotony of text, these visual aids have substantive purposes. The final three exercises in this chapter are designed to sharpen your awareness of illustrations. Tables, charts, and graphs are common features of history textbooks, and learning how to use them will enhance both your reading comprehension and your understanding of the historian's craft.

One of the primary tasks of historians is to study change — when, why, and how it occurs, and its impact on human beings. In studying change within a group or a society, historians must collect evidence expressed in numbers. After collecting evidence, historians often *quantify* information, meaning that they use mathematics to measure trends in the data. They may do this by computing an average or a mean or merely by comparing numbers and searching for patterns. Historians sometimes display their results in visual form, such as in a table, a chart, or a graph.

EXERCISE 5: *Reading Tables*

This exercise contains a table, which is simply an orderly presentation of numbers. The table compares by age group the percentage of African-Americans and European-Americans in the Deep South who were unable to write. The percentage 78.9 for African-Americans in 1870 means that in that year nearly 79 out of every 100 African-Americans in the five states covered could not write. Read through the table[10] carefully, and then complete the exercise.

Percentage of Persons in the Deep South Unable to Write, by Age Group, 1870–1890

	1870	1880	1890
Age 10–14			
African-American	78.9	74.1	49.2
European-American	33.2	34.5	18.7
Age 15–20			
African-American	85.3	73.0	54.1
European-American	24.2	21.0	14.3
Age over 20			
African-American	90.4	82.3	75.5
European-American	19.8	17.9	17.1

One conclusion consistent with the figures provided in this table is that the rates of illiteracy between 1870 and 1890 differed substantially among African-Americans and European-Americans. Six more conclusions follow. Circle the numbers of the conclusions that are consistent with the information in the table.

1. Rates of illiteracy among African-Americans steadily declined in the Deep South from 1870 to 1890.

2. Rates of decline in illiteracy were most pronounced among African-American adults.

3. The size of the decline among African-Americans exceeded that among European-Americans.

4. Throughout the period, a larger percentage of European-Americans were illiterate than African-Americans.

5. European-American adults were less likely to be illiterate than European-American youths; the opposite was true for African-Americans.

6. The rate of change for European-American and African-American youth was greater between 1880 and 1890 than between 1870 and 1880.

EXERCISE 6: *Reading Charts*

The presidential election of 1876–1877 is one of the most controversial in our history. Normally, the Electoral College determines the outcome of such elections, with each state having a number of votes equal to its representation in Congress. But if no candidate achieves a majority of the votes in the Electoral College, the issue is resolved in Congress. In 1876–1877, the Republican and Democratic parties initially could not agree on who had won 20 of the 369 Electoral College votes. As a result, neither Republican candidate Rutherford B. Hayes nor Democratic candidate Samuel J. Tilden emerged with a majority. Congress established a special commission to determine whether Democrats or Republicans should fill the contested seats. The commission's ruling in favor of the Republicans gave Hayes a one-vote majority in the Electoral College.

Historians and political scientists often use charts to show voting patterns in particular elections. The chart, or political map, in Figure 1.4 shows the winning party in each state in the election of 1876, except where the outcome was contested. If we were to place charts for several presidential elections side by side, you could use them to determine whether national politics had changed during the period covered. This exercise, however, asks you merely to pull information out of a single chart. Examine the chart closely and then respond to the questions that follow.

Questions on Figure 1.4

1. What do the numbers inside each state designate? (*Hint:* You may want to consult the U.S. Constitution at the end of your textbook to answer this question. Find Article II, Section 1, paragraph 2.) _____

_____

2. Why don't the unshaded areas have numbers in them? _____

_____

_____

3. Would the numbers be the same for a political map of the election of 1996? Explain.

_____

_____

_____

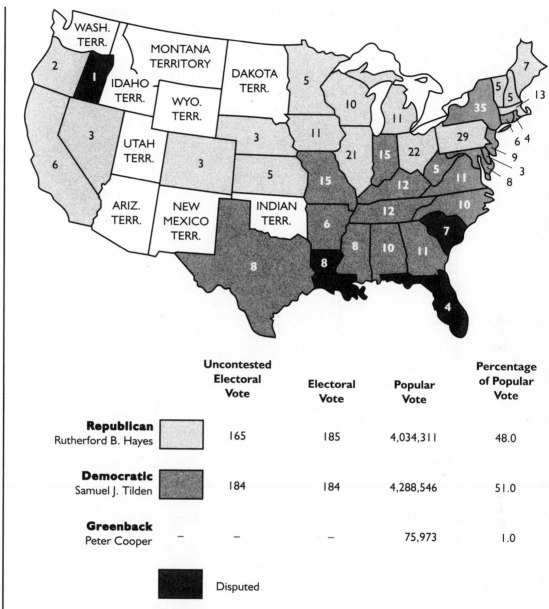

	Uncontested Electoral Vote	Electoral Vote	Popular Vote	Percentage of Popular Vote
Republican Rutherford B. Hayes	165	185	4,034,311	48.0
Democratic Samuel J. Tilden	184	184	4,288,546	51.0
Greenback Peter Cooper	–	–	75,973	1.0

Disputed

FIGURE 1.4 *The Disputed Election of 1876*

EXERCISE 7: *Reading Graphs*

You have read in your textbook about the tremendous devastation suffered by the South during the Civil War and about the difficult recovery in the war's immediate aftermath. The graph in this exercise (see Figure 1.5) shows developments in the South's economy from 1860 to the turn of the century. Like tables and charts, graphs provide visual displays of evidence. This graph shows changes in several economic indicators — that is, it measures change in aspects of the economy of a defined area over a particular period of time. It also addresses the question of whether change is primarily linear or cyclical. **Linear change** is indicated when a line on a graph always or nearly always moves in the same direction. **Cyclical change** is suggested when a line frequently changes direction. Three types of change are shown in Figure 1.6.

Examine the graph in Figure 1.5 carefully, and then complete the exercise. One conclusion derived from the graph is that substantial change occurred in the South's economy between 1860 and 1900. Circle the numbers of the conclusions that follow from information in the graph.

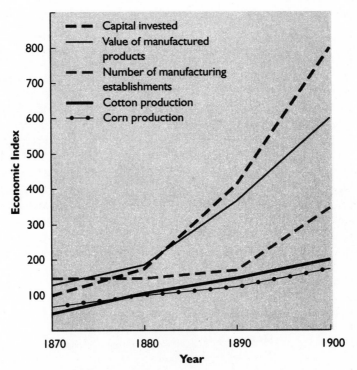

FIGURE 1.5 *The Economic Recovery of Former Confederate States, 1870–1900 (indexed at 1860 = 100)*
Source: *Twelfth Census of the United States, 1900: Agriculture.*

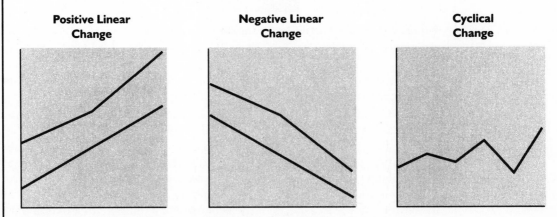

FIGURE 1.6 *Line Graphs Showing Three Kinds of Change*

1. Overall, change in the South's economy between 1870 and 1900 was basically cyclical.

2. Overall, change between 1860 and 1870 was basically linear. (*Hint:* To determine 1860 levels, carefully read the note below the graph.)

3. Of the *categories of production* represented, manufacturing showed the greatest increase between 1870 and 1900.

4. There is a correlation (mutual or reciprocal relation) between capital invested and the value of manufactured products.

5. Overall, the rate of increase in the number of manufacturing establishments was higher than the rate of increase for corn production.

This chapter has introduced you to history as a discipline — its nature, it uses, and some of the skills it requires. As your course proceeds, you will find yourself confronting many tasks, some drawing on familiar skills and others calling for new ones. Whether new or familiar, these abilities will serve you well in the world beyond this classroom. If you are asked to write an essay or to analyze a film in this course, you may be tempted to say to your teacher, "But this is a history course, not an English course"; or "This is a history course, not a film course." Keep in mind that the educated person possesses the capacity to integrate knowledge — that is, to apply it outside the context in which it was originally acquired. In the midst of constructing a coherent, grammatical narrative in Chapter 5 or contemplating the symbolism in the movie *Working Girl* in Chapter 8, remember that nowhere in your educational experience will you be expected to apply knowledge and skills from as wide a variety of subjects as in a course on the "universal discipline" — history.

We now turn to the exciting world of primary sources — documents that, as relics of a past age, are crucial to our understanding of times and places other than our own.

NOTES

1. *Congressional Globe,* 39th Cong., 1st sess., February 1, 1866, 589.

2. Ibid., 39th Cong., 2nd sess., December 11, 1866, 56.

3. W. H. Morgan, *Personal Reminiscences of the War of 1861–5* (Lynchburg, Va.: J. P. Bell and Co., n.d.), 272, 278–80.

4. Kenneth M. Stampp, *The Era of Reconstruction, 1865–1877* (New York: Knopf, 1965), 9–10.

5. Funk & Wagnalls, *New Comprehensive International Dictionary of the English Language,* Deluxe Reference Edition (Newark, N.J.: Publishers International Press, 1982), 1326.

6. Mark W. Summers, *Railroads, Reconstruction, and the Gospel of Prosperity* (Princeton: Princeton University Press, 1984), 300–301.

7. W. E. B. Du Bois, *Black Reconstruction in America* (New York: Russell and Russell, 1935), 722.

8. Hans L. Trefousse, *Andrew Johnson* (New York: Norton, 1989), 193.

9. David Donald, *Charles Sumner and the Rights of Man* (New York: Knopf, 1970), 586–587.

10. Roger Ransom and Richard Sutch, *One Kind of Freedom* (Cambridge: Cambridge University Press, 1978), 30.

2 EVIDENCE OF THE PAST: READING AND LOOKING AT PRIMARY SOURCES

Late-Nineteenth-Century America

In the 1950s television series "Dragnet," Sergeant Joe Friday always asked witnesses to give him "just the facts, please." He never got facts alone, however. What he got was different versions of the same event. On some points all witnesses may have agreed, but rarely did they concur on everything. Through careful investigation, Sergeant Friday attempted to separate the reliable evidence from the unreliable, and in so doing he pieced together an accurate version of the event. Historians work in much the same way, although their evidence tends to be written rather than oral.

The Variety of Primary Sources

Historians call the materials they use to determine the facts **primary sources.** By definition, primary sources are materials created during the period being studied. Newspapers and magazines are prominent among published primary sources, as are transcripts of legislative or court proceedings and presidential press conferences. Unpublished primary sources include private letters and diaries, among other things. Sometimes the private papers of prominent people get published, although normally not until many years after they were written. For example, both Harry S Truman and Dwight D. Eisenhower kept diaries while they served as president, and in the 1980s substantial portions of these writings appeared in print. Woodrow Wilson did not keep a diary, but he wrote many letters during his years as a professor and college president and later as a politician. The bulk of these have been published over the last thirty years. The vast majority of surviving letters and diaries, however, remain unpublished, stored in people's attics or cellars or in manuscript collections in research libraries.

Primary sources also include a wide variety of unwritten materials. Pictures, paintings, maps, buildings, and automobiles all qualify as primary sources. So do airplanes and space capsules like the ones on display at the Air and Space Museum in Washington, D.C. Historians of the recent past often interview people who participated in events, just as detectives question people who experienced, witnessed, or might have committed crimes. Even though many oral histories are made years after the event in question, they qualify as primary sources as long as the testimony is given by a person actually involved in that event. Thus spoken memoirs also belong in the category of primary sources.

The following exercises seek to develop your skills in identifying primary sources and evaluating their authenticity, reliability, and meaning. By the time you have completed this chapter, you will have worked with a variety of such sources, from traditional written materials to pictures and drawings.

EXERCISE 1: *Identifying Primary Sources*

The years after the Civil War and into the 1880s saw the "long drive" reach its height in the Southwest and plains states. During this drive, ranchers moved cattle from Texas, New Mexico, and Arizona to the Great Plains, from western Kansas northward, where the animals were loaded on trains and transported to slaughterhouses in Kansas City or Chicago. Two accounts of the long drive follow. The third selection describes the transition from the long drive to a more modern system of raising and marketing cattle.

Read the passages and write in the margin whether or not they are primary sources. If you are uncertain, say so. Be prepared to explain your answers.

A. Another offspring of the railroads and the Civil War was the cowboy of the Old West. The late 1860s saw . . . Texas crammed with 5,000,000 head of cattle raised under . . . conditions of open range, fancy roping and short shrift for the rustler. Their owners, eagerly seeking markets . . . , began to drive them northward to shipping points on the new railroad for loading into cars for the Kansas City and Chicago stockyards. . . . The traditional population of the country into which the Kansas Pacific and . . . the Union Pacific were pushing consisted of thousands of Indians living off millions of buffalo. Now Uncle Sam was herding the Indians into reservations and appallingly efficient professional buffalo hunters . . . were wiping out the great lumbering beasts. This left the grass and water of western Kansas free for cattlemen, and it was soon learned that . . . cattle could winter well enough on the Great Plains unsheltered. . . . Gradually the cattle country . . . spread into Wyoming and northward beyond the Canadian line.[1]

B. The [ranch] boss informed us that we were to take another herd of cattle north, away up in the northwestern part of Nebraska. . . . This announcement was met with exclamations of approval from the boys. . . . It did not take us long to round up the herd and the second day from the time we received the order we were off. . . . It was now late in the season and we had to hurry in order to get through in good weather, therefore we put the cattle to the limit of their traveling powers. . . . Our route lay over the old Hays and Elsworth trail, one of the best known cattle trails in the west, then by way of Olga [Oglala], Nebraska, at that time a very small and also a very tough place. It was a rendezvous of the tough element and the bad men of the cow country. There were a large number of cowboys there from the surrounding ranges and the place looked very enticing to our tired and thirsty crowd, but we had our herd to look after and deliver so we could not stop, but pushed on north crossing the Platte river, then up the trail that led by the Hole in the Wall country, near which place we went into camp. Then as now this Hole in the Wall country was the refuge of the train robbers, cattle thieves and bandits of the western country, and when we arrived the place was unusually full of them, and it was not long before trouble was brewing between our men and the natives which culminated in one of our men shooting and killing one of the bad men of the hole. . . . We broke camp at once and proceeded on our journey north. We arrived at the ranch where our herd were to be delivered without further incident.[2]

C. In the old days when the Chisholm Trail was new, it was the custom of some trail bosses to point the wagon pole at the North Star in the evening so that in the morning they had only to glance at it to know which direction to take. Those days were gone; after crossing Red River, a child could have found its way to Abilene without going astray.

Soon after the season of 1871 got into full swing, so many herds were moving toward Kansas that it was often difficult to keep them from treading on one another's heels. By midsummer overgrazing made it necessary to detour from the trail for a mile or two to find grass. . . .

As they moved into Dickinson County the drovers were harassed by fences and the organized resistance of the farmers. Still another herd law had been enacted, and this one had teeth in it. In some places the old brush fences had been replaced by a new invention . . . named, appropriately, barbed wire. It was cheap and it was deadly enough to turn back any critter. . . . The Texans . . . couldn't have surmised that in a few years it would be adopted by cattlemen north and south, and in time become the great safeguard for the orderly functioning of the livestock industry.[3]

You may have concluded from Exercise 1 that it is easier to determine what is a primary source than what is not. Sources written in the first person or in the present tense usually qualify as primary. Yet most memoirs (primary) and works by historians (secondary) are written in the past tense; newspaper articles (primary) and works by historians (secondary) generally use the third person. Although it is a good guess that sources written in both the past tense and the third person are secondary in nature, we frequently must do more than read a brief passage from them to tell for sure. The preface or introduction to a book often provides key information by revealing something about the author and the circumstances under which the document was written.

Survival of Primary Sources

Now let us consider the survival of primary sources. We saw in Chapter 1 that only a small portion of human events are ever recorded. Those that are documented often disappear from memory through the destruction of primary sources. War, fire, rain, insects, and rodents are among the great ravagers of historical evidence. So are humans. Just as we do today, people for centuries have been cleaning out their homes and places of business, discarding old newspapers, magazines, pamphlets, advertisements, and personal letters, many of which would have interested future historians. Thus only a tiny portion of what humans have created ultimately survives.

Are there common characteristics of the materials that survive? Or are survival rates merely a matter of chance? Not surprisingly, wealth and official position have a decided effect on the survival rate of evidence. What the government, its agents, and the wealthiest portion of a people leave behind has a much better chance of surviving the ravages of history than a poorer person's things. Letters and diaries are the products of people who can read and write and have some reason to put pen to paper. Until very recently, most poor people were illiterate. They were thus unlikely to leave behind letters or diaries. They did leave evidence of their lives, but this information must be carefully deciphered. Historians interested in social history — the lives of ordinary people — often have turned to anthropologists' and archeologists' methods to literally dig up evidence of how poor people lived. Historians working from the mid-nineteenth century on can make use of photographs, but pictures of ordinary people are far less plentiful than those of the rich and famous.

Despite the loss of so much information about the lives of ordinary people, historians still can piece together evidence of their experiences. This process is called history "from the bottom up" because these people were often on the bottom rung of society. Of course, most of the documents and other primary sources that have survived come from official sources and allow us to see government and society "from the top down."

The following exercises ask you to think about the survival prospects of various types of primary sources and to distinguish between public and private documents.

EXERCISE 2: *Survival Prospects*

Next to each item in the following list write an *S* if you think the item would be likely to survive for 100 years. If you think the item would not survive, write *NS*.

_____ diary of President McKinley

_____ southern sharecropper's home

_____ financial records of Andrew Carnegie's steel company

_____ mansion of the Vanderbilt family

_____ home of one of the workers in the Carnegie steel mill

_____ dress suit of a poor Italian immigrant

EXERCISE 3: *Private and Public Documents*

Examine each of the following documents. In the space provided, write *private* for those written by people acting as private individuals — that is, by people outside government or by people in government but acting outside their official capacity. Write *public* for documents that represent attempts to explain or make policy, and write *unclear* for those that do not quite fit either category.

A The following is a transcription of a handwritten letter.

My Dear Mrs. Felton:

I feel very grateful for your kind words of sympathy for me in my sorrow. Only those who have trodden the same path can understand what it is.

When I see you I want to tell you all about my little darling; her beautiful little life & her even beautiful death. She was <u>so lovely</u> — such an idol with all. But I cannot write about her the tears blind me so.

How is dear little Howard? I hope he will be hearty & well when I see him.

I was so sorry not to know when you were in Atlanta. Present me kindly to the Dr. and believe me

Your affectionate friend
Fanny Gordon[4]

Kirkwood
August 27th/77.

_____

B The following is from President Grover Cleveland's message to Congress of December 1885.

> The fact that our revenues are in excess of the actual needs of an economical administration of the government justifies a reduction in the amount exacted from the people for its support. Our government is . . . never better administered, and its true spirit is never better observed, than when the people's taxation for its support is scrupulously limited to the actual necessity of expenditure, and distributed according to a just and equitable plan.
>
> The proposition with which we have to deal is the reduction of the revenue received by the government, and indirectly paid by the people from customs duties. The question of free trade is not involved, nor is there now any occasion for the general discussion of the wisdom or expediency of a protective system.
>
> Justice and fairness dictate that . . . the industries and interests which have been encouraged by such laws, and in which our citizens have large investments, should not be ruthlessly injured or destroyed. We should also . . . protect the interests of American labor . . . ; its stability and proper remuneration furnish the most justifiable pretext for a protective policy. . . .
>
> I think the reduction should be made in the revenue derived from a tax upon the imported necessaries of life.
>
> We thus directly lessen the cost of living in every family of the land, and release to the people in every humble home a larger measure of the rewards of frugal industry.[5]

C The following document is a letter from Carl Schurz, the secretary of the interior, to a Republican ally, George William Curtis, dated December 29, 1879.

> I intended to answer your last note some time ago but the current business of the Department would not let me do so.
>
> It seems to me that it is time for the opponents of General Grant's nomination [by the Republican party for president] to act. The "boom business" has been so much overdone that the public mind is open for a reaction. . . . All that is necessary is that those who are earnestly opposed to the third term should openly say so. You strike the nail on the head in saying that the real danger consists in "the habituation of the popular mind to personal government." But I think you are not right in your apprehension that the people have no clear appreciation of that danger. It is just this appreciation, together with their remembrance of the corruptions and abuses of the Grant regime, that makes the Germans so unanimous in their opposition to the third term. I see this cropping out everywhere. Without the German Republican vote several of the Northwestern States, such as Wisconsin, Illinois and Ohio, cannot be carried. . . . Now let it be known that the Independent Republican element in New York is of the same mind . . . and the back of the Grant movement will be broken. . . .
>
> I write to you with entire frankness. . . . I hope you will communicate with me, of course, in entire confidence.[6]

Authenticity and Reliability

Exercise 3 was relatively uncomplicated. The texts themselves offered important clues as to their nature. Yet evaluating a primary source can be challenging. The first tasks are to determine its authenticity and reliability. Only after completing that step can we move on to assess its meaning.

Imagine that you have in your hands something that purports to be a primary source. You want to determine its genuineness. Is it what it claims to be? There are famous forgeries that still haunt historians. Not so long ago one of the most respected English historians authenticated Adolf Hitler's "diaries," which allegedly suggested that Hitler never intended to commit genocide. When the forger was revealed, this historian issued a qualified apology. The fact is that any historian can make a mistake.

The first clues to authenticity are physical. Is the document or artifact old enough to originate in the period from which it supposedly came? Was it found in an appropriate place? Does it use language or was it the product of tools from long ago? Is the handwriting genuine? One good way to authenticate a primary source is to compare it with similar sources that have already been authenticated. The problem with this method, though, is that the most interesting discoveries often contradict or add to existing sources.

Another good way to prove the legitimacy of a primary source is to find references to it in other well-established sources. It then fills a gap in our evidence. Of course, such gaps are often invitations to forgers. For example, a missing reply to a letter begs for a forgery. Entire sets of documents can be forged. Between 1861 and 1869, the Frenchman Vrain-Denis Lucas sold more than 27,000 forged letters, many of them supposedly written by famous scientists such as Galileo, Pascal, and Descartes. Two of the letters tried to show that the Frenchman Pascal, not the Englishman Newton, had discovered the law of gravity!

The issue of authenticity does not arise with the bulk of primary sources used by historians. Many documents, especially official ones, go into a specific collection soon after being created. For suspect documents, archivists frequently run standard checks before making them available to scholars. So despite an occasional notorious case, few historians, especially those who study recent American history, spend much of their time authenticating documents.

A far more common problem for historians of nineteenth- and twentieth-century America is the reliability of evidence in primary sources. Just because a source is authentic does not mean that it is reliable. After all, the authors of genuine primary sources may have been in a poor position to witness the events they describe. Their powers of observation may have been weak, or they may have possessed an ulterior motive for describing events as they did. Before relying on these sources as evidence, therefore, it is wise to ask a series of questions even of authenticated primary sources. These questions include the following: Was the author of the source well situated to see the event described? Was the author well acquainted with any or all of the people described? What was the character of the author — was he or she a truth teller or a fabricator of stories? Did the author have a personal interest in the event described? Is the language used in portraying the event calm and balanced or emotional and polemical? Was the source created immediately, within a short span of time, or after many years?

As you can see, determining the reliability of primary sources is often complex. It is a task, nonetheless, that is commonly performed by people outside the history profession, although they usually don't think of their evidence as primary sources. Recall the testimony of Professor Anita Hill and Judge Clarence Thomas before the Senate Judiciary Committee during the fall of 1991. Hill accused Thomas of sexual harassment during the time she worked for him several years earlier. Thomas adamantly denied her story. The senators on the committee had to decide which person to believe in order to determine how to vote on Thomas's nomination to the Supreme Court. Millions of Americans who watched the dramatic proceedings on television made judgments as well, even though they had no direct say regarding Thomas's fate. This is merely one case in which people confronted the task of evaluating evidence about the past as a means of reaching a conclusion in the present. Most of us engage in the same kind of activity on a regular basis in the normal course of our lives.

EXERCISE 4: *Evaluating the Reliability of Primary Sources*

The population grew rapidly in late-nineteenth-century America. Between 1860 and 1900, the number of people in the United States increased from 31.5 million to more than 76 million. During that time, over 13 million people came from other countries to live in America. As a result of this phenomenal growth, the center of population moved steadily westward, and cities expanded dramatically. Whereas in 1860 census takers classified only 16.1 percent of the population as urban, by the turn of the century they placed more than twice that percentage in this category. New York City grew more than threefold, Chicago more than tenfold. The increased crowding in cities and the growing diversity of their populations after 1880, as well as increasing disparities in wealth, created many problems, which in turn often led to conflict.

The two primary sources that follow are accounts by popular newspapers of an incident that resulted from friction between business and labor in Chicago. Known as the Haymarket Square incident, this event occurred on the evening of May 4, 1886. It grew out of a struggle by organized labor for the eight-hour workday. On the previous day, striking laborers and police had clashed near a McCormick Harvester plant in the city, leaving one laborer dead and several on both sides injured. To protest alleged police brutality, radicals in the labor movement called a mass meeting for the next night at Haymarket Square. As a result of a police effort to break up the meeting, eight policemen died, and dozens of civilians were killed or wounded. In the event's aftermath, conservative forces launched a nationwide campaign against labor organizers and socialists who sought to alter the structure of economic and political power in America. Chicago authorities arrested eight radicals for allegedly planning or provoking the incident. A jury convicted all eight, and seven received death sentences. Of the seven, four were hanged in November 1887, a fifth committed suicide the day before his scheduled execution, and the governor of Illinois commuted to life imprisonment the sentences of the other two. In 1893 a reform governor, John Peter Altgeld, pardoned the three remaining prisoners, declaring that they were innocent of the crimes for which they had been convicted.

Carefully read the following newspaper accounts of the actual incident and answer the questions that follow. (The map provided in Figure 2.1 of the Haymarket neighborhood may help you to visualize the event.)

 From the *Chicago Tribune,* May 5, 1886, p. 1:

A HELLISH DEED.

A DYNAMITE BOMB THROWN INTO A CROWD OF POLICEMEN. . . .

A dynamite bomb thrown into a squad of policemen sent to disperse a mob at the corner of Desplaines and Randolph streets last night exploded with terrific force, killing and injuring nearly fifty men. . . .

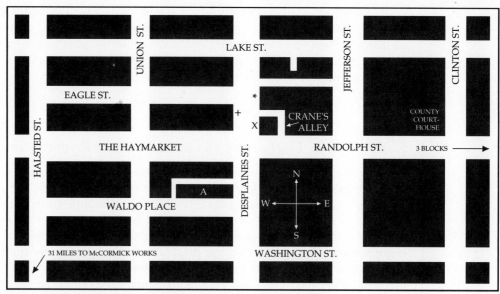

A–*Desplaines Street Police Station*   *–*Speakers' Wagon*
X–*Point from which bomb was thrown*   +–*Point at which bomb exploded*

FIGURE 2.1 *Map of Haymarket Neighborhood*

An Incendiary Speech

The following circular was distributed yesterday afternoon:

ATTENTION, WORKINGMEN!
GREAT MASS-MEETING
Tonight, at 7:30 o'clock,
At the
HAYMARKET, RANDOLPH STREET, BETWEEN
DES PLAINES AND HALSTED.

Good speakers will be present to denounce the latest atrocious act of the police —
the shooting of our fellow-workmen yesterday afternoon.

THE EXECUTIVE COMMITTEE.

In response to this about 1,500 people gathered, but a shower dispersed all but 600.
Several speeches had been made of a more or less rabid character when Sam Fielden,
the Socialist, put in an appearance.

"The Socialists," he said, "are not going to declare war; but I tell you war has been
declared upon us; and I ask you to get hold of anything that will help to resist the on-
slaught of the enemy and the usurper. The skirmish-lines have met. People have been
shot. Men, women, and children have not been spared by the ruthless minions of private capital. It had no mercy. So ought you. You are called upon to defend yourselves,
your lives, your future. What matters it whether you kill yourselves with work to get a
little relief or die on the battle-field resisting the enemy? (Applause.) What is the difference? Any animal, however loathsome, will resist when stepped upon. Are men less
than snails or worms? I have some resistance in me. I know that you have too. You
have been robbed. You will be starved into a worse condition."

At this point those on the outskirts of the crowd whispered "Police," and many of
them hastened to the corner of Randolph street. Six or eight companies of police, com-

manded by Inspector Bonfield, marched rapidly past the corner. Fielden saw them coming and stopped talking. When at the edge of the crowd Inspector Bonfield said in a loud voice: "In the name of the law I command you to disperse." The reply was a bomb, which exploded as soon as it struck. The first company of police answered with a volley right into the crowd, who scattered in all directions. . . .

What Another Reporter Saw.

Fielden was apparently about winding up his address when a dark line was seen to form north of Randolph street and in front of the Desplaines Street Station. For some time no attention was paid to it, but it gradually moved north. . . . As the line approached a cry arose in the crowd: "The police! The police!" and the south end of the crowd began to divide towards the sidewalk and walk south to Randolph street. But the wagon in front of the Crane Bros. Manufacturing Company was not vacated by the speaker and the other "leaders." Fielden continued speaking, raising his voice more and more as the police approached. . . . The police, marching slowly, were in a line with the east and west alley when something like a miniature rocket suddenly rose out of the crowd on the east sidewalk, in a line with the police. It . . . fell right in the middle of the street and among the marching police. . . . The bomb lay on the ground a few seconds, then a loud explosion occurred, and the crowd took to their heels, scattering in all directions. Immediately after the explosion the police pulled their revolvers and fired on the crowd. An incessant fire was kept up for nearly two minutes. . . .

Questions to Consider

1. Does the headline of the article suggest any point of view? If so, what? _____

   _____

   _____

2. Is the word *mob,* used in the first paragraph, a neutral word, or does it suggest a bias?

   How about *rabid* later on? _____

   _____

3. Does the article merely describe Sam Fielden's speech, or does it purport to quote it?

   Does your answer suggest that the reporter was present at the incident? _____

   _____

   _____

4. How does the description of events under the heading "What Another Reporter Saw" compare with the description before it? Is it more or less biased, or about the same?

   Are there any factual discrepancies? _____

   _____

5. Does the fact that the newspaper published both of the reports suggest anything

   about its point of view and reliability? _____

   _____

   _____

B From the *New York Times,* May 5, 1886, p. 1:

ANARCHY'S RED HAND

RIOTING AND BLOODSHED IN THE STREETS OF CHICAGO

POLICE MOWED DOWN WITH DYNAMITE

STRIKERS KILLED WITH VOLLEYS FROM REVOLVERS. . . .

Chicago, May 4. — The villainous, [sic] teachings of the Anarchists bore bloody fruit in Chicago tonight, and before daylight at least a dozen stalwart men will have laid down their lives as a tribute to the doctrine of Herr Johann Most [an anarchist leader]. There had been skirmishes all day between the police and various sections of the mob, which had no head and no organization. In every instance the police won. In the afternoon a handbill, printed in German and English, called upon "workingmen" to meet at Des Plaines and Randolph streets this evening. "Good speakers," it was promised, "will be present to denounce the latest atrocious act of the police — the shooting of our fellow-workmen yesterday afternoon."

In response to this invitation 1,400 men, including those most active in the Anarchist riots of the past 48 hours, gathered at the point designated. At Des Plaines street, Randolph street, which runs east and west, widens out, and is known as the Old Haymarket. . . . It was just off the northeastern corner of the plaza and around the corner into Des Plaines street, 100 feet north of Randolph, that the crowd gathered. A light rainstorm came up and about 800 people went away. The 600 who remained listened to speeches from the lips of August Spies . . . and A. H. Parsons, an Anarchist with a negro wife. The speeches were rather mild in tone, but when Sam Fielden, another Anarchist leader, mounted the wagon from which the orators spoke, the crowd pressed nearer, knowing that something different was coming.

They were not disappointed. Fielden spoke for 20 minutes, growing wilder and more violent as he proceeded. Police Inspector Bonfield had heard the early part of the speech, and, walking down the street to the Des Plaines street police station, not 300 feet south of where Fielden stood, called out a reserve of 60 policemen and started them up the street toward the crowd. The men were formed into lines stretching from curb to curb. The Inspector hurried on ahead, and, forcing his way through the crowd, reached a point close to the wagon. Fielden had just uttered an incendiary sentence, when Bonfield cried:

"I command you in the name of the law to desist, and you," turning to the crowd, "to disperse."

Just as he began to speak[,] . . . from a little group of men standing at the entrance to an alley opening on Des Plaines street, opposite where Fielden was speaking, some thing rose up into the air, carrying with it a slender tail of fire, squarely in front of the advancing line of policemen. It struck and sputtered mildly for a moment. Then, as they were so close to it that the nearest man could have stepped upon the thing, it exploded with terrible effect.

The men in the center of the line went down with shrieks and groans, dying together. Then from the Anarchists on every side, a deadly fire was poured in on the stricken lines of police, and more men fell to the ground. . . . The police answered the fire of the rioters with deadly effect. In two minutes the ground was strewn with wounded men. Then the shots straggled, and all was quiet and the police were the masters of the situation.

Questions to Consider

1. How does the headline of article B compare with that of article A? _____

   _____

2. What does use of the word *villainous* in the first sentence suggest about the point of

   view of the article? _____

   _____

3. Why do you think the article mentions that one of the speakers had "a negro

   wife"? _____

   _____

   _____

4. How do articles A and B compare in their coverage of Fielden's speech? _____

   _____

   _____

5. Is there any point on which article B provides more detail than article A? _____

   _____

   _____

6. How do the two articles differ on who first fired guns? _____

   _____

7. Now it is time for you to evaluate the reliability of these articles. Using your answers
   to the preceding questions, as well as the reliability questions provided on page 24,
   evaluate the accounts. (Some of the reliability questions will be more useful than others.) Identify at least three points of similarity in the articles and three points on which
   they differ.

   Similarities:

   a. _____

   _____

   b. _____

   _____

   c. _____

   _____

   Differences:

   a. _____

   _____

   b. _____

   _____

c. _____

_____

8. If you had to provide an account of the Haymarket Square incident on the basis of one of the two articles alone, which one would you choose? _____

    Why? _____

    _____

    _____

    _____

9. What additional evidence would you seek if you were a historian writing an article on the incident? What kind of useful evidence would you expect might have survived?

    _____

    _____

    _____

10. Explain how these documents take you out of the present. What sets them apart

    from articles on the front page of today's major newspapers? _____

    _____

    _____

    _____

    _____

The Interpretation of Primary Sources

Evaluating primary sources involves more than just questioning their authenticity and reliability. It also requires you to judge their meaning. In interpreting the past, historians think extensively about what the available primary sources mean. What are the authors of the sources trying to say? What was the meaning of their choice of particular words or phrases? How important was their message to others of their time? Why was their message important or unimportant? Did it help to shape opinion, official or otherwise, or did it merely reflect it? If the sources are nontextual — pictures, paintings, or drawings — what do they say about the society of the time? For example, does the clothing worn by people in a picture reflect the prevailing style of a particular time and place or class? If so, what does it suggest about economic and social conditions? These are only a few of the questions historians ask once they have confirmed the authenticity and reliability of their sources.

The remaining six exercises ask you to analyze drawings as well as written materials. They will expand your understanding of changes that were taking place in late-nineteenth-century America, especially in relation to gender, and perhaps help you comprehend changes that have occurred since the late nineteenth century.

EXERCISE 5: *Women and Economic Change*

Industrialization ushered in rapid changes in late-nineteenth-century America. Advances in technology made possible major savings in the human labor required to produce most finished goods, from processed food to machinery. This development led to reductions in the average workweek among laborers in manufacturing from sixty-six hours in 1860 to sixty in 1890 and forty-seven in 1920. Labor-saving devices also appeared in the home, cutting sharply the time required to carry out many household tasks. One result was more time available to Americans, especially in the growing and increasingly prosperous middle class, for nonproductive activities such as leisure and education. Another result was to give women a wider range of activities outside the home.

The passage below is from *Women and Economics*, a book published in 1898. Its author, Charlotte Perkins Gilman (1860–1935), wrote extensively about women and their inferior position to men in American society. Here she discusses the impact of economic change on women's status. Read the passage and answer the questions that follow. Keep in mind that Exercise 10, the final exercise in this chapter, asks you to write a paragraph about middle-class women in late-nineteenth-century America based on this document and the documents in Exercises 6, 7, 8, and 9. You will find the exercises helpful as you ponder linkages among the documents.

> The change in education is in large part a cause of this . . . slow emergence of the long-subverted human female to full racial [sic] equality . . ., and progressively a consequence. Day by day the bars go down. More and more the field lies open for the mind of women to glean all it can, and it has responded most eagerly. Not only our pupils, but our teachers, are mainly women. And the clearness and strength of the brain of the woman prove continually the injustice of the clamorous contempt long poured upon what was scornfully called "the female mind.". . .
>
> No sociological change equal in importance to this clearly marked improvement of an entire sex has ever taken place in one century. Under it all . . . goes . . . the one great change, that of the economic relation. . . . Just as the development of machinery constantly lowers the importance of mere brute strength of body and raises that of mental power and skill, so the pressure of industrial conditions demands an ever-higher specialization, and tends to break up that relic of the patriarchal age, — the family as an economic unit.
>
> Women have been led under pressure of necessity into a most reluctant entrance upon fields of economic activity. The sluggish and greedy disposition bred of long ages of dependence has by no means welcomed the change. Most women still work only as they "have to," until they can marry and "be supported." Men, too, liking the power that goes with money, and the poor quality of gratitude and affection bought with it, resent and oppose the change; but all this disturbs very little the course of social progress.
>
> A truer spirit is the increasing desire of young girls to be independent, to have a career of their own, at least for a while, and the growing objection of countless wives to the pitiful asking for money, to the beggary of their position. . . .
>
> For a while the introduction of machinery which took away from the home so many industries deprived women of any importance as an economic factor; but presently she arose, and followed her lost wheel and loom to their new place, the mill. To-day there is hardly an industry in the land in which some women are not found. . . .
>
> Consider, too, the altered family relation which attends this movement. Entirely aside from the strained relation in marriage, the other branches of family life feel the strange new forces, and respond to them. "When I was a girl," sighs the gray-haired

mother, "we sisters all sat and sewed while mother read to us. Now every one of my daughters has a different club!". . . We invariably object to changed conditions in those departments of life where we have established ethical values. For all the daughters to sew while the mother read aloud to them was esteemed right; and, therefore, the radiating diffusion of daughters among clubs is esteemed wrong, — a danger to home life. . . .

The growing individualization of democratic life brings inevitable change to our daughters. . . . Girls do not all like to sew. . . . Now to sit sewing together, instead of being a harmonizing process, would generate different degrees of restlessness, of distaste, of irritation. . . . As the race become more specialized, more differentiated, the simple lines of relation in family life draw with less force, and the more complex lines of relation in social life draw with more force; and this is a perfectly natural and desirable process for women as well as for men.[7]

1. What, according to Gilman, had happened to the status of women in the United States over the past century? _____

_____

2. Why did the change occur? _____

_____

_____

_____

3. Identify one specific manifestation of the change in the workplace. _____

_____

_____

_____

4. How did men react to the change and why? _____

_____

_____

_____

5. How did mothers react to the change and why? _____

_____

6. What does Gilman mean by the "growing individualization of democratic life"? _____

_____

_____

7. How did the change influence family life? _____

_____

_____

_____

_____

EXERCISE 6: *Mothers and Daughters in an Era of Change*

The passage below was written by Jane Addams (1860–1935), founder of the Chicago welfare settlement Hull House in 1889. In it she speaks to some of the emotional costs to women of changes that were occurring in the late nineteenth century, especially among the increasing number of women raised in prosperous middle-class families. The daughter of a successful merchant in Rockford, Illinois, Addams was the first woman in her family to graduate from college. Unlike the vast majority of women of her background, she never married. After nearly a decade of uncertainty and anxiety she decided on the course that would make her one of the most influential women in American history. Here she reflects on her thoughts during the 1880s as she searched for her calling. Read the passage, taken from her memoir *Twenty Years at Hull House* (1911), and answer the questions that follow.

I gradually reached a conviction that the first generation of college women had taken their learning too quickly, had departed too suddenly from the active, emotional life led by their grandmothers and great-grandmothers; that the contemporary education of young women had developed too exclusively the power of acquiring knowledge and of merely receiving impressions; that somewhere in the process of "being educated" they had lost that simple and almost automatic response to the human appeal, that old healthful reaction resulting in activity from the mere presence of suffering or of helplessness; that they are so sheltered and pampered they have no chance even to make "the great refusal." . . .

I remember a happy busy mother who, complacent with the knowledge that her daughter daily devoted four hours to her music, looked up from her knitting to say, "If I had had your opportunities when I was young, my dear, I should have been a very happy girl. I always had musical talent, but such training as I had, foolish little songs and waltzes and not time for half an hour's practice a day."

The mother did not dream of the sting her words left and that the sensitive girl appreciated only too well that her opportunities were fine and unusual, but she also knew that in spite of some faculty and much good teaching she had no genuine talent and never would fulfill the expectations of her friends. She looked back upon her mother's girlhood with positive envy because it was so full of happy industry and extenuating obstacles, with undisturbed opportunity to believe that her talents were unusual. The girl looked wistfully at her mother, but had not the courage to cry out what was in her heart: "I might believe I had unusual talent if I did not know what good music was; I might enjoy half an hour's practice a day if I were busy and happy the rest of the time. You do not know what life means when all the difficulties are removed! I am simply smothered and sickened with advantages. It is like eating a sweet dessert the first thing in the morning."[8]

1. What did Addams conclude about the deficiencies of the first generation of college women? _____

   _____

   _____

   _____

2. What does Addams mean by "the great refusal"? _____

   _____

   _____

3. In what sense does Addams view the mother of the 1880s as ambivalent regarding the position of her daughter? _____

_____

_____

_____

4. In what sense does the daughter envy her mother? _____

_____

_____

_____

5. Identify three points that the Addams passage has in common with the Gilman passage in Exercise 5.

a. _____

_____

_____

b. _____

_____

_____

_____

c. _____

_____

_____

6. Gilman talks about a broader range of women than does Addams. In what way is this so?

_____

_____

_____

_____

EXERCISE 7: *Cartoons as Social Satire*

In Chapter 1 you analyzed a political cartoon from the Reconstruction era to distinguish between past and present. Here you will evaluate a cartoon that constitutes social satire. Social satire employs sarcasm, irony, or ridicule to denounce a group's values or way of doing things. The cartoon in Figure 2.2 appeared during the early 1890s in *Harper's New Monthly Magazine*.

Questions on Figure 2.2

1. What group (class or gender) do you think is being satirized? _____

_____

ANTE-POSTHUMOUS JEALOUSY.—Drawn by GEORGE DU MAURIER.

"*Isn't* Emily Firkinson a darling, Reginald?"
"A—ahem—no doubt. I can't say much for her *singing*, you know!"
"Ah! but she's so good and true—a perfect angel! I've known her all my life! I want you to *promise* me something, Reginald!"
"Certainly, my love!"
"If I should die young, and you should ever marry again, promise, oh! promise me that it shall be Emily Firkinson!"

FIGURE 2.2 *The Cartoon as Social Satire*

2. How are the women and the man portrayed? _____

_____

3. What is the significance of the title and the setting of the cartoon? _____

_____

_____

4. See whether you can explain the cartoon's message. (*Hint:* Does it relate to changes

discussed in Exercises 5 and 6?) _____

_____

_____

EXERCISE 8: *Gender and Class, Sport and Courtship*

We saw in Exercises 5, 6, and 7 how economic change altered the balance of indoor activities for women. In this exercise, we use a primary source to explore the expanded range of outdoor activities available to men and women alike, and we examine how this development influenced dress and courtship patterns.

With the increase in leisure time in late-nineteenth-century America, sporting activity grew sharply. Baseball became the most popular sport, and in the decade following the founding of the National League of Professional Baseball Clubs in 1876 it emerged as a major business enterprise. Baseball appealed primarily to men, but other sports, such as croquet, bicycling, and golf, attracted both sexes. These sports provided new ways for

A LITTLE INCIDENT

SHOWING THAT EVEN INANIMATE OBJECTS CAN ENTER INTO THE SPIRIT OF THE GAME

FIGURE 2.3 *1890s Drawing of the "Gibson Girl"*

men and women to interact, thus affecting courtship patterns and, in the last two cases, ushering in major changes in women's dress. If a woman was to ride a bicycle comfortably or swing a golf club efficiently, she had to rid herself of constraining undergarments, particularly the corset. By 1900, when the population of the country stood at 76 million, there were over 10 million bicycles. For the most part, golf was reserved for the wealthy, but this group always influenced popular fashions well out of proportion to its numbers.

Figure 2.3, a drawing by Charles Dana Gibson, who produced many sketches for *Life* magazine during the 1890s, shows a man and a woman interacting in a setting very different from the setting portrayed in Figure 2.2. Think about those differences before responding to the questions that follow.

1. Given what is stated above, would the incident in Figure 2.3 or the incident in Figure 2.2 be more likely to have occurred before the 1890s? Explain. _____

    _____

    _____

    _____

    _____

2. How does the clothing of the principal women in Figures 2.2 and 2.3 differ? How do you explain the difference? _____

    _____

    _____

    _____

    _____

3. The man and the woman in Figure 2.3 are courting. How do you think the changes occurring in the late nineteenth century described above influenced courtship patterns?

_____

_____

_____

_____

_____

4. What is the difference in demeanor of the two principal women in Figures 2.2 and 2.3? How do you explain the difference? Is one woman more traditional in her demeanor than the other? Which one? How do you explain the difference? What answer does the excerpt by Charlotte Perkins Gilman in Exercise 5 suggest? _____

_____

_____

_____

_____

_____

_____

_____

5. Does the woman in Figure 2.3 fit the portrayal of young women of the 1880s described by Jane Addams in Exercise 6? Why or why not? _____

_____

_____

_____

_____

6. The different portrayals of women in Figures 2.2 and 2.3 were made at roughly the same time. Some of the difference may be explained by the fact that the creators of the scenes were two different people. Can you think of one or two other explanations? What explanation do you think Gilman might offer? _____

_____

_____

_____

_____

_____

Advertisements as Historical Documents

Although primitive advertisements existed centuries before the birth of Christ, scholars usually say that the fifteenth century, when Europeans began to use movable type, or the seventeenth century, when newspapers first carried advertisements, marks the beginning of modern advertising. The first modern advertising agency did not appear until 1869 in the United States. That same year also saw the completion of the transcontinental railroad, a fact that was more than just a coincidence. The development of a national transportation network vastly increased the readership of newspapers and magazines. This growth, in turn, greatly expanded the market for advertising. By the end of the century, agencies not only were placing advertisements but preparing them as well.

Because advertisers try to convince consumers that a product will help them achieve desirable goals, advertisements are a useful source for identifying the prevailing values of a bygone age. One key to assessing the implications of individual advertisements is to identify their intended audience. Usually they are directed toward one or two groups of people rather than toward the population as a whole. Only by examining advertisements aimed at a wide variety of groups can historians draw definitive conclusions about the values of an entire society. Yet analyzing advertisements directed toward one group can be extremely suggestive, especially if that group has substantial influence in a society.

EXERCISE 9: *Advertisements and Attitudes Toward Gender*

This exercise asks you to analyze two advertisements. Both of them appeared in the June 1895 issue of *The Chautauquan,* a monthly magazine, and sought to appeal to people who wanted their children to attend a private school. These people constituted a small portion of the adult population, but, because of their above-average wealth and social standing, they wielded considerable influence on contemporary values.

Examine closely the advertisements shown in Figure 2.4. Notice that one school is a boys' school and one is for girls only. Pay particular attention to how this difference influences the advertisements' content and how the contents reflect attitudes toward gender roles in American society at the time. Then answer the questions that follow.

Questions on Figure 2.4

1. How do the drawings in the advertisements differ? _____

   _____

   _____

2. How might the difference between the drawing in B and that in A be explained by the fact that Lasell Seminary was exclusively for females and the Berkeley School was for males?

   _____

   _____

3. What are the differences in the advertisements regarding the curriculum and activities

   offered at the schools? _____

   _____

   _____

A.

Berkeley

School,

Nos 18, 20, 22 and 24 West 44th Street,

New York,

Named to commemorate the work of BISHOP GEORGE BERKELEY, the greatest benefactor of early education in America, was opened in 1880.

"THE OVAL COTTAGE"

In 1891 it took possession of its new building, one of the largest and most beautiful school buildings in the world. The schoolhouse is absolutely fire-proof, is heated by hot water, and all the rooms are supplied with fresh air by a system of enforced ventilation carried on by means of fans.

The full course of the school is eight years, ages 10 to 18 with a preparatory department for little boys, 7 to 9. The school has a staff of twenty-six able masters and assistants (an average of one instructor for every ten pupils), and affords thorough preparation for the leading colleges and scientific schools, two hundred and thirty graduates having been sent to college in fifteen years. Besides an admirable equipment for manual training, the school employs the military drill, using its own armory and gymnasium, measuring 85 by 100 feet, the members being organized into two battalions of three companies each. It has systematic instruction in gymnastics, supplemented by unequalled opportunities for out-door exercise, possessing ten acres of playgrounds at Morris Heights, called the Berkeley Oval, fifteen minutes distant by train from 42nd Street. Seventeen resident pupils are received in the school building on 44th Street, and seventeen more in the new cottage at the Oval. Tuition $250 to $350 per annum. Boarding pupils, JOHN S. WHITE, LL. D., *Head Master*. J. CLARK READ, A. M., *Registrar*.

B.

Lasell Seminary for Young Women, Auburndale, Massachusetts.
(ten miles from Boston).

Suggests to parents seeking a good school consideration of the following points in its method :

1st. Its special care of the health of growing girls.
Resident Nurse supervising work, diet, and exercise ; *abundant food in good variety* and *well cooked* ; early and long sleep ; a fine gymnasium furnished by Dr. Sargent, of Harvard ; bowling alley and swimming-bath ; no regular or foreknown examination, etc.

2d. Its broadly planned course of study.
Boston proximity both necessitates and helps to furnish the best of teachers, including many specialists ; with one hundred and twenty pupils, a faculty of thirty. Four years' course ; *in some things equal to college work ; in others, planned rather for home and womanly life.* Two studies required, and two to be chosen from a list of eight or ten electives. One preparatory year. Special students admitted.

3d. Its home-like air and character.
Training in self-government ; limited number (many declined every fall for lack of room) ; personal oversight in habits, manners, care of person, room, etc.; comforts not stinted.

4th. Its handiwork and other unusual departments.
Pioneer school in scientific teaching of Cooking, Millinery, Dress-cutting, Business Law for Women, Home Sanitation, Swimming.

Regular expense for school year, $500. For illustrated catalogue address (mentioning THE CHAUTAUQUAN) C. C. BRAGDON, Principal.

Jennie June says : " It is the brightest, most home-like and progressive boarding-school I ever saw."
Mary J. Safford, M.D., of Boston, says : " I believe you are honestly trying to *educate and not veneer* young women for life's duties."

FIGURE 2.4 *Advertisements for Children's Private Schools*

4. How do you think these differences are related to gender attitudes? _____

_____

_____

5. What other differences in the advertisements could reflect attitudes toward gender

roles in America? _____

_____

_____

6. When placed in the context of materials in Exercises 5 through 8, what do these advertisements suggest about change and continuity in gender roles in late-nineteenth-century America? _____

_____

_____

_____

_____

_____

EXERCISE 10: *Synthesizing Primary Sources*

Now we ask you to use the material in Exercises 5 through 9 as the basis for a synthesis on change and continuity in the status of middle-class women at the end of the nineteenth century. *Synthesis* is defined as "the combination of separate elements or substances so as to form a whole."[9] Like the history you read in a book, synthesis involves condensing a body of material — attempting to capture its essence rather than its totality.

To help you structure your effort, we set the following ground rules. Your synthesis must be in the form of a single paragraph containing between four and six sentences and written (or typed) on a separate sheet of paper. The paragraph must have a clear topic sentence at the beginning. (A topic sentence states the main idea you seek to communicate.) As you write, make sure that you constantly refer to your topic sentence to see whether it covers what you are saying. If it does not, you must change either the topic sentence or what you are saying.

Pieces of historical evidence have much in common with objects you encounter in your everyday life. Likewise, the way historians assemble data and decipher their meaning requires skills that you can use to solve problems in the present. In addition to interpreting and evaluating primary documents, historians must contend with secondary sources, or accounts that they themselves produce. The skills you learned in Chapter 2 will prove of considerable use in Chapter 3, which introduces you to these products of historians' labors.

NOTES

1. J. C. Furnas, *The Americans: A Social History of the United States, 1587–1914* (New York: Putnam, 1969), 683.

2. Nat Love, *The Life and Adventures of Nat Love* (New York: Arno Press, 1969), 66–67, 69.

3. Harry Sinclair Drago, *Great American Cattle Trails* (New York: Bramhall House, 1965), 126–127.

4. Fanny Gordon to Mrs. Rebecca L. Felton, August 27, 1877, Box 1, Rebecca L. Felton Collection, Georgia Room, University of Georgia Library, Athens, Ga.

5. George F. Parker, ed., *The Writings and Speeches of Grover Cleveland* (New York: Casell, 1892), 67–68.

6. Frederic Bancroft, ed., *Speeches, Correspondence and Political Papers of Carl Schurz,* vol. 3 (New York: Putnam, 1913), 494–495.

7. Charlotte Perkins Gilman, *Women and Economics* (New York: Harper & Row, 1966), 151–155.

8. Jane Addams, *Twenty Years at Hull House with Autobiographical Notes* (Urbana, Ill.: University of Illinois Press, 1990), 44–45.

9. Copyright © 1996 by Houghton Mifflin Company. Adapted and reprinted by permission of *The American Heritage Dictionary of the English Language*, Third Edition.

3 THE HISTORIAN'S WORK: SECONDARY SOURCES

American Expansion During the 1890s

The primary source is raw material for the historian; the secondary source is the product of his or her efforts. The distinction seems obvious, but the boundary between primary and secondary sources can get confusing. In Chapter 2, we defined primary sources as materials created during the period being studied. Typically, **secondary sources** are created after the period being studied. Yet oral histories and written memoirs are primary sources even if they are recorded years after the events recalled. There is one qualification, however: the testifier must have been involved in the events he or she discusses. What about sources that come from the period being studied but that are *not* created by someone actually involved in the events discussed? Such a person may recount the events shortly after they occurred, but only on the basis of testimony from others or of physical evidence from the scene. Should we classify a source by this person as primary or secondary?

This dilemma commonly applies to journalists' accounts. Consider the famous book *The Final Days,* written by *Washington Post* reporters Bob Woodward and Carl Bernstein. Published in 1976, the book came from the period of the Watergate scandals it described, but its authors did not actually participate in those events. They pieced together their story largely from the oral statements of participants, many of whom insisted that their identities not be revealed. We would place *The Final Days* in the category of primary sources because its authors reconstructed events within months, sometimes even days, of their occurrence and on the basis of direct contact with people who participated in them. Some historians would disagree, arguing that the failure to participate directly in or observe the event automatically disqualifies a person from being a primary source. Thus, although we define a secondary source as one created long after the events described and by someone who did not participate in them, others would drop the first qualification.

The distinction between primary and secondary sources becomes even more complex once we realize that some sources qualify as both, depending on how we use them. For example, more than a decade before Henry Kissinger became President Richard Nixon's leading adviser on foreign affairs, he wrote a book on European diplomacy in the aftermath of the Napoleonic Wars. Kissinger based his book on a wide array of documents surviving from the early nineteenth century. To a biographer of Kissinger analyzing Kissinger's attitudes toward international politics, this book is an important primary source. Yet if you took a course on nineteenth-century European diplomacy and found the book on your list of assigned reading, you would be using it as a secondary source.

Books and articles by historians also qualify as primary sources when they are the subject of studies of the evolution of historical thought. We refer to such studies as **historiography.** If you wrote a paper on how historians have interpreted late-nineteenth-century American expansion, you would be doing historiography, and your primary sources would be books and articles by historians on that particular topic. But if you read an account by a historian of late-nineteenth-century American expansion to enhance your knowledge and understanding of that topic, you would be using the account as a secondary source.

Historiography can be an engaging and important endeavor, in part because over time historians have offered varying interpretations of the same events. Studying those interpretations can reveal a good deal about the personalities of individual historians as well as the times during which they wrote. Perhaps you already have picked up differences in interpretation between class lectures and your textbook. If so, your discovery may have produced a bit of anxiety. Who is right, you may have asked yourself, my instructor or my textbook author? The question probably has deeper roots than idle curiosity. After all, how are you supposed to answer an examination question if historians interpret events differently? We cannot answer the last question for you, although it is a fair one to ask your instructor. On the question of who is right, however, we can say that, on matters of interpretation, often no one is absolutely right or wrong. Different historians frequently read the same evidence in different ways, and there is no way to prove which view is correct.

Your anxiety may extend beyond concern over your coursework. It would be comforting to know that, once you have established the credentials of a historian, you could place trust in his or her account. In truth, the vast bulk of the data presented in works by reputable historians can be relied on as accurate. When you move into the realm of interpretation, however, uncertainty becomes unavoidable.

This fact may bother you, but it hardly makes history unique as a discipline. Think, for example, of the field of medicine. Medicine qualifies as a science, and most people think of scientists as detached pursuers of truth. Yet physicians often disagree with each other. If they did not, there would be no reason to seek a second opinion about an illness or a treatment. Uncertainty pervades most aspects of human life, and more often than not we refuse to let it immobilize us. Although we should read secondary sources with a critical eye, always watching for bias and judgments based on incomplete information, our uncertainty should not prevent us from using these resources to study history.

Much of your reading and verbal communication in everyday life requires you to evaluate secondary sources. Think of articles or statements on television news programs about the past records of political candidates or of similar accounts of what caused a particular problem in the present. Because we do not have time to study primary sources on most of the issues we face, we look to others for assistance. The quality of our decisions often depends on whether we have chosen and evaluated our secondary sources wisely. In short, our skill in this area can be every bit as important as it is in judging primary sources.

The exercises in this chapter will develop your ability to evaluate secondary sources, just as those in Chapter 2 improved your skill in working with primary sources. Two of the exercises involve identifying passages from secondary writings as representative of particular schools and subfields in history. Then you will examine a selection from an important book on American imperialism during the 1890s to see how the historian used evidence to develop an interpretation. This exercise not only will help you to grasp how historians create secondary sources, but also will advance your ability to evaluate such sources critically.

Types of History

One method of categorizing secondary works is by subfield. Historians usually concentrate on particular aspects of the past, each of which has appropriate sources. A historian who decides to write political history will be very interested in election results, voting patterns in a legislature, or the letters of politicians but not so interested in the average age at which women give birth for the first time. A historian studying the changing American family will be very interested in childbirth and marriage statistics and not at all concerned about what politicians did or said. The types of history flow from the types of evidence the author has chosen, and the author in turn chooses types of evidence that fit his or her subject. Some of the different types of history are the following:

Political history: the story of government, political leaders, electoral activities, the making of policy, and the interaction of branches of government

Diplomatic history: the study of the relations between nations, diplomats, and ideas of diplomacy

Social history: the study of ways and customs, family, education, children, demography (population change), and voluntary institutions (such as churches)

Cultural history: the study of language and its uses, the arts and literature, sport, and entertainment

Economic history: the study of how an entire system of production and consumption (or any of its parts) works, and of markets, industry, credit, and working people at all levels of the system

These conventional categories are neither airtight compartments nor are they exhaustive. For example, where does a history of newspapers belong — social, economic, or cultural history? An account of the founding and early years of Stanford University may be political as well as social and cultural history.

EXERCISE 1: *Distinguishing Among Types of History*

The following passages are examples of types of history. Write in the space at the end of each passage the type it best represents. Also write a brief explanation of your answer.

A The 1890s saw a burgeoning of sporting activity at the collegiate and even the professional level. In part, this development was an outgrowth of the economy's improved efficiency. With Americans having to spend less time producing the necessities of life, more and more activity could be devoted to other endeavors. Also, the rapid industrialization and bureaucratization of American life sparked concern about physical fitness that drew attention as never before to the positive dimensions of organized sport. Predictably, this concern generated new interest in recreational sport as well.

Type: _____ Explanation: _____

_____

B The 1896 election was a watershed in American history. The outcome ended the balance between the two parties that had existed in national politics over the past twenty years. Bearing the misfortune of holding the White House during the worst depression the nation had ever faced, the Democrats held only the solid South and the plains and mountain states while the Republicans swept the more populous Northeast and Midwest. Of the ethnic groups that previously had voted overwhelmingly Democratic, only the Irish retained their loyalty to the party of Jefferson. Republican domination of national politics would continue with only one interruption until the 1930s, when a depression even worse than that of the 1890s swept the GOP out of power.

Type: _____   Explanation: _____

_____

C Childbearing in America at the turn of the century revealed some interesting patterns. Overall, American families had become small, as women bore fewer and fewer children. The drop-off was not evenly distributed, however; women living on farms and in working-class families in the city gave birth to more children than did urban middle- or upper-class women. The reason for this was partly economic, as farm and urban working-class families often depended upon children to provide labor and income from an early age.

Type: _____   Explanation: _____

_____

Historical Schools

Another way to categorize historians is through their distinctive interpretations of particular events or subfields. Until recently, much writing in American history could be grouped into two schools. The first, which we label the **conservative-consensus school,** viewed our history in terms of broad continuities over time. Consensus historians believed that Americans agreed on basic ideas about politics and society — they argued over details but concurred on principles. To representatives of this tradition, American history is largely a success story. Although the school's leading practitioners criticize numerous incidents in our past, they generally approve of our nations's society, economy, and politics, and regard them as flexible enough to adapt to new realities without major internal disruption.

The conservative-consensus tradition had its roots in the mid-nineteenth century. Then, "amateur" historians — people who did not teach history or receive postgraduate training in the field — promoted the romantic vision of America as unique and special. In their view, our forebears were carrying out a spiritual mission to bring democracy to the world. The consensus school reached its heyday in the 1950s. Since then it has declined in influence, but historians who emphasize the country's pluralism carry forward its legacy today. For pluralists, American history features interaction among a variety of groups and institutions, and major events grow out of a multiplicity of causes rather than single factors such as economics or ideology. The pluralists' link with the consensus school derives from their view that institutions in the United States, both public and private, have provided a framework within which conflict can be channeled without major social disruption.

The second school, which we call the **Progressive — New Left school,** views our nation's history predominantly as a series of conflicts between groups with different economic interests and stresses the way power and property have been used to repress weaker minorities at home and abroad. Representatives of this school tend to criticize capitalism and support a variety of reform causes. Blossoming shortly after the turn of the century, this school was initially labeled "Progressive" after the 1900–1920 era in which it appeared. Progressive historians flourished through the 1930s but fell into temporary eclipse during World War II and its aftermath, when sharp criticism of the United States' past was discouraged. This tradition resurfaced forcefully in the reform climate of the 1960s and often was labeled "New Left" to distinguish it from an older group of communist or socialist writers.

In addition to presenting a sharp critique of capitalism and emphasizing the prevalence of conflict throughout American history, members of the Progressive–New Left school drew new attention to many groups that were left out of conservative-consensus history, including immigrants, women, African-Americans, Native Americans, and the very poor. New Left historians generally portrayed these groups as victims of dominant elites, abused as cheap labor and denied equal treatment in the public arena. These historians also emphasized the role of economic motivation in the nation's politics and foreign policy. Although the New Left did not maintain its momentum in the more conservative trend that arose during the 1970s and 1980s, many of its central ideas, particularly the need to include minority and women's history in textbooks, have enriched every history survey course.

The current generation of historians does not show the dominance of any one or two doctrines. Indeed, a major complaint of older historians is that historical writing today is too fragmented and diverse. Yet ideas from the two schools continue to appear in many of the historical works of recent years.

EXERCISE 2: *Identifying Schools of Interpretation: American Foreign Policy During the 1890s*

The historiography of American foreign policy at the end of the nineteenth century is rich in differing opinions on why the United States went to war in 1898 and then expanded its overseas territories. Not all scholarship on these questions fits neatly into the two schools discussed earlier. Although the Progressive–New Left tradition is apparent among historians who emphasize economic motives in American expansion, opposing interpretations do not converge around something identifiable as conservative-consensus. In considering the following selections, therefore, we will keep **Progressive–New Left** as one classification while adding several others:

Psychological-emotional: emphasizes a particular state of mind of a people at a given time

Reactive: views American action as a response to foreign influences

Domestic politics: dwells on public pressures at home on U.S. leaders

Nationalist: exalts the virtue of the United States in its actions abroad

Read the following example, note the "school" it falls into, and read the explanation of why.

> . . . [war with Spain might have been avoided] if diplomacy could have been conducted in a vacuum. . . . But the tidal wave of war sentiment in America, especially after the *Maine* report, would not wait. Within the President's own Republican party a

group of young jingoes [aggressive patriots] was making a commotion out of all proportion to its numbers.

The cry for blood was not confined to a few bellicose groups. Following the official report on the *Maine*, the masses were on fire for war. . . .

McKinley, an astute politician, was not blind to political realities. If he tried to thwart the popular will, he would jeopardize, perhaps ruin, his chances of re-election in 1900.[1]

School(s) of interpretation: <u>psychological-emotional and domestic politics</u>

Explanation: The passage combines the two interpretations by stressing, on the one hand, the psychological and emotional state of "a group of young jingoes" and "the masses" and, on the other hand, the impact of those groups on President William McKinley ("McKinley . . . was not blind to political realities") because of his political ambition ("re-election in 1900").

Now examine the following four selections and decide which school(s) of thought each reflects. Write your choice(s) in the space provided, and circle the key phrases or sentences that led you to your conclusion.

A. When the United States demanded the withdrawal of Spain from Cuba, it was with the declaration that "The United States hereby disclaims any disposition or intervention to exercise sovereignty, jurisdiction, or control over said island except for the pacification thereof, and asserts its determination, when that is accomplished, to leave the government and control of the island to its people." Never has a pledge made by a nation under such circumstances been more faithfully carried out. The administration of Cuba during the period of American military occupation was a model of its kind. General Leonard Wood, the military governor, and his associates . . . established order, relieved distress, organized hospitals and charitable institutions, undertook extensive public works, reorganized the system of public schools, and put Havana, Santiago, and other cities in a sanitary condition. In a hospital near Havana, Major Walter Reed, a surgeon in the United States army, demonstrated the fact that yellow fever is transmitted by the bite of a mosquito. This discovery was at once put to the test in Havana, and the city was rendered free from yellow fever for the first time in one hundred and forty years.[2]

School(s) of interpretation: _____

B. . . . It is often said that the 1890's, unlike the 1870's, form a "watershed" in American history. The difference between the emotional and intellectual impact of these two depressions [of the 1870's and 1890's] can be measured . . . by reference to a number of singular events that in the 1890's converged with the depression to heighten its impact on the public mind.

First in importance was the Populist movement, the free silver agitation, the heated campaign of 1896. For the first time in our history a depression had created a protest movement strong enough to capture a major party and raise the specter, however unreal, of drastic social convulsion. Second was the maturation and bureaucratization of American business . . . and the development of trusts on a scale sufficient to stir the anxiety that the old order of competitive opportunities was approaching an eclipse. Third . . . was the apparent filling up of the continent and the disappearance of the frontier line. . . . To the mind of the 1890's it seemed that the resource that had engaged the energies of the people for three centuries had been used up. The frightening possibility suggested itself that a serious juncture in the nation's history had come.[3]

School(s) of interpretation: _____

C. International fashions in thought and events on the world scene could have had a decisive influence on men of the establishment. . . . Knowledge of foreign thought affected their ideas about America's world mission and their understanding of Social Darwinism. Observation of foreign experience suggested to them alternative methods of promoting national prosperity and dealing with social discontent. Above all, the foreign scene provided models for imitation (reference groups and reference idols, in social science jargon). The well-traveled and well-read American could select a position on the colonial issue by identifying it with, on the one hand, [such anti-imperialists as] Bright, Gladstone, Morley, and Richter or, on the other, [imperialists like] Roseberry, Chamberlain, Ferry, Bismarck, or Wilhelm II. Neither the American past nor an assessment of American economic needs nor Social Darwinism nor the domestic political scene offered such guidance.[4]

School(s) of interpretation: _____

D. The primary force producing the war against Spain was the marketplace-expansionist outlook generated by the agricultural majority of the country. . . . However they differed over the means — among themselves, and with their metropolitan counterparts — the farm businessmen had never been thinking simply or only about Cuba. Cuba was but the temporary focus and symbol of their general, inclusive drive for overseas economic expansion.[5]

School(s) of interpretation: _____

Secondary Sources in Historical Context

It is possible to explain some of the differing interpretations of historians by looking at the period in which they lived. Current political and intellectual trends frequently influence the way people interpret the past, and historians, after all, are just people. Not surprisingly, a school emphasizing the economic motives of elites in American history emerged during the first two decades of the twentieth century, when big business increasingly came under attack in our national politics. Yet America is a pluralistic society, and the historical profession mirrors that quality. So along with reform-minded historians, the early twentieth century produced conservative scholars as well, people who espoused the nationalist interpretation of American history mentioned in Exercise 2.

If personal experiences condition the way historians see the past, must we conclude that all historical writing is colored by the time and place in which it was produced? Those who would answer *yes* — that is, those who believe that all written history is conditioned, if not dictated, by the period in which the historian lives — are **historical relativists.** Others believe that scholars can approach, if never quite reach, objectivity in their writing and are **historical objectivists.**

The only way that we as readers can alert ourselves to a historian's point of view, hidden or overt, is to hone our critical skills: Does the historian's choice of words reveal bias, or is it balanced? Does the selection of primary materials appear one-sided, or is it thorough and appropriate? Does the construction of fact from evidence betray a slant, or is it sensible? Does the argument rest on prejudgment, or is it fully supported by the facts? These are the same kinds of questions we should ask in evaluating the platform of a political candidate, a legal brief, or a business report.

EXERCISE 3: *Evaluating a Secondary Source*

Now that you have been introduced to bias, interpretation, and various schools of historical thought, you are ready to try your hand at evaluating a secondary source. The selections that follow[6] are by a distinguished diplomatic historian, Ernest May of Harvard University. In them, May offers an explanation for President McKinley's decision to demand that Spain cede the Philippines to the United States. Each paragraph is lettered. After each paragraph, write a one-sentence summary of the paragraph's major point. The questions following the selection require you to identify May's overall argument, or thesis, and to consider the evidence on which he bases that thesis.

A. The President must have recognized at a very early date that he could not simply return to Spain ground that had been occupied by American troops. No voice in the land had spoken except against such a course. . . . Nearly all evidence filtering back to the White House pictured Spanish rule as worse in the Philippines than in Cuba. . . . Hardly a popular magazine in either the United States or England failed to print someone's reminiscence or comment on Spanish iniquity.

Paragraph's major point: _____

_____

B. Nor could he have believed for long that sale or transfer was a feasible alternative. While the war was still in progress, the British and Japanese governments both said that if the United States did not want the islands, they did. The German ambassador in London told [U.S. ambassador to Great Britain John] Hay of Germany's desire for at least a base or coaling station. The New York *Herald* reported on July 3 a rumor that France and Russia had agreed to support Germany if she sought the whole archipelago. For the United States to offer the islands to any one power would surely bring protests, if nothing worse, from the rest. At home, the Germans and Irish would fight transfer to England, while others would oppose sale to anyone else. Moreover, as McKinley later observed, any such transaction might prove "bad business." The Philippines were reputed not only to offer advantageous bases for trade and navigation but also to possess rich resources, including quantities of gold. . . .

Paragraph's major point: _____

_____

C. His one real option was to insist on independence for the islands, and he may have postponed [his] final decision partly in order to collect information on the character and disposition of the natives. Early data painted a depressing picture. John Foreman, an Englishman regarded as the foremost expert on the islands, wrote in the July *Contemporary Review,* "The Philippine islands . . . would not remain one year peaceful under an independent native government. It is an utter impossibility." McKinley saw this article, for he obtained a copy from his private secretary. . . . He may also have read other, similar writings, of which magazines and newspapers were full. At any rate, he saw little to contradict Foreman; hardly anyone claiming firsthand knowledge disputed his conclusions. . . .

Paragraph's major point: _____

_____

D. . . . If doubt lingered in his mind, it was because his thoughts were not really rational alternatives. His advisers talked of what would be wise, statesmanlike, and in the national interest. He did not.

Paragraph's major point: _____

_____

E. In his explanation to the French ambassador of why he could not offer precise armistice terms, the President said, "The American people would not accept it if we did not obtain some advantage from our great victories at Manila and from the sacrifices we have made in sending to the Philippines a large body of troops." When Oscar Straus advised him early in August not to take the islands, "he seemed," Straus noted in his diary, "to fear public opinion would not approve such a course." When McKinley first drafted a final directive to his commissioners, he did not mention information newly come or any other such consideration. He wrote simply, "There is a very general feeling that the United States, whatever it might prefer as to the Philippines, is in a situation where it can not let go . . . , and it is my judgment that the well-considered opinion of the majority would be that duty requires we should take the archipelago." The sole concern of the President was with the mood and whim of public opinion. . . .

Paragraph's major point: _____

_____

F. In order to [gauge public sentiment] . . . , he arranged a speaking tour that would carry him through Indiana, Illinois, and Iowa, three states whose electoral votes had made the difference between victory and defeat in 1896, and through Nebraska and Missouri, where he had lost narrowly to Bryan. Considered either in terms of the contest for the House of Representatives or the approaching 1900 campaign, these were the areas that mattered. [See Figure 3.1.]

Paragraph's major point: _____

_____

G. In the course of each speech, McKinley said something that could be interpreted as referring to the Philippines. At Tama, Iowa, on October 11, he asserted, "We want to preserve carefully all the old life of the nation, — the dear old life of the nation and our cherished institutions — "; there was scattered clapping. He went on, "but we do not want to shirk a single responsibility that has been put upon us by the results of the war"; and there was great applause. Yet at Arcola, Illinois, on October 15, he won a similar rousing response with these words: "We have had great glory out of the war, and in its settlements we must be guided only by the demands of right and conscience and duty."

Paragraph's major point: _____

_____

H. He tried imperialism out at Ames, Iowa, from whence had come innumerable petitions to Congress in favor of pacifist causes. He experimented with anti-imperialism in Denison, the home of the state's war-hawk governor, Leslie M. Shaw. On each occasion, a

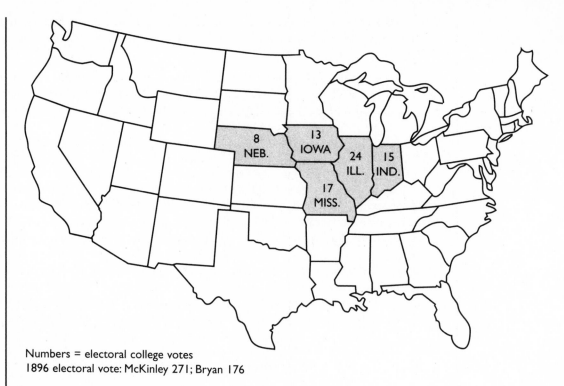

Numbers = electoral college votes
1896 electoral vote: McKinley 271; Bryan 176

FIGURE 3.1 *McKinley's 1898 Tour*

stenographer made careful notes on the intensity and duration of applause. McKinley's own ears presumably registered the more subtle sounds.

Paragraph's major point: _____

_____

I. By the time he had circled to Omaha, Nebraska, and started back through Iowa, the President had found his answer. At the Trans-Mississippi Exposition in Omaha, he asked, "Shall we deny to ourselves what the rest of the world so freely and so justly accords to us?" From the audience came a loud cry of "No!" He went on amid great applause to speak of "a peace whose great gain to civilization is yet unknown and unwritten" and to declare, "The war was not more invited by us than were the questions which are laid at our door by its results. Now as then we will do our duty."

Paragraph's major point: _____

_____

J. . . . After the reception given these words, he virtually ceased to sound the cautious note. . . . The President had heard the voice of the people. There can be no doubt that this was what he had waited for. . . . Earlier, when dealing with the Cuban issue, he had sought to escape public clamor and pursue safe, cautious courses defined by himself and conservative statesmen and businessmen around him. After the crisis that brought on the war, he wanted only to hear the wishes and obey.

Paragraph's major point: _____

_____

The following eight questions include five multiple choice and three short answer. For the multiple-choice questions, circle the letter(s) beside the answer(s) that correctly complete(s) the statement or respond(s) to the question. For the short-answer questions, write your response in the space provided.

1. May's thesis is that McKinley supported annexation of the Philippines
   a. for economic reasons.
   b. because of public opinion.
   c. because he feared that Germany would take over the islands.
   d. because he was a racist.

2. A piece of evidence in paragraph B that could be used to support a thesis other than May's is that
   a. the Germans and Irish in the United States would not tolerate annexation of the Philippines by England.
   b. France and Russia supported German annexation of the islands.
   c. the Philippines supposedly would provide good bases for trade and navigation.
   d. the Spanish treated Filipinos harshly.

3. May presents *direct* evidence to support his thesis for the first time in paragraph
   a. E.
   b. A.
   c. C.
   d. H.

4. Why is it fair to assume that in October 1898 McKinley was *more* concerned about public opinion than he was at the same time during the previous year?
   a. The year 1898 was a congressional election year; 1897 was not.
   b. A presidential election was just around the corner in October 1898.
   c. Public opinion naturally tends to be more emotional after a war has started than before.
   d. The Republican party was weaker in the fall of 1898 than it had been the year before.

5. Why, according to May, did McKinley choose on his speaking tour (paragraphs G–I) to visit states such as Indiana, Illinois, Iowa, Missouri, and Nebraska?
   a. These states all had hotly contested races in the upcoming congressional elections.
   b. McKinley had lived in all these states at one time or another.
   c. All these states were likely to be important in McKinley's bid for reelection in 1900.
   d. Several key U.S. senators were from these states, and McKinley was trying to influence their votes on a peace treaty with Spain by shaping public opinion in their states.

6. Does May believe that McKinley went on a speaking tour to the Midwest and

   Plains states primarily to gauge public opinion or to shape it? _____

   _____ On what basis do you reach your conclusion? _____

_____

On what evidence does May reach his conclusion? _____

_____

7. Copy a sentence in which May clearly goes beyond — but does not contradict — the evidence he presents in attributing a motive or a reaction to McKinley during his speaking tour. _____

_____

_____

8. Do you think that May draws a reasonable inference from his evidence here? _____ Explain. _____

_____

_____

You are now familiar with some of the ways in which historians interpret the past and with some of the critical methods with which you should approach their works. You probably considered Exercise 3 as requiring a meticulous examination of a secondary source, yet there are other steps you could take to evaluate the selection. For example, you could go to the primary sources cited by May and read them to determine whether or not he characterized them accurately and interpreted them wisely. You also could compare his interpretation of McKinley's decision with other secondary sources. Such a comparison might bring to light evidence that May chose not to include. In executing such tasks, you would need first to know your way around the library. Only then could you find the primary and secondary sources you needed. In the next chapter, we take you on a journey through the library to familiarize you with its many resources for the historian.

NOTES

1. Thomas A. Bailey, *A Diplomatic History of the American People,* 6th ed. (New York: Appleton-Century-Crofts, 1958), 460–461.
2. John Holladay Latane and David W. Wainhouse, *A History of American Foreign Policy,* 2nd ed. (New York: Odyssey Press, 1940), 511.
3. Richard Hofstadter, *The Paranoid Style in American Politics* (New York: Knopf, 1966), 148–149.
4. Ernest R. May, *American Imperialism* (New York: Atheneum, 1968), 228–229.
5. William Appleman Williams, *The Roots of the Modern American Empire* (New York: Random House, 1969), 408, 432.
6. Excerpt from Ernest R. May, *Imperial Democracy: The Emergence of America as a Great Power,* (Chicago: Imprint Publications, 1991), pp. 253–260.

4 FINDING EVIDENCE: LIBRARY SKILLS

The Progressive Era, World War I, and the 1920s

The library is the most crucial resource on any college campus. It houses the vast range of materials you will need in your coursework, provides space for individual or group study, and offers basic information on local and regional activities — political, cultural, and recreational — that may occupy your time outside academic pursuits. This resource will remain useful to you, both in the workplace and during leisure time, throughout your adult life. The acquisition of library skills is thus an important part of your college experience.

Such skills are best developed not by reading about them in a textbook but by going to the library and exploring its holdings. This chapter provides a series of exercises designed to take you through the library and show you how to benefit from its offerings. First you will find a list of user areas common to most libraries. Then a series of assignments will take you to several of those areas. At the same time, you will enhance your knowledge of the Progressive era, World War I, and the 1920s. The early exercises deal with primary sources, the later ones with secondary sources.

Although all libraries have certain common qualities, they also possess many idiosyncracies. Your library will have some or all of the areas listed in Exercise 1, yet their precise location will vary a good deal from one library to another. Whenever you enter any library for the first time, you should pick up a map of its rooms and areas of interest. Accordingly, the first exercise asks you to find and examine a library map. The remaining exercises require you to use several of the library's offerings.

Hunting for Primary Sources

Libraries possess a wide array of primary sources, from published materials such as books, magazines, and newspapers, to unpublished manuscript collections. To save space, libraries increasingly order microform versions of back issues of magazines and newspapers — on microfilm, microfiche, or microcards (microprint). Libraries sometimes do the same with important manuscript collections. Because libraries possess materials in various sizes, shapes, and conditions, some of which require special handling or machines for use, they always have separate sections. To find what you want, you will need to become familiar with these sections and their holdings.

EXERCISE 1: *Orienting Yourself in the Library*

The first step in developing library skills is to approach the library in an inquisitive state of mind. Few people, even noted research historians, get through most visits to the library without asking its staff for help. Sometimes library visitors check out books or order manuscript materials. On other occasions they need to ask questions. Begin your library experience by asking a staff member for a map of the premises. This map may be in a pamphlet introducing you to library facilities or may simply be hanging on a wall. Check off the areas in the list that appear on your map. If you do not find an area, go to the reference desk and ask a librarian if it exists in your library. Your map may be incomplete, or your campus may have another library that houses additional user areas. Once you have found the map, examine it carefully for the rooms or areas in the following list:

1. Reference desk
2. Card catalog or computer terminals
3. Circulation desk — where books are checked out
4. Reserve desk or room
5. Periodicals room or section
6. Stacks — where most books are located
7. Government-documents room or area
8. Rooms housing special collections of primary sources
9. Interlibrary loan area
10. Microfilm and microform reading area
11. Map room or area

Once you know where to find the main user areas in your library, you should be ready to go to work. Exercises 2 and 3 take you to the card catalog or the computer-assisted search terminal to track down books on various topics.

EXERCISE 2: *Using the Card Catalog or Computer Terminal to Find a Book (Part I)*

This exercise utilizes the card catalog or the computer-assisted search terminal to locate books in the stacks or shelving area of the library. Many college and university libraries no longer use card catalogs. Instead, all new acquisitions receive an entry in a computer. You can access this information by following a series of instructions on screens displayed by a computer terminal. Most library computer systems provide a list of possible commands — a menu — on the screen. The "GALIN" system at the University of Georgia Library is one such facility. Below we walk you through a search in the GALIN system. Then we examine a sample card from a card catalog.

Theodore Roosevelt is the first president of the Progressive era. One of the stronger and more colorful presidents in our nation's history, he has attracted more than his share of biographers. Let us turn to a computer terminal in the University of Georgia Library in search of a "life and times" biography of Roosevelt. We choose this kind of biography because it tends to be comprehensive.

```
        xXXXXXXXXx           xxXXXXXXxx
    xXXXX          XXXx      XXX      XX
   xXX              XXx     XXX
XXXXXXXXXXXXXXXXXXXXX     XXX            X
   XXXX     XXXX     XXXX  XXX    XXXXX    XXX
    XX      XX      XX     XXX    XXX    XX XX
    XX      XX      XX     XXXXXXXX  XX    XX
    XX      XX      XX              XXXXXXXXX    XXXX
    XX      XX      XX           XX       XX    XX
    XX      XX      XX           XX      XX    XX
    XX      XX      XX           XXXX       XXXX  XX
    XX      XX      XX                            XX    XXXX
    XX      XX      XX                          XX  XX  XX
    XX      XX      XX     Georgia          XXXXXXXX  XX
XXXXXXXXXXXXXXXXXXXXXXX      Academic           XX   XXXX    XXXX
XXXXXXXXXXXXXXXXXXXXXXX      Library             XX   XXXX   XX
                            Information          XX   XXXXX  XX
                            Network            XXXX  XX XXX XX
                                                     XX  XXXXX
                                                     XX   XXXX
         This is the University of Georgia Libraries' new     XXXX    XXX
         online access system.  Every display has instructions,
         and many help screens are available.
------------------------------------------------------------------------
Press the ENTER key to begin.
```

FIGURE 4.1 *The Welcome Screen*
Reprinted courtesy of University of Georgia Library.

Figure 4.1 shows the home page, the first screen you will see in the computer cataloging system. The screen welcomes you and invites you to begin your search.

When you press "enter" (sometimes the keyboard uses the left-handed arrow symbol or "return" instead of *enter*), you move to a screen displaying choices of library or other finding aids. Figure 4.2 shows this screen.

Since we want to find a book, rather than a newspaper, periodical, or reference volume, we pressed "1" for the "UGA Libraries' Catalog" and pressed "enter." Figure 4.3 shows the display.

```
                    Welcome to GALIN:
            Georgia Academic Library Information Network
-------------------------------------------------------------------
     Make a selection by typing its NUMBER, then press the ENTER key.
     (You may choose any of the first four categories from other screens
     by typing cho and the three-letter code, for example: cho ind )

       1.  UGA Libraries' Catalog                               uga

       2.  Indexes of journal'newspaper articles (8 databases)  ind

       3.  Reference sources (1 database)                       ref

       4.  Other library catalogs and statewide serials list    lib

       5.  News about the Libraries and GALIN                   news


--- OPTIONS ----------------------- UGA - UGA Library Catalog ---------
SUGgest    Quit

Command:

                                                        -LPAMOOBMS
```

FIGURE 4.2 *Selecting a Library: Finding Aids*
Reprinted courtesy of University of Georgia Library.

```
-------------------- THE UGA LIBRARIES' CATALOG --------------------
Type your command on the command line on the bottom of the screen, then
press the ENTER key.

FOR:                        TYPE:        ,--- Example command searches ---,
                                         |
 - User's guide/Help menu     h          | BROwse au walker, a
                                         | Find au hemingway ernest
 - Learn how to search        learn      | bro ti newsweek
                                         | f ti tale of two cities
 - Scope of this database     scope      | bro su georgia--history
                                         | f su animal and su ecolog?
                                         | f au walker and ti purple
 - Choose other databases     cho        | f su fusion and pd 1991-
                                         | f all cyberspace
 - Guided searching           guided     '--------------------------------'


        --- Names of commands and options can be abbreviated to only
            the letters shown in uppercase. (Type in lowercase.) ---

--- OPTIONS ------------------------- UGA - UGA Library Catalog -------
Back    Help    LEARN    SCOPE    CHOose    GUIDED    SUGgest    Quit
Command:

                                                        -LPAMOOUGA
```

FIGURE 4.3 *Help with Catalog: Command Choices*
Reprinted courtesy of University of Georgia Library.

We want to find a book on the subject "Theodore Roosevelt," so we typed in "f su Roosevelt, Theodore" and pressed "enter." Notice that we typed in Roosevelt's last name first. We do the same thing when we are doing author searches. In some systems, you must type an "=" after the "su" and you do not have to type in "f" (for "find"). Your system's menu will tell you which symbols to use. Figure 4.4 shows the first sixteen listed headings in the University of Georgia Library under the subject "Theodore Roosevelt." If

```
YOUR SEARCH: f su roosevelt, theodore              MATCHES:

---------------- SUBJECT HEADING ------------------------# of TITLES
  1. Roosevelt, Theodore, 1858-1918.                          1
  2. Roosevelt, Theodore, 1858-1919.                        135
  3. Roosevelt, Theodore, 1858-1919--Anniversaries, etc.      1
  4. Roosevelt, Theodore, 1858-1919--Archives--Catalogs.      1
  5. Roosevelt, Theodore, 1858-1919--Books and reading.       1
  6. Roosevelt, Theodore, 1858-1919--Cartoons, satire, etc.   1
  7. Roosevelt, Theodore, 1858-1919--Childhood and youth.     1
  8. Roosevelt, Theodore, 1858-1919--Correspondence.          2
  9. Roosevelt, Theodore, 1858-1919--Drama.                   1
 10. Roosevelt, Theodore, 1858-1919--Dwellings--North Dakota. 1
 11. Roosevelt, Theodore, 1858-1919--Family.                  4
 12. Roosevelt, Theodore, 1858-1919--Fiction.                 1
 13. Roosevelt, Theodore, 1858-1919--Iconography.             1
 14. Roosevelt, Theodore, 1858-1919--Journeys--Brazil.        1
 15. Roosevelt, Theodore, 1858-1919--Juvenile literature.     4
 16. Roosevelt, Theodore, 1858-1919--Knowledge and learning.  1

--- OPTIONS ----------------------- UGA - UGA Library Catalog ---------
More    Back    COMbine    Help    NEW    Quit
To display, type line number(s).  For example:  1 or 1,3-5
Command:
Enter "More" to See Additional Items.                -LIL01KWSU
```

FIGURE 4.4 *Subject Headings*
Reprinted courtesy of University of Georgia Library.

```
Command:
Enter "More" to See Additional Items                      -LIL01SBSU
YOUR SEARCH: f su Roosevelt, Theodore          MATCHES:         32
--------------- TITLE ------------------------ AUTHOR ---------- DATE -
Subject: Roosevelt, Theodore, 1858-1919.  {  135 Titles}
   16. Marquis de Mores in North Dakota.        Droulers, Charles   1979
   17. The Roosevelt chronicles                 Miller, Nathan, 19  1979
   18. Velvet on iron : the diplomacy of Theodor Marks, Frederick W  1979
   19. The rise of Theodore Roosevelt           Morris, Edmund.     1979
   20. The Bull Moose years : Theodore Roosevelt Gable, John A.      1978
   21. Chinese exclusion versus the open door po McKee, Delber L.,   1977
   22. Neither socialism nor monopoly : Theodore Chalmers, David Ma  1976
   23. The life and times of Theodore Roosevelt Harbaugh, William   1975
   24. The autobiography of Theodore Roosevelt : Roosevelt, Theodor  1975
   25. The real versus the rhetorical Theodore R Reter, Ronald Fran  1973
   26. Departing glory: Theodore Roosevelt as ex Gardner, Joseph La  1973
   27. Theodore Roosevelt and Afro-Americans, 19 Haney, James E.     1972
   28. The Rhetoric of the 1896 and 1900 Republi Nelson, Jeffrey Ar  1972
   29. Theodore Roosevelt,                       Burton, David Henr  1972
   30. Theodore Roosevelt: outdoorsman,          Wilson, R. L. (Rob  1971

--- OPTIONS ----------------------- UGA - UGA Library Catalog ---------
More    Back    List    Help    NEW    Quit
To display, type a line number.  For example:  1
Command:
Enter "More" to See Additional Items.                      -LIL01SBSU
```

FIGURE 4.5 *Listings Under "Roosevelt, Theodore"*
Reprinted courtesy of University of Georgia Library.

we wanted to see the remaining sixteen headings, we would type "more" and press "enter." However, number "2," with its 135 listings appears to be a promising place to find biographies. Thus we press "2" and then "enter."

The first page showed two possibilities for biographies, but since we were looking specifically for a "life and times" biography, we decided to examine the second page of fifteen listings by pressing "more" and then "enter." Figure 4.5 shows what we found.

```
YOUR SEARCH: f su Roosevelt, Theodore              MATCHES: 32
--------------------------- BRIEF DISPLAY -------------- 23 of 135 ---


          TITLE:    The life and times of Theodore Rooosevelt / William H.
                    Harbaugh.

         AUTHOR:    Harbaugh, William Henry, 1920-

        EDITION:    New, rev. ed.
      PUBLISHED:    Oxford : New York : Oxford University Press, c1975.
    DESCRIPTION:    xiv, 542 p. ; 21cm.

       SUBJECTS:    Roosevelt, Theodore, 1858-1919.
---LOCATION ----------------- CALL NUMBER ----------------- STATUS --
Main (4th)                    E757.H28 1975b               AVAILABLE



--- OPTIONS ----------------------- UGA - UGA Library Catalog ---------
More    Back    FUll    Next    PRevious    List    Help    NEW    Quit
For related titles, type either RAUthor, RSUbject, RSEries
Command:
                                                          -LITD01PB
```

FIGURE 4.6 *A Book Entry*
Reprinted courtesy of University of Georgia Library.

```
E757            Roosevelt, Theodore, president U. S.,
W817r           1858-1919
                Wister, Owen, 1860-1938.
                ...Roosevelt, the story of a friendship,
                1880-1919. New York, The Macmillan company,
                1930.

                v, 372, p., 1 1. front., illus., plates,
                ports., facsim. 24½cm.


                1. Roosevelt, Theodore, pres. U. S., 1858-
                1919. I. Title.

                        6           r       GU46-3250
                       ED                               6
```

FIGURE 4.7 *Card from the Card Catalog*

Number "23" appears to be exactly what we want, so we type in "23" and press "enter." Figure 4.6 displays the result.

The key for finding the actual book described in Figure 4.6 is to look under "location," "call number," and "status." In this case, the entry tells us that the book is located on the fourth floor under the call number E757.H28 1975b and that it is available (that is, it is not checked out of the library or on reserve). If we wanted to find the book, we could either write down the call number or copy a printout by pressing the "shift" and "alt" keys simultaneously and then the "ident" key.

Even if your library possesses a computer system for searches of its holdings, a card catalog may offer the only method for looking up older acquisitions. Figure 4.7 shows a card for a primary source on Theodore Roosevelt, a book published by a friend in 1930, eleven years after Roosevelt's death. Notice that the call number is in the upper lefthand corner and that the floor on which the book is located and the book's availability are not included.

You are now ready to do a search of your own.

EXERCISE 3: *Using the Card Catalog or Computer Terminal to Find a Book (Part II)*

This exercise has three options, all of which ask you to find a book on a particular topic in the stacks. Complete one of the options. (*Note:* If your library is small, you may have to try more than one before you are successful.)

Option A: Political History

In the library, find a volume that includes the papers of a president of the United States during the period 1900–1920. This volume may contain speeches, messages, letters, or any combination of the three. If you are not sure who the presidents were from 1900 to 1920, look up the chapters in your textbook that discuss politics during the Progressive era. Once you have a list of the presidents (there were four), go to the card catalog or computer terminal and find one of the presidents' names in the subject and, if necessary, the author index. The books probably will have the words *papers* or *letters* in their titles. On the write-on lines provided, write the full citation of this source (author, title, city: publisher, date). Here is a sample citation of a collection of a famous late-nineteenth-century politician:

> Allan Nevins, ed., *Letters of Grover Cleveland 1850–1908* (Boston: Houghton Mifflin Co., 1933).

Notice that the editor is listed as the author, even though he did not actually write the documents. The card catalog usually will list the book (or books, if they are a series) under both the author and the editor. Also make a note of the call number(s) for the book(s).

Source citation: _____

_____

Go to the stacks and find your source. If it is a series of volumes, select one. Using the index at the back of the volume, find a subject entry on a major issue of the day (examples: the tariff or other taxes, antitrust legislation, conservation, government regulation of banking). Go to the pages indicated, select one document, photocopy the statement, and clip it to this page of your workbook. Your instructor may call on you to discuss the document in class.

Option B: Social History

Using the subject index of the card catalog or computer terminal, find a book that is a primary source for one of the following topics on the early twentieth century (1900–1930):

> abortion
> birth control
> divorce
> sexual practices, including homosexuality
> prostitution
> the role of women

You usually can identify a primary source by its initial publication date. A primary source for the Progressive era thus will have been published between 1900 and 1930, or shortly thereafter. Sometimes, however, the initial publication date will not appear in the card catalog or computer terminal listing, so you may have to check the book's copyright page to be certain.

Provide a full citation of your source in the space following. Look through the source for a statement that reflects an attitude strikingly different from views that prevail today. (For example, if your source is on birth control, a statement opposing the use of birth control devices would be very different from prevailing views in the present.) Identify that attitude, and explain how it differs from present-day attitudes.

Source citation: _____

_____

Differing attitude: _____

_____

_____

_____

Option C: Science and Technology

Find a book that describes how a scientific or technological advance altered life in America between 1870 and 1930. If the book itself is not a primary source, be sure that it reproduces one or more primary sources from that period (pictures as well as written documents are acceptable). Provide a full citation for your source. Briefly describe the change. If the book is a secondary source, photocopy an example of a primary source from it, and clip the copy to this page. Your instructor may ask you to discuss the primary source in class.

Source citation: _____

_____

Resulting change: _____

_____

_____

_____

EXERCISE 4: *Using Census Records*

The U.S. government conducts a national census during the first year of every decade. Its results appear in print between one and four years later. The more recent the census is, the more elaborate detail it provides. The following assignments familiarize you with census records and increase your knowledge of population change in America between 1900 and 1920.

Go to the government-documents section of the library. Ask a librarian to help you find the census records. Pull off the shelf Volume 1 on population for the 1900 census and Volumes 1 and 2 for the 1920 census. Use the table of contents and index of each volume to find the information you need to answer the following questions.

1. Identify the center of population in the United States in 1900 and in 1920. How did the center change over the twenty-year period? _____

   _____

2. What was the total population of the forty-five states in 1900? _____

3. What territories became states between 1900 and 1920? _____

   _____

4. What present-day states remained territories in 1920? _____

5. Name one territory that was acquired by the United States between 1900 and 1920.

   _____

6. Was a larger percentage of blacks classified as urban in 1900 or 1920? _____

   Did this pattern follow the overall national trend toward urbanization during those

   two decades? _____

7. How is the concept "urban" defined in the 1900 census? _____

   _____

In the 1920 census? _____

_____

What is the significance of this change? _____

_____

8. The census of 1920 shows a huge number of immigrants coming to the United States over the previous ten years. From what continent did most of those immigrants travel? _____

If we divided this continent into four regions — northwestern, central, eastern, and southern — which would have the *fewest* people moving to the United States between 1900 and 1920? _____

_____

Which country outside Europe (excluding Canada) had the most people moving to the United States between 1900 and 1920? _____
Explain why, based on information in your textbook. (*Hint:* Look up the country in the index of your textbook.) _____

_____

9. In both 1910 and 1920, there were more males than females in the U.S. population, with a larger disparity in 1910. How does the 1920 census explain the actual reduction in the disparity between 1910 and 1920? _____

_____

_____

EXERCISE 5: *Using Microfilm*

Space is a precious commodity in the modern library. Thus microform editions of documents are increasingly useful. Microform is a method of reproducing greatly reduced images. Microfilm is the most common type of microform. Using any type of microform requires special magnifying machines, which libraries generally place, along with the microforms, in a separate room.

After taking you briefly to the reference area, this exercise introduces you to the microfilm reading room, where you will use some back issues of a newspaper. First, ask your reference librarian to help you find the *Encyclopedia of American History,* edited by Richard B. Morris. In the encyclopedia, look up the dates of the outbreak of war in Europe in 1914, the U.S. declaration of war against Germany in 1917, and President Woodrow Wilson's 14 points in 1918. Write the dates here. _____

_____

Now go to the *New York Times Index.* (Ask the reference librarian for help if necessary.) Find three articles that discuss, first, the outbreak of war and its implications for the United States, second, the debate in Congress on whether or not to declare war, and, third, the reaction to Wilson's 14 points. Write down the articles' dates and page numbers.

_____

_____

_____

_____

Ask a reference librarian to direct you to the serials catalog, which lists all the newspapers and periodicals held by your library. This catalog may be in the main reference room or in the periodicals room. Find the card for the *New York Times*. Write down the call number and ask a librarian where the *New York Times* is stored. It probably will be in or near the microfilm reading area. Back issues of newspapers are usually available only on microfilm because it is far less bulky to store than the actual papers. Normally, each reel covers ten or more issues. If the microfilm is in an open area, you can go right to it. If not, you will have to fill out an order slip that lists the dates of the issues you want to examine. When you have the microfilm in hand, ask a librarian to show you how to use a microfilm reader. Once your microfilm is set up in the machine, you are ready to do your assignment.

Find and read the articles that discuss the pertinent issues. Take notes on the articles on a separate sheet of paper to answer such questions as these: What concerns do the articles on each one of the issues discuss? Do the articles simply outline the views of others, or do they offer their own opinions? What are the opinions outlined or expressed? Are any biases revealed in the articles, in the title or in the body? If so, what are they? At the top of your notes on each article, write down the article's date, title and author (if identified), and page number(s). Be prepared to discuss the articles and the issues in class.

EXERCISE 6: *Using the Internet*

Most college and university libraries have computers with access to the Internet, a worldwide database. Sometimes it is faster and easier to look up information on the Internet than in the stacks. At times, there is information on the Internet that is not available in hard copy in your library. It is useful, therefore, to be familiar with the Internet. This exercise introduces you to this valuable source.

Below we walk you through an abbreviated search for an important document from the World War I era, the Covenant of the League of Nations. The search is abbreviated because we give you an address on the World Wide Web without which you would have to go through at least two more steps. Despite the relative simplicity of this search, if you have not used the Internet before, you may want to ask a reference librarian to help you, especially if your library computer system does not possess "Netscape," the most widely used Web browser. Also, Web site addresses can change, and if this has happened to the address for "The World War I Document Archive," you certainly will want to ask for assistance.

Call up "Netscape" on your computer. Then hold down the left mouse button, and move the mouse arrow on the screen to the selection "Open" at the top of the screen. When the new screen appears, type in the following address (make sure every character is accurate):

   http://www.lib.byu.edu/~rdh/wwi/

Then press "enter."

The next screen to appear should be the beginning of "The World War I Document Archive." (If it is not, either the address has changed or you have made a mistake.) The document we seek is listed under "Conventions, Treaties, & Official Papers," which does not appear on the first screen. Thus you must move to subsequent screens until you find that category (it is on the second screen). To do this, move the mouse arrow to the down scroll arrow on the right side of the screen. Then hold down the left mouse button until the next screen appears. When you see the desired category, move the mouse arrow to the text, and click the left mouse button. The procedure will take you to a list of agreements of the World War I era. Go through the procedure you used to find "Conventions, Treaties, & Official Papers"; only now look for "The Peace Treaty of Versailles." Click the mouse arrow on this title, which will take you to a list of the parts of that treaty. Find "The Covenant of the League of Nations," and click the mouse arrow on that listing. This will bring the beginning of that document to the screen.

In the United States, the League of Nations was the most controversial part of the Treaty of Versailles. Article 10 of the Covenant was the most controversial section of the document. The treaty was rejected by the Senate, partly because President Wilson refused to compromise on that article. Move down the document until Article 10 appears on the screen. Print a copy of this article by moving the mouse arrow to the "Print" option at the top. Read the article carefully, and try to think of why many members of the Senate might have objected to it. Keep your copy of the article, and be prepared to discuss it in class.

You have now completed your search. If you wish to exit from the Internet, put the mouse arrow on the "File" option at the top of the screen, click the left mouse button, and then hold the button down until you are on "Exit" and click again.

Finding Secondary Sources

Your experience in finding and using primary sources should ease the task of finding secondary sources. Such sources often are housed in the same areas as primary sources. The stacks, for example, include printed primary and secondary sources. So does the periodicals section. There are exceptions, however. The government-documents, special collections, and microfilm sections of the library hold largely primary sources, whereas the reference section holds mostly secondary sources. In some libraries, both primary and secondary sources are listed in the main card catalog or the computer terminal. Ask a reference librarian if this is so in your library.

Review the following list and brief description of some useful secondary works in American history. Some of these offer basic data in American history; others are bibliographies. Notice the date of publication of these tools for historical research.

Historical Dictionaries and Encyclopedias

An Encyclopedia of World History (Boston: Hougton Mifflin, 1972), ed. William Langer. This is an impressive compilation of facts from ancient times to the modern world. In American history, it is useful primarily in dealing with U.S. involvement in major world events.

Dictionary of American Biography (New York: Charles Scribner's Sons, 1928–1988). This multivolume work provides invaluable information on more than 18,000 important Americans who died before 1970.

Notable American Women (Cambridge, Mass.: Harvard University Press, 1971–1980), ed. Edward T. James. Three of the four volumes in this set appeared in 1971 and covered prominent American women who died before 1951. The fourth volume appeared in 1980 and included women who died between January 1, 1951, and December 31, 1975. The volumes include many more women than does the *Dictionary of American Biography.*

Encyclopedia of American History, 7th ed. (New York: HarperCollins, 1982), eds. Richard B. Morris and Jeffrey B. Morris. You used this source in Exercise 5. It is extremely useful for basic facts in American history.

A note about historical dictionaries and encyclopedias: these sources frequently overlap in the information they provide, yet they always have different emphases. Some are extremely broad in their coverage but provide limited detail on any given topic. Others cover a relatively narrow area but in considerable detail. Sometimes you can get a good idea of the depth of information provided merely by looking at the title and length of the source. The narrower the subject matter covered in the title and the lengthier the source, the more detailed is the information you are likely to find there. In other cases, however, you will need to go to the source itself. Two historical dictionaries of World War I, for example, might be of relatively equal length, but one might place emphasis on military events while another centers on politics and diplomacy. To discover this difference, you might have to read the preface of each source or perhaps even study their contents.

Statistical Compilations

Historical Statistics of the United States, Colonial Times to 1970 (Washington, D.C.: Bureau of the Census, 1976).

Statistical Abstract of the United States (Washington, D.C.: Government Printing Office, 1878–present). Annual.

Indexes and Bibliographies

American History and Life. This is a wonderful source for periodical literature on American history published since 1954. It includes articles and book reviews. Multiple volumes have appeared annually since 1974, the last being an index to all the others. Because this source can be difficult to use, ask a reference librarian to assist you on your first try.

Arts and Humanities Citation Index. This source is especially useful in finding reviews of books.

Book Review Digest. This annual volume has been published continuously since 1905 and provides a particularly good list of the short book reviews that appear within a year of a book's publication.

Book Review Index. Since 1965 this source has listed book reviews, mostly those that have appeared within a year of a book's publication.

Harvard Guide to American History, 2 vols. (Cambridge, Mass.: Harvard University Press, 1974), ed. Frank Friedel and Richard Showman. This is a standard bibliographical guide to American history, but it needs updating.

Humanities Index. Since 1974 this series has provided a monthly index to scholarly American and British journals, including book reviews. Previous titles of this index were *Reader's Guide to Periodical Literature Supplement* (1907–1919), *International Index* (1920–1965), and *Social Sciences and Humanities Index* (1965–1974).

Index to Book Reviews in the Humanities. Since 1960 this source has indexed several hundred English-language periodicals, including history titles and book reviews.

Journal of American History. Recent issues of this journal will probably be in the periodicals area, old ones in the stacks. Each issue includes listings of recent articles and doctoral dissertations in American history.

Writings in American History. This series began in 1903, skipped 1904 and 1905, but then was published continuously through 1961. Each volume covers books and articles on American history published over the one- or two-year period included in the volume title. Suspended after 1961 for financial reasons, it resumed publication in 1974 with a volume covering articles published on American history during 1973 and 1974. A four-volume set appeared listing articles published between 1962 and 1973.

Comprehensive Guides to Reference Sources in History

Jules R. Benjamin, *A Student's Guide to History,* 4th ed. (New York: St. Martin's Press, 1991). See especially Chapter 4, "How to Research a History Topic"; Appendix A, "Basic Reference Sources for History Study and Research"; and Appendix B, "Useful Information for the Historian."

Helen J. Poulton, *The Historian's Handbook: A Descriptive Guide to Reference Works* (Norman: University of Oklahoma Press, 1972). Chapter 3, "Guides, Manuals, and Bibliographies of History"; Chapter 4, "Encyclopedias and Dictionaries"; Chapter 8, "Biographical Materials"; and Chapter 11, "Government Publications," are particularly useful.

In what often seems like an attempt to confuse users, some libraries do not place all volumes of reference sources in the same place. If you become frustrated in your search for some of these, ask a librarian for help.

The following exercises send you to some of the previously mentioned reference works or to the stacks and periodicals area. They will develop your skills both in using the library and in working with secondary sources.

EXERCISE 7: *The Reference Section Revisited*

This two-part exercise exposes you to some of the differences among various historical dictionaries and encyclopedias. Your instructor may give you the option of doing Part I or Part II.

Part I

Jane Addams, Carrie Chapman Catt, and Margaret Sanger all contributed mightily to reform during the Progressive era and the 1920s. Choose *one* of these three prominent Americans and look up her biography in the *Dictionary of American Biography, Notable American Women,* and either the *Encyclopaedia Britannica* or the *Encyclopedia Americana.* After reading the biographical sketch, answer the following questions.

1. Outline two things that the articles have in common, besides being about the same individual.

   a. _____

   _____

   b. _____

   _____

2. Outline two ways in which the pieces differ. For example, do they differ in the amount of information provided?

a. _____

_____

b. _____

_____

You now have some familiarity with the three reference sources. You might have to complete the two following assignments in a future history class. Which source would you begin with in each case, and why?

3. A term paper on woman's suffragist Carrie Chapman Catt.

Source: _____

Why? _____

_____

4. A five-page paper providing sketches on a dozen leading politicians during the Progressive era.

Source: _____

Why? _____

_____

_____

Part II

Take the *Encyclopedia of American History* and *An Encyclopedia of World History* off the shelf. Open each to the section that discusses the United States and World War I. Read through the sections and answer the following questions.

1. Which source helps you more in understanding U.S. policy during the first two and a half years of the war?

Source: _____

Explain: _____

_____

_____

2. Which source gives you a better sense of the progression of the fighting after the United States entered the war?

Source: _____

Explain: _____

_____

_____

3. Which source gives you a better sense of the diplomacy of peacemaking among the European belligerents during 1918 and 1919?

Source: _____

Explain: _____

_____

_____

4. Which source gives you a better sense of the politics of peacemaking *within* the United States?

Source: _____

Explain: _____

_____

5. After doing this assignment, which of the two sources would you consult first if you were looking for basic facts on the origins of the Cold War?

Source: _____

Explain: _____

_____

_____

Just as individual reference sources have distinctive purposes, so do secondary works of a more interpretive nature. In Chapter 3, we listed and defined various types of history. The Progressive era has stimulated a rich historiography in all of the categories mentioned. The next two exercises introduce you to some of the historical literature on that period. These exercises not only will improve your skills in using a library, but also will develop your ability to evaluate secondary sources.

EXERCISE 8: *Finding Secondary Sources for Different Types of History*

Following are listed two of the seven types of history identified in Chapter 3. Using the subject index of the card catalog or computer terminal, find a book on the 1920s for each of the two types. (Refer to Chapter 3 if you need to refresh your memory of social and cultural history topics.) Your sources must qualify as secondary sources and possess a publication date after 1939. Write a full citation for the books in the space provided. Remember that full citations include the following information: author's first name, then last name, *full title* (city: publisher, year of publication).

Social history: _____

_____

Cultural history: _____

_____

Now, using the reference guides *American History and Life, Writings in American History,* and the *Journal of American History,* find a journal article on the 1920s for each of these two types of history. The first two of those sources may be available in your library in both hard and computerized copies or in only one or the other. Again, list the full citations for the articles. Journal citations include the author's first name, then last name, full article title, *journal title,* volume (date): page numbers.

Social history: _____

_____

Cultural history: _____

_____

Evaluating Secondary Sources

The books and articles you listed in Exercise 8 may vary a good deal in quality. One way to judge quality is to read the materials yourself. There are certain standards by which historians normally judge each other's work. Although historians often disagree, they generally accept originality and persuasiveness of argument, adequacy of research, and clarity and felicity of writing style as key elements in any evaluation. The significance of the topic covered also is important. A book or article may be outstanding in all the criteria mentioned above and still be a minor contribution to the literature because of its limited scope.

Historians spend a good deal of time evaluating each other's work. Such evaluations can help you not only to judge the quality of secondary sources but also to comprehend the debates that occur among historians. The book review is a major source of historians' evaluations of each other. Exercise 9 asks you to find two book reviews and examine them as instruments of evaluation and debate.

EXERCISE 9: *Locating and Examining Book Reviews*

Find two reviews of *one* of the books in the following list. For the most part, reviews appear within two years of a book's publication, so check listings in *American History and Life* for the year of publication and the three years following. *Each review you choose must be at least 400 words long, and you should give priority to longer reviews.*

Ellis W. Hawley, *The Great War and the Search for a Modern Order: A History of the American People and Their Institutions, 1917–1933* (1979).

William E. Leuchtenberg, *The Perils of Prosperity, 1914–1932* (1958).

Robert Sobel, *The Great Bull Market: Wall Street in the 1920s* (1968).

Joan Hoff Wilson, *Herbert Hoover: Forgotten Progressive* (1975).

Reviews:

1. _____

_____

2. _____

_____

Go to the journals, find the reviews, and photocopy them. Remember that in most libraries the periodical room holds journals for only a year or so after their publication; they are then bound and placed in the stacks.

Read each review carefully, highlighting each statement that constitutes a judgment about one of the five categories of evaluation mentioned earlier: originality, persuasiveness, adequacy of research, writing style, and significance. Be prepared to discuss the reviews in class and to hand them in if your instructor desires.

We hope that these exercises have familiarized you with your library. The thought of going there to find something should be a bit less intimidating than before. Now you can enter the library feeling like a veteran detective seeking information that will solve a puzzle, rather than like a person stranded for the first time in a new city. Searching for materials in a library represents an early stage in producing history, however; only after you write about what you found is your task completed. In Chapter 5, we turn to the final stage: narrative and expository writing.

5 NARRATIVE AND EXPOSITION: TELLING THE STORY

The Great Depression

Narrative, according to one dictionary, is "an orderly, continuous account of an event or series of events." **Exposition** is "an explanation" of or "commentary" on an event, series of events, or issue. Most historical writing combines the two: it both tells a story and explains events.

Writing can be fun, but it is nearly always hard work. You cannot avoid the latter, but this chapter offers some guidelines and exercises that, along with the analytical skills you have already learned in this book, will improve the final product of your efforts. Because the rest of this volume includes substantial writing assignments, it is critical that you develop basic writing skills here.

Making Your Point

A historical essay must have an identifiable beginning, middle, and end. The beginning, or *introduction*, should tell the reader what the essay is about. In a short essay of the kind you would write for an examination, the introduction should be no more than one short paragraph. In a longer essay, such as one you might write as a term paper in an upper-level class, the introduction might be a page or slightly longer. In addition to informing readers, the ideal introduction will engage them, enticing them to read on.

The middle, or *body*, of the essay should continue to engage readers, but primarily it develops the major theme. A theme is the writer's argument or interpretation of an event. In an essay on the origins of the Great Depression, for example, the theme would explain why that event occurred. If the essay author subscribed to the monetarist interpretation, he or she would center the theme on the ill-advised policies of the Federal Reserve Board. The essay's body contains both descriptive and explanatory detail; thus it is normally several times as long as each of the other sections.

The end, or *conclusion*, pulls together the material in the body. In some cases, it merely summarizes key points made in the body; in other cases, it goes beyond anything stated explicitly in the body to develop the full implications of the material covered. Although the conclusion should be much shorter than the body, it is not as restricted in length as the introduction.

One thing common to beginnings, middles, and ends is that they are divided into paragraphs. Paragraphs contain the basic units of thought in an essay and carry the reader forward in a logical sequence from one point to the next. In turn, the central organizing device in a paragraph is the *topic sentence*, which states the paragraph's main idea. Sometimes the topic sentence offers a generalization that takes two or even several paragraphs to discuss. The third paragraph in this chapter, for instance, begins with a topic sentence about essays that serves three paragraphs. We could have combined the third, fourth, and fifth paragraphs into one, but we thought that dividing up the material on the beginnings, middles, and ends of essays would help you understand the material more easily.

Our choice demonstrates the fact that writers possess a good deal of freedom within broad guidelines. Topic sentences usually cover one paragraph and come at the beginning of paragraphs, but there are exceptions. We prefer to keep our paragraphs from a quarter to a third of a page in length, long enough to develop a thought but not so long as to tire or confuse the reader. Yet some paragraphs in this workbook are shorter than that, and others are longer. Furthermore, when we write for an audience of fellow professional historians, we use somewhat different rules than we do here. Guidelines are not hard and fast: sometimes they are broken or adapted to different circumstances. Nonetheless, you need to keep them in mind and remember that the fundamental purpose of writing is to communicate with your audience.

The first four exercises in this chapter give you some practice in analyzing paragraphs. They will help you to distinguish among paragraphs that appear at the beginning, middle, or end of narratives; to identify information that does or does not fit together; to grasp the conclusions that may be drawn from a narrative; and to spot qualifiers, or statements that limit generalizations. By the end of the chapter, you will be ready to write an essay that combines narration and exposition.

EXERCISE 1: *Beginnings, Middles, and Ends*

The following excerpts from a book by a distinguished historian are chosen to help you learn about narrative. Each comes from the introduction, the body, or the conclusion of a book on the Depression and the New Deal. Comparing them reveals some of the differences between beginnings, middles, and ends, as well as some of the characteristics of good historical writing.

Ⓐ The following excerpt is the first paragraph in *The Crisis of the Old Order, 1919–1933*, by Arthur M. Schlesinger, Jr. The book focuses on American politics from the end of World War I to Franklin D. Roosevelt's assumption of the presidency in March 1933. Read the passage and answer the questions that follow.

The White House, midnight, Friday, March 3, 1933. Across the country the banks of the nation had gradually shuttered their windows and locked their doors. The very machinery of the American economy seemed to be coming to a stop. The rich and fertile nation, overflowing with natural wealth in its fields and forests and mines, equipped with unsurpassed technology, endowed with boundless resources in its men and women, lay stricken. "We are at the end of our rope," the weary President at last said, as the striking clock announced the day of his retirement. "There is nothing more we can do."[1]

1. Why do you suppose Schlesinger opens with a scene from 1933, chronologically the termination point of the book? _____

   _____

2. The topic sentence of the paragraph is the third sentence, not the first. Why do you think Schlesinger chose to place that sentence third rather than first? _____

   _____

   _____

3. Do you find the paragraph engaging? Why or why not? _____

   _____

4. What role does the quotation at the end of the paragraph play? _____

   _____

5. What effect does Schlesinger seek by referring to Herbert Hoover as the "President" rather than using his name? _____

   _____

6. What qualities does the paragraph possess that mark it as a beginning? _____

   _____

   B The next paragraph is from the middle of Schlesinger's book. Read it and answer the questions that follow.

   At the breadlines and soup kitchens, hours of waiting would produce a bowl of mush, often without milk or sugar, and a tin cup of coffee. The vapors from the huge steam cookers mingling with the stench of wet clothes and sweating bodies made the air foul. But waiting in the soup kitchen was better than the scavenging in the dump. Citizens of Chicago, in this second winter, could be seen digging into heaps of refuse with sticks and hands as soon as the garbage trucks pulled out. On June 30, 1931, the Pennsylvania Department of Labor and Industry reported that nearly one-quarter of the labor force of the state was out of work. Clarence Pickett of the Friends found schools where 85, 90, even 99 per cent of the children were underweight, and, in consequence, drowsy and lethargic. "Have you ever heard a hungry child cry?" asked Lillian Wald of Henry Street. "Have you seen the uncontrollable trembling of parents who have gone half starved for weeks so that the children may have food?"[2]

1. Does the paragraph capture your interest? Why or why not? _____

   _____

2. What are some of the words Schlesinger uses that help capture your attention? _____

   _____

   _____

3. Schlesinger uses direct quotations at the end of paragraphs A and B. What purpose do they serve? _____

   _____

4. There is no topic sentence in paragraph B. Do you think the paragraph is strengthened or weakened by the absence of a topic sentence? _____

   Why? _____

   _____

5. Write a topic sentence for the paragraph. _____

   _____

   Where would you put it? _____

   Why? _____

6. Do you think paragraph B could be used effectively at the beginning or end of an article or book? Explain your answer. _____

   _____

   C The following passage is the last paragraph in Schlesinger's book. Read it and answer the questions that follow.

> Many had deserted freedom, many more had lost their nerve. But Roosevelt, armored in some inner faith, remained calm and inscrutable, confident that American improvisation could meet the future on its own terms. And so on March 4, as he took the silent ride in the presidential limousine down the packed streets to the Capitol, he was grim and unafraid. Deep within, he seemed to know that the nation had resources beyond its banks and exchanges; that the collapse of the older order meant catharsis [purging and cleansing] rather than catastrophe; that the common disaster could make the people see themselves for a season as a community, as a family; that catastrophe could provide the indispensable setting for democratic experiment and for presidential leadership. If this were so, then crisis could change from calamity to challenge. The only thing Americans had to fear was fear itself. And so he serenely awaited the morrow. The event was in the hand of God.[3]

1. Which is the topic sentence of the paragraph? _____

   _____

   Why doesn't Schlesinger place it first? _____

   _____

2. What distinguishes this paragraph as a last rather than a first paragraph? If you wish, compare this paragraph with paragraph A. _____

   _____

3. Although this paragraph serves as the book's conclusion, the book is the first in a multivolume study entitled *The Age of Roosevelt.* In what way does the paragraph serve as both an end to one volume and a lead-in to another? _____

   _____

4. As in paragraphs A and B, Schlesinger paints a mental picture in paragraph C, an image in the reader's mind of a past situation. Identify one method he uses to create that picture. _____

   _____

5. Summarize the qualities that Schlesinger displays in the three quoted paragraphs that make him an effective writer. _____

_____

EXERCISE 2: *Detecting "Ringers"*

Each paragraph of a narrative tells part of a story, and every part is the result of a series of decisions by the author about what to include and what to leave out. Think of a narrative as a dish of fine cuisine. Behind that dish is a recipe with a variety of ingredients in very precise amounts. If those ingredients changed, so would the flavors in the dish. If the amounts fluctuated, so would the balance of flavors. In crafting a narrative, you must constantly ask yourself what material belongs, what does not, and, for the material that does belong, what portion of it should be included. Every sentence in a narrative could be made longer by the insertion of more information. Every paragraph could be extended in the same way. You have to decide what kinds of information fit together, and in what proportion.

Read the following three passages on the Great Depression. Each one has a sentence that should be removed — a "ringer"—because it is not essential to the narrative or contradicts the other sentences. Underline the sentence that should be deleted. Explain your answer in the space provided after each passage. The first passage is completed for you as an example.

A. The United States of the 1930s remained a giant step from the nation that, in the aftermath of World War II, took over Great Britain's nineteenth-century role as international balancer. Early in the decade, Washington did little to stem the tide of economic collapse abroad. Indeed, the Hawley-Smoot tariff adopted in mid-1930 produced the highest barriers to imports into the United States of the entire twentieth century; the stubborn insistence on continuing payments on war debts into the following year played havoc with Europe's need for capital; and the refusal to cooperate with the British at the London Economic Conference during the summer of 1933 prevented any stabilization of exchange rates. Politically, the United States did little to cultivate a multilateral response to the aggressions of Japan, Germany, and Italy. <u>Mussolini's rise to power in the last country in the 1920s produced only a marginal response in Paris, London, and Washington</u>. Even with the outbreak of war in Europe in September 1939, American policymakers remained determined to avoid direct involvement on the eastern shores of the Atlantic.

Explanation: The sentence deals with the 1920s rather than the 1930s and involves the responses of Great Britain and France as well as the United States.

B. Americans in the early 1930s yearned for a dynamic, self-assured leader in the White House, a man who could restore the nation's confidence in the aftermath of the stock market crash and the subsequent nose dive of the economy. Herbert Hoover proved unequal to the task. An engineer by training and an introvert by disposition, he lacked the intellectual flexibility and the personal flair to guide a democratic, pluralistic nation through its time of trial. To him, the ideal vacation was a weekend of fly fishing in a trout stream in the Virginia mountains. Only after Franklin D. Roosevelt, a seemingly shallow New York patrician, took the oath of office in March of 1933 did the national mood begin to shift.

Explanation: _____

_____

_____

C. The most powerful political asset that African-Americans and women held in Washington, D.C., during the New Deal years was the president's wife, Eleanor. An activist in a variety of reform causes since World War I, Eleanor Roosevelt was determined as First Lady to be more than the keeper of her husband's social calendar. During the 1940s, she would become an enthusiastic supporter of U.S. involvement in the United Nations. She called her own press conferences and permitted entry only to female reporters. She met frequently with relief administrator Harry Hopkins, taking special interest in jobs for women and African-Americans. She nudged FDR leftward on appointments for these underrepresented groups. For her efforts, she gained a special place in the hearts of the downtrodden, but she also sparked criticism and nasty rumors, especially among tradition-minded white southerners.

Explanation: _____

_____

_____

EXERCISE 3: *Drawing Inferences*

In the end, the purpose of an essay is to persuade the reader to accept the author's point. To do so, a story has to make sense. The following exercise asks you to determine whether a passage supports a series of inferences, or conclusions, drawn from evidence. If we know that a river flows from north to south, for example, we can infer that most boats traveling on the river will move faster when going southward than when going northward. This conclusion might not turn out to be true, but it still would be reasonable, given the available evidence.

After each of the following passages, you will find four statements. Each statement purports to be true. Decide which can be sustained by the passage. If you think that the statement follows logically from the narrative, write *true* in the space provided. If the statement is contradicted by what you have read, write *false*. If there is no evidence one way or the other, write *cannot determine*. Be prepared to justify your answers in class.

A. As late as 1940 there were still 1,250,000 women seeking work, and another 450,000 women were employed on public emergency work. Along with unemployment, women workers had to face the additional obstacle of prejudice and discrimination on the part of their prospective employers and coworkers. The antagonism toward the woman worker, which had always been present, even in times of prosperity, was greatly intensified by the Depression. Its most severe impact was felt by the white-collar woman worker, especially if she happened to be married.[4]

1. During the Depression, more women than men were seeking work. _____

2. Antagonism toward married women in the workplace was greater than antagonism toward unmarried women. _____

3. Antagonism toward women in the workplace was greater during the Depression than during previous times of prosperity. _____

4. During the Depression, more women were employed in the private than in the public sector. _____

B. Watching the bureaucratic history of [Civilian Conservation Corps] camps for unemployed women was a frustrating experience for Hilda Washington Smith and her colleagues in the [women's] network. Expectations for camps for women were always far below the scale proposed for camps for men. Hilda Smith felt this discrepancy keenly: "The CCC camps with their millions of dollars for wages, educational work, travel, and supervision constantly remind me of what we might do for women from these same families. *As [is] so often the case, the boys get the breaks, the girls are neglected.* Even though similar plans for women are more difficult to develop, I do not believe they should be discarded as impossible" [emphasis added]. Yet as a result of the efforts of women like Smith, Eleanor Roosevelt, and other prominent women administrators, the government at least made a token effort to meet the needs of these young women. While not a stunning achievement in numbers (8,500 women compared to 2.5 million men), the camps might not have materialized at all without the dedication and persistence of certain members of the network.[5]

1. During the 1930s, well-connected women played a crucial role in getting some government assistance for less fortunate women. _____

2. New Deal programs provided just as many benefits for women as for men. _____

3. Civilian Conservation Corps camps for women were less well equipped than those for men. _____

4. The New Deal served more men than women, but those women who did get government aid got just as much as their male counterparts. _____

EXERCISE 4: *Qualifiers*

It is difficult to know why one narrative is more convincing than another. Certainly, detail and logic are important. So is a graceful style of storytelling. Most important, however, is conveying to your readers a sense that you have given all the points of view on your subject a fair hearing. You cannot take all of them equally into account; if you did, your narrative would degenerate into a mass of conflicting statements. The challenge is to choose among them while reassuring your reader that you have not ignored the ones you ultimately reject.

One way to convince your reader that your account is balanced and reasonable is through the use of *qualifiers*, words that modify or limit your claims. *Many, few, some, usually, sometimes, increasing, decreasing, liberal, conservative,* and the like are all qualifiers. Phrases as well as single words can serve as qualifiers. The following passage on unemployment during the Depression is filled with qualifiers. Three of them are underlined. Underline six more.

Men of <u>old-fashioned</u> principles <u>really</u> believed that the less said about the unemployed, the faster they would get jobs. They really believed that public relief was bad for the poor because it discouraged them from looking for work or from taking it at wages that would tempt business to start up again. <u>According to their theory</u>, permanent mass unemployment was impossible, because there was work at some wage for every able-bodied man, if he would only find and do it. Charity was necessary, of course, for those who were really disabled through no fault of their own, but there could never be very many of these, and they should be screened carefully and given help of a kind and in a way that would keep them from asking for it as long as possible. Those who held this view were not necessarily hardhearted or self-interested.

Josephine Lowell, a woman who devoted her life to the poor, issued the bluntest warn-ing: "The presence in the community of certain persons living on public relief has the tendency to tempt others to sink to their degraded level." That was in 1884, when cities were smaller, and fewer people depended on the ups and downs of factory work.[6]

Some Qualities of Good Writing: A Review

Good writing is not always easy to define, but the first four exercises in this chapter pro-vide some guidelines. In general, a well-written essay has an identifiable structure — an introduction, body, and conclusion — as well as paragraphs containing clear topic sen-tences. The structure helps the reader follow the development of the story or argument. A well-written essay also contains words and phrases that capture and hold the reader's attention. Active verbs, colorful quotations from primary sources, and short, crisp sen-tences all engage the reader. A plausible thesis based on the logical presentation of evi-dence is also important. Opinions develop from the evidence presented and, although they need not be restricted to a narrow interpretation of the facts, are qualified suffi-ciently to prevent the reader from suspecting excessive bias. Keep these points in mind as you work on Exercise 5.

EXERCISE 5: *Writing an Essay*

This exercise asks you to write an essay. The topic has been chosen for you, as have the documents on which you must base your story. Nonetheless, the story is yours to write, and your choice of themes and emphasis makes it your own. Do not be afraid to reach your own conclusions. Originality is an important part of any essay, whether written by a historian or by a student of history.

Following is a series of documents from the 1930s by people who lived through that decade. Read the introductory materials and the documents carefully, thinking about how you can use them to construct a narrative on the experience of the Great Depression. The questions that accompany the documents will help you to focus your thoughts. As you read, highlight passages in each document that suggest a theme or that you could use to enliven your narrative. In the space provided at the end of each passage, jot down some notes for future reference: What theme does the document suggest? How does the document relate to the other passages? Do not hesitate to write ideas in the margins.

A The son of a West Virginia coal miner, Tom Kromer spent three years in college but never finished for lack of funds. Twenty-three years old in 1930, Kromer became a vagrant during the Depression, traveling from city to city across the country on freight trains, begging for a few dimes for a meal or a flop (a bed on which to sleep the night). As often as not, he wound up sleeping on a park bench and going for days without food. Figure 5.1 conveys the hopelessness of many men (and women) in his situation. Eventu-ally Kromer found work for fifteen months with the Civilian Conservation Corps, a New Deal agency. In 1935 he was able to publish an autobiographical novel, *Waiting for Noth-ing*, from which the following is excerpted.

It is night, and we are in . . . a garbage heap. Around us are piles of tin cans and broken bottles. Between the piles are fires. A man and a woman huddle by the fire to our right. A baby gasps in the woman's arms. It has the croup. It coughs until it is black in the face. The woman . . . pounds it on the back. It catches its breath for a little while, but

FIGURE 5.1 *Hoboes During the 1930s*

that is all. You cannot cure a baby of the croup by pounding it on the back with your hand.

The man walks back and forth between the piles of garbage. His shoulders are hunched. He clasps his hands behind him. Up and down he walks. Up and down. He has a look on his face. I know that look. I have had that look on my own face. You can tell what a stiff is thinking when you see that look on his face. He . . . wishes to Jesus Christ he could get his hands on a gat [gun]. But . . . a gat costs money. He has no money. He is a lousy stiff. He will never have any money.

Where are they going? . . . They do not know. He hunts for work, and he is a damn fool. There is no work. He cannot leave his wife and kids to starve to death alone, so he brings them with him. Now he can watch them starve to death. What can he do? Nothing but what he is doing. If he hides out on a dark street and gives it to some bastard on the head, they will put him in and throw the keys away if they catch him. . . . So he stays away from dark streets and cooks up jungle slop for his wife and kid between the piles of garbage.

I look around this jungle filled with fires. They are a pitiful sight, these stiffs with their ragged clothes and their sunken cheeks. They crouch around their fires. They are cooking up. They take their baloney butts out of their packs and put them in their skillets to cook. They huddle around their fires in the night. Tomorrow they will huddle around their fires, and the next night, and the next. It will not be here. The bulls [police] will not let a stiff stay in one place for long. . . .

We are five men at this fire I am at. We take turns stumbling into the dark in search of wood. . . . I am groping my way through the dark in search of wood when I stumble into this barbed wire fence. . . . A couple of good stout poles will burn a long time. What do I care if this is someone's fence? . . . We are five men. We are cold. We must have a fire. It takes wood to make a fire. I take this piece of iron pipe and pry the staples loose.

This is good wood. It makes a good blaze. We do not have to huddle so close now. It is warm, too, except when the wind whistles hard against our backs. Then we shiver and turn our backs to the fire and watch these rats that scamper back and forth in the shadows. These are no ordinary rats. They are big rats. But I am too smart for these rats. I have me a big piece of canvas. This is not to keep me warm. It is to keep these rats from biting a chunk out of my nose when I sleep. But it does not keep out the sound and the feel of them as they sprawl all over you.[7]

Questions to Consider

What group of people does Kromer describe? What sets them apart from other poor people? Did traditional gender roles survive the harsh conditions that these people faced? How can you tell from the document? How do these people feel about the law? Why? Is their view of the law similar to that of poor people today? Why or why not? _____

_____

_____

_____

_____

B Born in Iowa in 1900, Meridel Le Sueur grew up in an atmosphere of political radicalism. During the 1920s, she joined the Communist Party of the United States. An essayist, novelist, and poet, Le Sueur published extensively during the 1920s and 1930s, especially on the lives of middle- and lower-middle-class women. The next excerpt is from "Women Are Hungry," which appeared in 1934 in the journal *American Mercury.* Le Sueur spent most of the 1930s in Minneapolis raising two children, writing, and working in a variety of menial jobs. Partly from her personal experiences and partly from extensive interaction with other poor women, she creates a poignant vision of the Depression's impact on her gender and the family.

When you look at the unemployed women and girls you think instantly that there must be some kind of war. The men are gone away from the family; the family is disintegrating; the women try to hold it together, because women have most to do with the vivid life of procreation, food, shelter. Deprived of their participation in that, they are beggars.

. . . poverty is more personal to them than to men. The women looking for jobs or bumming on the road, or that you see waiting for a hand-out from the charities, are already mental cases as well as physical ones. A man can always get drunk, or talk to other men, no matter how broken he is in body and spirit; but a woman, ten to one, will starve alone in a hall bedroom until she is thrown out, and then she will sleep alone in some alley until she is picked up.

When the social fabric begins to give way it gives way from the bottom first. . . . The working-class family is going fast. The lower-middle-class family is also going, though not so fast. It is like a landslide. It is like a great chasm opening beneath the feet and swallowing the bottom classes first. The worker who lives from hand to mouth goes first, and then his family goes. The family rots, decays and goes to pieces with the woman standing last, trying to hold it together, and then going too. The man loses his job, cannot find another, then leaves. The older children try to get money, fail, and leave or are taken to the community farms. The mother stays with the little children helped by charity, until they too are sucked under by the diminishing dole and the growing terror.

Where are the women? There is the old woman who has raised her children, and they have all left her now, under the lash of hunger. There is the unattached woman, and the professional one, and the domestic servant. The latter went down two years ago. The professional woman began going down only recently. They are the young school girls — more than a million of them — who were graduated into unemployment two or three years ago. Many of them, particularly those coming from the industrial centers, who never went beyond grammar school, are now hoboes riding on the freights. Their ages run from eight to eighteen.[8]

Questions to Consider

How does this document compare to the three others authored by women (documents C, D, and F)? How does Le Sueur compare in status, occupation, residence, and political outlook (insofar as you can tell) to the other women authors? Can you envision Le Sueur writing any of the other three documents? _____

_____

_____

_____

_____

C The following letter, dated January 2, 1935, was addressed to First Lady Eleanor Roosevelt by a woman in Troy, New York, a small city near the state capital at Albany.

About a month ago I wrote you asking if you would buy some baby clothes for me with the understanding that I was to repay you as soon as my husband got enough work. Several weeks later I received a reply to apply to a Welfare Association so I might receive the aid I needed. . . .

Please Mrs. Roosevelt, I do not want charity, only a chance from someone who will trust me until we can get enough money to repay the amount spent for the things I need. As a proof that I really am sincere, I am sending you two of my dearest possessions to keep as security, a ring my husband gave me before we were married, and a ring my mother used to wear. Perhaps the actual value of them is not high, but they are worth a lot to me. If you will consider buying the baby clothes, please keep them [rings] until I send you the money you spent. It is very hard to face bearing a baby we cannot afford to have, and the fact that it is due to arrive soon, and still there is no money for the hospital or clothing, does not make it any easier. . . .

If you still feel you cannot trust me, it is allright and I can only say I do not blame you, but if you decide my word is worth anything with so small a security, here is a list of what I will need — but I will need it very soon. . . . [There follows a list of eleven different pieces of infant clothing.]

If you will get these for me I would rather no one knew about it. I promise to repay the cost of the layette as soon as possible.[9]

Questions to Consider

Why do you suppose the woman wrote to Mrs. Roosevelt instead of to the president? Why did the wife rather than the husband write for help? Why doesn't the woman want charity? Why does she not want others to know about her approaching Mrs. Roosevelt? Do this woman's values appear to differ from those of Le Sueur in document B? If so,

how do they differ? _____

_____

_____

_____

_____

D The next document also was addressed to Mrs. Roosevelt. The letter was from a woman living in Winnsboro, a small town in Louisiana. It was dated October 29, 1935. Figure 5.2 shows a woman posing for the photographer with her husband and sons.

> I read your letter telling me to write to the relif office for help I did they wrote me that they was puting people off the relif now instead of takin them on and I dont want on the relif if I can help it I want to work for my livin but the last thing we have is gone my cow that I ask you to send me some money to save her for my little children to have milk has bin taken and we only ge $17.50 on our debt for her we picked cotton at 40 cents per 100 lbs till it was all gone now there isnt one thing here that we can do to get bread to eat my sick child is still livin and takin medicine but the Dr says he cannot keep letting us have medicine unless we pay him some for he is in debt for it and the man that has let us have a house and land to work wont let us stay in the house if we cant get a mill plow the land with. . . . dont you know its aful to have to get out and no place to have a roof over your sick child and noting to eat I cant tell all my troubles there isnt any use we only have a few days to stay here in the house. . . . please send me some money and please dont write me like you did before my Husban is in bad condishion and if you write me a letter like you did before it will hurt him so much so wont you please send it and say nothing about it.[10]

Questions to Consider

What is the most noticeable difference between this letter and document C? Can you explain this difference? If so, how? Like the woman in document C, the writer of this letter does not want others to know that she has written to Mrs. Roosevelt. Are their reasons similar? Does this suggest anything about American values at the time? Do you think

such values continue to prevail today? _____

_____

_____

_____

_____

E The following letter to President Roosevelt, dated October 19, 1935, was from an unidentified person living in Reidsville, Georgia. Figure 5.3 shows three generations of an impoverished rural family posing for the photographer.

FIGURE 5.2 *Poor Farmers in the Deep South During the 1930s*

Would you please direct the people in charge of the relief work in Georgia to issue the provisions + other supplies to our suffering colored people. I am sorry to worrie you with this Mr. President but . . . the relief officials here are using up most every thing that you send for them self + their friends. they give out the releaf supplies here on Wednesday . . . and give us black folks, each one, nothing but a few cans of pickle meet and to white folks they give blankets, bolts of cloth and things like that . . . the witto Nancy Hendrics own lands, stock holder in the Bank in this town and she is being supplied with Blankets cloth and gets a supply of cans goods regular this is only one case but I could tell you many.

Please help us mr President because we cant help our self and we know you is the president and a good Christian man we is praying for you. Yours truly cant sign my name Mr President they will beat me up and run me away from here and this is my home[11]

Questions to Consider

Do you think the letter is by a man or a woman? Why? What is similar in the actual texts of documents D and E? How do you explain the similarity? What is different about the writers of the two letters? Is the author of document E concerned about townpeople discovering his or her appeal to the president for the same reason that the authors of documents C and D don't want others to know of their appeals to Mrs. Roosevelt? How is the appeal in document E different from that in documents C and D? Can you explain the difference? If so, how? _____

_____

FIGURE 5.3 *A Rural Family in the South During the 1930s*

_____

_____

_____

F The following letter to Mrs. Roosevelt, from a woman in Mancelona, Michigan, was dated August 6, 1934.

> I am writing you to ask you to help me and my old Father to live I am in a farm which he owns and has planted or farmed all he was able to do we havnt any stock nothing to feed them untill his corn is through growing we have a fuw chickens this is what I would like to ask of you and the President if I could have a small pinsion each month so we would not starve my father is seventy six to old to work at the Antriim Co furnace I cant go away and leave him alone to look for work and to stay here in such poverty I am so disturbed trying to know what to do.[12]

Questions to Consider

What do the authors of documents D and F have in common? In what ways are the two letters similar? What group of people is introduced in this document? How has the condition of most people in that group changed since the 1930s? Why has the change

occurred? _____

_____

FIGURE 5.4 *A Soup Kitchen in Chicago During the 1930s*

_____

_____

_____

(G) The following letter to the president was from a boy living in Chicago, Illinois, and was written sometime in February 1936. Figure 5.4 shows men down on their luck in Chicago receiving a free meal.

> I'm a boy of 12 years. . . . My father hasn't worked for 5 months He went plenty times to relief. . . . They won't give us anything. I don't know why. Please you do something. We haven't paid 4 months rent, Everyday the landlord rings the door bell, we don't open the door for him. We are afraid that we will be put out, been put out before, and don't want to happen again. We haven't paid the gas bill, and the electric bill, haven't paid grocery bill for 3 months. My brother goes to . . . High School. . . . hasn't gone to school for 2 weeks because he got no carfare. I have a sister she's twenty years, she can't find work. My father is staying home. All the time he's crying because he can't find work. I told him why are you crying daddy, and daddy said why shouldn't I cry when there is nothing in the house. I feel sorry for him. That night I couldn't sleep. The next morning I wrote this letter to you. . . . Please answer right away because we need it. will starve Thank you.[13]

Questions to Consider

How does the father in this document differ from the author of document C? How do you think the father would react if he knew about his son's letter? How are the conditions described in this document similar to those described in the other documents?

Would the family described in document G find it easier to get help today? If so, from whom? _____

_____

_____

_____

_____

H Not everyone suffered during the Great Depression, as this and the next document reveal. Both are excerpts from oral histories recorded in the late 1960s of people who either got rich or stayed rich during the 1930s. The first speaker is William Benton, who, after his business successes of the 1930s, became a United States senator from Connecticut.

> I left Chicago in June of '29. . . . Chester Bowles and I started a business with seventeen hundred square feet, just the two of us and a couple of girls. . . .
>
> I was only twenty-nine, and Bowles was only twenty-eight. . . . We didn't know the Depression was going on. Except that our clients' products were plummeting, and they were willing to talk to us about new ideas. They wouldn't have let us in the door if times were good. So the Depression benefited me. My income doubled every year. . . .
>
> . . . I contributed enormously to the "Maxwell House Show Boat," which later became the Number One program in broadcasting. . . .
>
> "Show Boat" went on in 1933, really the bottom of the Depression. Maxwell House Coffee went up eighty-five percent within six months. And kept zooming. . . . The chain stores were selling coffee that was almost as good — the difference was indetectable — for a much lower price. But advertising so gave a glamor and verve to Maxwell House that it made everybody think it was a whale of a lot better.[14]

Questions to Consider

How do you explain Benton's success in the 1930s in contrast to the failure of others? What percentage of the American people do Benton and Martin DeVries, the author of document I, represent? What does the success of Maxwell House Coffee during the 1930s suggest? _____

_____

_____

_____

_____

I Martin DeVries, a wealthy businessman, showed limited sympathy for those who suffered in the Depression.

> People were speculating. Now who are they gonna blame aside from themselves? It's their fault. . . . If you gamble and make a mistake, why pick on somebody else? It's your fault. . . .
>
> It's like many people on the bread lines. I certainly felt sorry for them. But many of them hadn't lived properly when they were making it. They hadn't saved

anything. . . . Way back in the '20s, people were wearing $20 silk shirts and throwing their money around like crazy. If they had been buying Arrow $2 shirts and putting the other eighteen in the bank, when the trouble came, they wouldn't have been in the condition they were in. . . .

Most people today are living beyond their means. They don't give a damn. The Government'll take care of them. People today don't want to work. . . .

These New Dealers felt they had a mission to perform. . . . My friends and I often spoke about it. . . . Here we were paying taxes and not asking for anything. Everybody else was asking for relief, for our money to help them out. . . . A certain amount of that is O.K., but when they strip you clean and still don't accomplish anything, it's unfair.[15]

Questions to Consider

Do you think the people about whom DeVries complains represent a large percentage of the American people? Do you think they are characteristic of the people writing and being described in documents A through G? How do DeVries's values compare with those of the people represented in those documents? How do you explain any differences?

_____

_____

_____

_____

_____

Now that you have read the documents, it is time to write the first draft of your essay. In following the steps below, keep in mind a length limit. All writing involves making decisions about what material to include and what to omit. This assignment is no different. Your final essay should be no longer than three typewritten (double spaced) pages or nine handwritten (single spaced) pages.

Step 1. Look over your notes for each passage, and think about a theme that you would like to develop. What would you like to say about life during the Great Depression? Write your theme in one sentence below.

_____

_____

_____

Step 2. How will you support your theme? In the space provided, list the points that you will use to support your argument. After each point, include some details, taken from the documents, that will flesh out the point. These points, with their details, will form the paragraphs of your essay's body.

_____

_____

_____

_____

_____

_____

_____

_____

_____

_____

_____

_____

_____

Step 3. On a separate sheet of paper, write the introduction to your essay. Remember that the introduction should do three things: grab the reader's attention, state your theme, and briefly preview the supporting points that you will cover in your essay body.

Step 4. Draft the body of your essay. Look at your list from Step 2 and expand each point into a full paragraph. Be sure that each paragraph begins with a clear topic sentence that announces the paragraph's main point. Also check that each paragraph contains interesting details that support the topic sentence. Finally, be sure that each paragraph flows smoothly into the next paragraph.

Step 5. Write the conclusion of your essay. Recap your main points, and firmly restate your theme. If you wish, raise any larger questions that may have come to mind as you thought about the Depression.

Step 6. Set aside your first draft for a few hours or for a day or two.

Step 7. Reread your essay, asking yourself the following questions:

Does my introduction state my thesis?
Will it grab the reader's attention?
Does each paragraph in the essay body contain only one main idea, and does that main idea back up my thesis?
Does each paragraph have enough supporting, interesting details to flesh out the topic sentence?
Does each paragraph flow smoothly into the next one?
Throughout my essay, do I express my ideas clearly and vividly?
Will my readers want to keep reading my paper?
Does my paper end in a satisfying conclusion that restates my thesis?

You may want to have a friend read your first draft, too, and give you his or her impressions.

Step 8. Revise your essay to resolve any problems that came up in Step 7. Do not hesitate to make extensive changes; most authors revise their work several times before being satisfied.

Step 9. Read through your second draft again, and correct any spelling, punctuation, or grammatical errors.

Step 10. Hand in your final essay with pride.

You have completed the first major writing assignment in this book. Rather than emphasizing style and organization, the assignments in the remaining chapters will center on more specific aspects of historical writing. For example, Chapter 6 focuses on causation, or the question of why events occur. Still, to complete these assignments, you will have to read and take notes on primary documents, organize an essay, and then write several paragraphs of clear and lively prose, just as you did in this chapter. All this effort devoted to writing is not wasted. Good writing takes much practice, but these skills will prove valuable to you for the rest of your life. Whether you become a historian, a novelist, a journalist, a businessperson, a doctor, or a teacher, your ability to communicate persuasively and engagingly through the written word will have considerable impact on your attainments.

NOTES

1. Excerpts from *The Crisis of the Old Order* by Arthur M. Schlesinger. Copyright © 1957 by Arthur M. Schlesinger. Reprinted by permission of Houghton Mifflin Company. All rights reserved.
2. Ibid., 171.
3. Ibid., 485.
4. Winifred D. Wandersee, *Women's Work and Family Values, 1920–1940* (Cambridge, Mass.: Harvard University Press, 1981), 97.
5. Susan Ware, *Beyond Suffrage: Women in the New Deal* (Cambridge, Mass.: Harvard University Press, 1981), 114.
6. Caroline Bird, *The Invisible Scar* (New York: McKay, 1966), 30–31.
7. Text by Tom Kromer from *Waiting for Nothing & Other Writings,* edited by Arthur D. Casciato and James L. West. Copyright © 1986. Reprinted by permission of the University of Georgia Press.
8. The article was republished in Meridel Le Sueur, *Ripening Selected Work, 1927–1980,* edited with an introduction by Elaine Hedges (Old Westbury, N.Y.: Feminist Press, 1934), 144–157.
9. From *Down and Out in the Great Depression: Letters from the "Forgotten Man"* by Robert S. McElvaine. Copyright © 1983 by the University of North Carolina Press. Used by permission of the publisher.
10. Ibid., 69–70.
11. Ibid., 83.
12. Ibid., 100–101.
13. Ibid., 117.
14. Studs Terkel, *Hard Times: An Oral History of the Great Depression* (New York: Pantheon, 1970), 60–62.
15. Ibid., 74–75.

6 CAUSATION: WHY EVENTS HAPPEN

World War II and the Origins of the Cold War

E. H. Carr wrote in his widely acclaimed book *What Is History?* that "the study of history is the study of causes. The historian . . . continuously asks the question: Why?; and so long as he hopes for an answer, he cannot rest."[1] Although historians often substitute for *causes* words such as *roots, origins, influences, foundations,* and *factors,* causal analysis continues to play a central role in their enterprise. Indeed, the same can be said for the rest of us as well. Rarely do we go through a day without asking why something happened the way it did.

The study of causation, though important, is complicated. Historians usually divide causes into the underlying and the immediate. **Underlying causes** are long-term factors that tend to move events in a particular direction, such as toward war or peace between nations. **Immediate causes** are short-term factors that spark an event. In analyzing the Cuban missile crisis of 1962, for example, historians generally identify the long-standing tension and competition between the Soviet Union and the United States as an underlying cause and the impulsive personality of Soviet leader Nikita Khrushchev as an immediate one. Deciding how much weight to give to these two types of causes is one of the primary tasks that historians face in explaining the past. This challenge is also essential for anyone attempting to anticipate the future.

To understand this principle, imagine a person, Jane Doe, who recently inherited a portfolio with thousands of shares of stock in oil companies that have major holdings in the Middle East. The date is August 3, 1990, and Iraqi forces just invaded Kuwait, sending the region into a state of heightened uncertainty. Should Jane sell her oil stocks? Chances are, Jane will base her decision on an assessment of what caused past fluctuations of her stocks' value and how likely those forces are to arise in the future, in both the short and the long term. If her oil stocks are showing a long-term upward trend, despite occasional downward shifts, and if her financial needs are mainly long-term, then she probably will hold on to those investments. If, however, her needs are primarily short-term, and if past crises in the Middle East led to sharp dips in the value of her stocks, she is likely to sell them quickly.

The nature of the event or phenomenon being analyzed may further complicate the study of causation. The Cuban missile crisis is a readily identifiable event with a limited duration; but other phenomena are more diffuse, both in character and in duration. The Cold War, of which the Cuban missile crisis was a part, is a prime example.

You have seen and heard the phrase "Cold War" many times, usually to refer to the intense and often bitter competition between the United States and the Soviet Union that ended in the late 1980s. Historians sometimes disagree over when the Cold War started, although they acknowledge that it emerged in the aftermath of World War II and to some degree as a result of that most monumental of conflicts. Tensions subsided temporarily during the mid-1950s and again in the early 1970s, but not until Mikhail Gorbachev rose to leadership in the Soviet Union and American president Ronald Reagan welcomed his overtures did relations between Moscow and Washington relax to a point where the two countries' leaders could consistently negotiate major issues short of crisis conditions.

Despite the high level of animosity characteristic of the Cold War, actual fighting between American and Soviet forces never occurred. For a long time, historians studying the conflict's causes preoccupied themselves with explaining Soviet-American enmity. More recently, scholars have devoted greater attention to the absence of a "hot" war between the two nations. Whatever the emphasis, the peculiar nature of the Cold War has presented numerous challenges to historians asking *why?* This chapter focuses on historical causation, with the Cold War serving as the example and World War II as the background. For additional information on these events, consult your textbook.

The following exercises provide you with the opportunity to hone your skills, first in comprehending the historical background leading up to a major event, second in summarizing and categorizing causal statements, and third in developing your own causal explanation based on primary sources.

EXERCISE 1: *Western Strategy in World War II and the Political Configuration of Europe and Asia Later On*

The great nineteenth-century Prussian strategist Karl von Clausewitz once characterized war as "politics by other means." In fact, whether intended or not, military events and strategies in wartime usually play a major role in determining subsequent political developments. By studying the maps in Figures 6.1 through 6.4, you should be able to make this connection in the context of World War II. Section A deals with the European theater, section B with Asia and the Pacific. Section C asks you to integrate the two.

(A) The United States and its ally, Great Britain, pursued a Europe-first strategy in World War II, believing that Germany was a greater threat to their interests than was Japan. Yet Japan's attack on American possessions in the Pacific and British possessions in Southeast Asia in December 1941 meant that these two nations had to fight in Asia and the Pacific as well as in Europe. The Soviet Union, in contrast, did not enter the war against Japan until August 1945. Thus its entire war effort until Germany surrendered on May 8, 1945, was in Europe. Examine the map in Figure 6.1 carefully. How do you think the movement of forces against Germany was influenced by the fact that the United States and Great Britain were fighting in Asia and the Pacific at the same time while the

Soviet Union was fighting only in Europe? _____

_____

_____

_____

_____

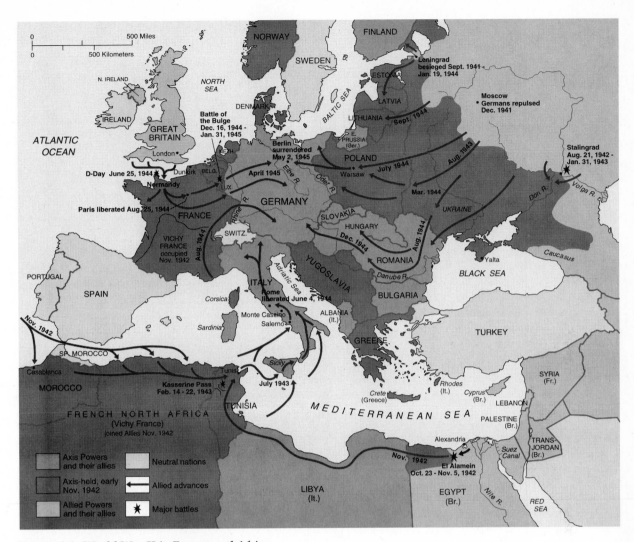

FIGURE 6.1 *World War II in Europe and Africa*

Boyer, et al., *The Enduring Vision,* Second Edition, Volume 2. Copyright © 1993 by D. C. Heath and Company. Adapted by permission of Houghton Mifflin Company.

Now compare the movements of Allied forces in Figure 6.1 with the map in Figure 6.2, which shows Soviet territorial expansion and the emergence of Communist governments during and after the war. What pattern does this comparison suggest? _____

_____

_____

_____

_____

Outside the eastern front against the Soviet Union, the main concentration of German military power was in France and Belgium in the west. Keeping this in mind, examine the dates of the military movements of Anglo-American forces on the map in Figure 6.1.

Additional areas in which communist
governments were established, 1944–1948

Soviet territorial gains in
Europe during World War II

FIGURE 6.2 *Communism's Advance in Europe As a Result of World War II*

Do these help to explain the positions of British and American forces in relation to Soviet

forces at the end of the war? If, so how? _____

_____

_____

_____

_____

_____

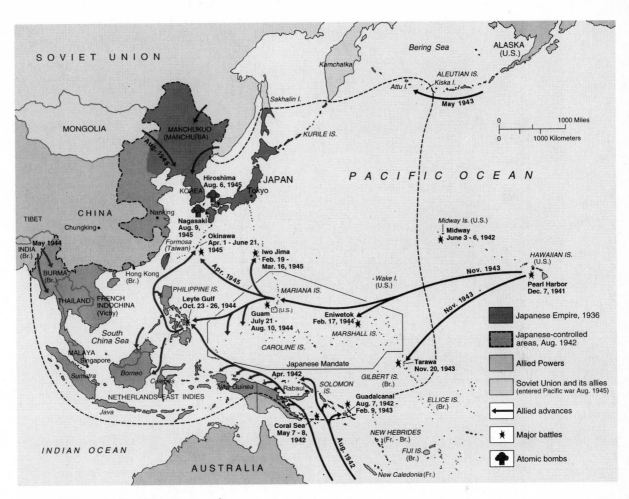

FIGURE 6.3 *World War II in the Pacific*
Boyer, et al., *The Enduring Vision*, Second Edition, Volume 2. Copyright © 1993 by D. C. Heath and Company. Adapted by permission of Houghton Mifflin Company.

B Although the United States and Great Britain emphasized the European theater of operations in World War II, they put considerable effort into the struggle against Japan. The map in Figure 6.3 shows the dates and places of major allied military operations in the Pacific and Asian theaters. What do these operations suggest to you about allied military strategy against Japan and its empire? _____

_____

_____

_____

Notice where the Soviet Union moved its forces in August 1945 when it declared war against Japan. Now examine the map in Figure 6.4, which shows areas governed by Communists at the beginning of 1950. What does this comparison suggest to you about the connection between military operations in wartime and political developments later on?

_____

_____

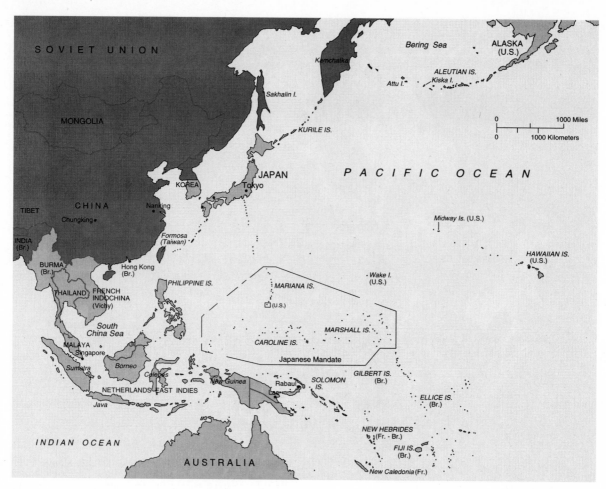

FIGURE 6.4 *Communist-governed territories in Asia (1950)*

C Write a paragraph below pulling together conclusions you reached in sections A and B about the linkage between military events during World War II and political developments in its aftermath. _____

_____

_____

_____

_____

_____

_____

EXERCISE 2: *Identifying Causal Statements*

An event as complicated as the Cold War is bound to generate disagreement among historians. In fact, scholars have offered a wide variety of explanations as to why the Cold War developed as it did. The following excerpts present a few of those explanations. Read the excerpts and in the space provided summarize in no more than two sentences the author's causal statement about the Cold War. Also indicate whether the causal statement is essentially long-term or short-term. If you are not sure, write *uncertain*.

A. Washington policymakers mistook [Soviet leader Joseph] Stalin's determination to ensure Russian security through spheres of influence [in eastern Europe, Iran, and northeast Asia] for a renewed effort to spread communism outside the borders of the Soviet Union. The Russians did not immediately impose communist regimes on all the countries they occupied after the war, and Stalin showed notoriously little interest in promoting the fortunes of communist parties in areas beyond his control. But the Soviet leader failed to make the limited nature of his objectives clear.[2]

The Cold War occurred because _____

_____

Is this a long-term or a short-term cause? _____

B. . . . the fundamental explanation of the speed with which the Cold War escalated . . . lies precisely in the fact that the Soviet Union was not a traditional national state . . . : it was a totalitarian state, endowed with an all-explanatory, all-consuming ideology, committed to the infallibility of government and party, . . . and ruled by a dictator who . . . had his paranoid moments. . . .

   Stalin and his associates . . . were bound to regard the United States as the enemy not because of this deed or that, but because of the primordial fact that America was the leading capitalist power and thus, by Leninist syllogism, unappeasably hostile, driven by the logic of its system to oppose, encircle, and destroy Soviet Russia.[3]

The Cold War occurred because _____

_____

Is this a long-term or a short-term cause? _____

C. Stalin's effort to solve Russia's problem of security and recovery short of widespread conflict with the United States was not matched by American leaders who acceded to power upon the death of Roosevelt. The President bequeathed them little . . . beyond the traditional outlook of open-door expansion. They proceeded rapidly . . . to translate that conception of America and the world into a series of actions and policies which closed the door to any result but the cold war. . . . [Fundamental to their thinking] was the fear that America's economic system would suffer a serious depression if it did not continue to expand overseas.[4]

The Cold War occurred because _____

_____

Is this a long-term or a short-term cause? _____

Causal Statements and Historical Schools

Now that you are familiar with some theories about what caused the Cold War, you are ready to examine how they fit into interpretive schools.

Most causal statements in history, particularly about phenomena as large and as recent as the Cold War, derive in part from their authors' political or ideological attitude. Political orientation — reactionary, conservative, liberal, radical, revolutionary—affects how a historian determines cause. During the 1950s, conservatives and liberals usually agreed on the origins of the Cold War. Members of these groups argued intensely over specific issues, but they accepted the broad view that the Cold War grew out of a necessary U.S. response to Soviet expansionism — that is, the Soviet Union started the conflict, and the United States reacted. Behind this **traditional explanation** of the Cold War was a consensus that applauded capitalism and democracy as practiced in the United States and that rejected the authoritarian, socialist system of the Soviet Union.

Only a few radicals departed from this traditional interpretation. These **revisionist thinkers** were extremely critical of American capitalism, and, if not advocates of the Soviet system in its entirety, they were at least sympathetic to aspects of its government-controlled economy. During the 1960s, with the rise of opposition to U.S. involvement in Vietnam, revisionist historians became more numerous. Radicals gained a substantial following, and many liberals and moderates began to question the Cold War consensus of the 1950s. Revisionists argued that American leaders sometimes had overreacted to Soviet moves abroad and on occasion had held the Soviets to standards of behavior that they themselves did not always uphold.

The challenge to the traditional view led not to a new consensus rallying around the revisionists but to an effort to pull together aspects of both interpretations into a **postrevisionist synthesis**. Subscribers to this approach, which emerged in the more conservative 1970s, refused to place sole blame for the Cold War on one side and were keenly sensitive to post–World War II conditions that sparked tension between the Soviet Union and the United States.

Given the pluralism of political views within American academe, all three of these interpretations are likely to continue to be well represented.

EXERCISE 3: *Categorizing Causal Statements*

Go back to the selections in Exercise 2 and, using the discussion of Cold War historiography in the preceding section, categorize them as *traditionalist, revisionist,* or *postrevisionist.* In each case, explain your choice.

Selection A

Interpretation: _____

Explanation: _____

_____

Selection B

Interpretation: _____

Explanation: _____

_____

Selection C

Interpretation: _____

Explanation: _____

_____

The Atomic Bomb: A Causal Analysis

Exercises 2 and 3 focused on the work of others. With the experience gained in examining and categorizing causal statements, you are now ready to do some causal analysis of your own. Exercise 4 introduces you to this task through a selection of primary documents relating to the American decision to use the atomic bomb against Japan in 1945. Before you plunge into the exercise, read the following background information. You may want to supplement this material by reading pertinent sections in your textbook or in an encyclopedia.

Historians have long argued over why President Truman used the bomb against Japan, and in the mid-1990s controversy spilled over into the public arena over an exhibit on the event at the Air and Space Museum in Washington, D.C. On the surface, the reason seems obvious: to induce Japan to surrender quickly, thus eliminating the need for an American invasion of its home islands and the hundreds of thousands of U.S. casualties that would result. This was the most popular explanation in the United States for the first generation after the dropping of the bomb. In the mid-1960s, another interpretation emerged—namely, that Truman ordered the bomb's use against Japan primarily to impress the Soviets. Relations between Washington and Moscow had deteriorated after President Franklin D. Roosevelt's death in April, and, by demonstrating the power of the new weapon, Truman hoped to increase his bargaining power on a variety of unresolved issues.

During the 1970s, as new documentation pertinent to the bombing became available, scholars began to acknowledge that there may have been a number of reasons driving Truman's decision. For one thing, historians pointed out that the desires to save American lives and to influence the Soviets were not mutually exclusive. Both may have entered Truman's calculations. Emotion and momentum also may have played a role. Americans had not forgotten Japan's surprise attack on Pearl Harbor in 1941 or the atrocities of Japanese soldiers during the ensuing war in the western Pacific and China. To most Americans of the time, the Japanese seemed to be an alien people with devious and barbarous inclinations. The desire for revenge against what many believed to be a lower order of human beings was deeply ingrained in people's minds. Furthermore, virtually everyone involved with the Manhattan Project since its inception in 1942 had been assuming that the bomb would be used against the enemy as soon as it was ready. For Truman, a decision not to use the weapon against Japan would have required a reversal of the past thinking of responsible officials. The new president, who did not even learn of the Manhattan Project until late April 1945, was not in a strong position to adopt such a course.

Whatever cause or causes one chooses to emphasize, it is clear that the final decision to drop the bomb came only after much deliberation. In early May 1945, the president approved the establishment, under Secretary of War Henry L. Stimson, of an Interim Committee of top scientists and government officials. This group was to make recommendations on possible use of the weapon once it was ready. (An atomic device was not actually tested in the New Mexico desert until July 16.) On June 1 the committee recommended using the bomb against Japan without warning, a decision that reflected what Stimson and Truman already believed. Later in June, in response to a plea from scientists directly involved in the Manhattan Project, the committee considered providing the Japanese with a technical demonstration of the weapon's power before using it on a live target. However, the committee remained unpersuaded that anything other than its actual deployment against the enemy would have the desired effect. There is no evidence that Truman subsequently reconsidered his view that the bomb should be used as soon as practicable. With the technical and logistical tasks completed around August 1, all that remained was to wait for clear weather over a target city. The United States dropped one bomb on Hiroshima on August 6 and one bomb on Nagasaki three days later.

EXERCISE 4: *Writing a Causal Analysis*

The excerpts from the primary sources that follow include evidence as to why President Truman decided to use the atomic bomb against Japan. Examine this evidence and make up your own mind about what caused Truman to take the course he did. A brief introduction precedes each excerpt to place it in context. Figure 6.3 shows a map of the western Pacific. After each excerpt space is provided for you to comment on the significance of the passage. Think about which of the reasons outlined earlier fits each document. Specifically, does the document support the interpretation that Truman bombed Japan to end the war or to impress the Soviets, or for one or any of the reasons previously mentioned? Do any other explanations not discussed seem plausible? Ask yourself how important each document is in explaining Truman's decision. Remember that, in the end, the decision was the president's alone to make.

Consider the author of the source and the circumstances under which it was produced, as well as its content. Did the author possess an obvious bias in recounting events the way he did? Was he in a good position to describe the events mentioned? How long after the event was the document created? Feel free to highlight portions of the documents and to write notes in the margins.

Ⓐ This excerpt, dated May 15, 1945, is from the diary of Secretary of War Stimson. The excerpt relates a meeting held by the Committee of Three, a top-level group of U.S. officials that sought to coordinate policy among the War, Navy, and State departments. Winston Churchill was prime minister of the United Kingdom, and Joseph Stalin was Soviet premier and secretary of the ruling Communist party. The map in Figure 6.2 will help you to understand the concern over the Soviets' territorial gains. W. Averell Harriman was the U.S. ambassador to the Soviet Union.

> . . . the President has now promised apparently to meet Stalin and Churchill on the first of July and at that time . . . it may be necessary to have it out with Russia on her relations to Manchuria and Port Arthur and various other parts of North China, and also the relations of China to us. Over any such tangled wave of problems the S-1 [the code name for the atomic bomb] secret would be dominant and yet we will not know until after that time probably, until after that meeting, whether this is a weapon in our hands or not. We think it will be shortly afterwards, but it seems a terrible thing to gamble with such big stakes in diplomacy without having your master card in your hand. The best we could do today was to persuade Harriman not to go back until we had had time to think over these things a little bit harder.[5]

Questions to Consider

What does the excerpt suggest about the state of U.S. relations with the Soviet Union (Russia)? Do the meeting participants make a connection between the Soviet-American relationship and the atomic bomb? _____

_____

_____

_____

_____

B This excerpt is from the "Reminiscences" of Leo Szilard, a scientist in the Manhattan Project who doubted the prudence of using the atomic bomb against Japan. The meeting outlined in this excerpt occurred on May 28, 1945. James Byrnes was the president's representative on the Interim Committee. On July 3 he became secretary of state.

Byrnes agreed that if we refrained from testing the bomb, people would conclude that its development did not succeed. However, he said that we had spent two billion dollars on developing the bomb, and Congress would want to know what we got for the money spent. "How would you get Congress to appropriate money for atomic energy research if you do not show results for the money which has been spent already?" . . .

Byrnes thought that the war would be over in about six months, and this proved to be a fairly accurate estimate. He was concerned about Russia's postwar behavior. Russian troops had moved into Hungary and Rumania; Byrnes thought it would be very difficult to persuade Russia to withdraw her troops from these countries, and that Russia might be more manageable if impressed by American military might.[6]

Questions to Consider

Why is Byrnes concerned about views in Congress? Does his concern seem to be pushing him toward or away from using the bomb against Japan? Is Byrnes's concern about the Soviet Union an argument for or against using the bomb against Japan? _____

_____

_____

_____

_____

C Here is another excerpt from Stimson's diary, this time for June 6, 1945. The excerpt describes a meeting with President Truman.

I then took up the matters on my agenda, telling him first of the work of the Interim Committee meetings last week. He said that Byrnes had reported to him already about it and that Byrnes seemed to be highly pleased with what had been done. I then said that the points of agreement and views arrived at were substantially as follows:

That there should be no revelation to Russia or anyone else of our work in S-1 until the first bomb had been successfully laid on Japan.

That the greatest complication was what might happen at the meeting of the Big Three. He told me he had postponed that until the 15th of July on purpose to give us more time. I pointed out that there might still be delay and if there was and the Russians should bring up the subject and ask us to take them in as partners, I thought that our attitude was to do just what the Russians had done to us, namely to make the simple statement that as yet we were not quite ready to do it.

Questions to Consider

Does a basic decision appear to have been made to use the atomic bomb against Japan? What was Truman's reason for postponing the meeting with the Soviet Union and Great

Britain? _____

_____

_____

_____

_____

D The next excerpt is from a memo from Secretary of War Stimson to President Truman. The president read the memo during a meeting with Stimson on July 2 and, according to Stimson, "was apparently aquiescent with my attitude."

Proposed Program for Japan

1. The plans of operation up to and including the first landing have been authorized and the preparations for the operation are now actually going on. This situation was accepted by all members of your conference on Monday, June 18th.

2. There is reason to believe that the operation for the occupation of Japan following the landing may be a very long, costly and arduous struggle on our part. . . .

3. If we once land on one of the main islands and begin a forceful occupation of Japan, we shall probably have cast the die of last ditch resistance. The Japanese are highly patriotic and certainly susceptible to calls for fanatical resistance to repel an invasion. . . .

4. A question then comes: Is there any alternative to such a forceful occupation of Japan which will secure for us the equivalent of an unconditional surrender of her forces and a permanent destruction of her power again to strike an aggressive blow at the "peace of the Pacific"? I am inclined to think that there is enough such chance to make it well worthwhile our giving them a warning of what is to come and a definite opportunity to capitulate. . . .

We have . . . enormously favorable factors on our side. . . .

The problem is to translate these advantages into prompt and economical achievement of our objectives. I believe Japan *is* susceptible to reason in such a crisis to a much greater extent than is indicated by our current press and other current comment. Japan is not a nation composed wholly of mad fanatics of an entirely different mentality from ours.

On the other hand, I think that the attempt to exterminate her armies and her population by gunfire or other means will tend to produce a fusion of race solidity and antipathy which had no analogy in the case of Germany. We have a national interest in creating, if possible, a condition wherein the Japanese nation may live as a peaceful and useful member of the future Pacific community.

5. It is therefore my conclusion that a carefully timed warning be given to Japan by the chief representatives of the United States, Great Britain, China and, if then a bel-

ligerent, Russia, calling upon Japan to surrender and permit the occupation of her country in order to insure its complete demilitarization for the sake of the future peace. . . .

6. Success of course will depend on the potency of the warning which we give her. She has an extremely sensitive national pride and, as we are now seeing every day, when actually locked with the enemy will fight to the very death. For that reason the warning must be tendered before the actual invasion has occurred and while the impending destruction, though clear beyond peradventure, has not yet reduced her to fanatical despair. If Russia is a part of the threat, the Russian attack, if actual, must not have progressed too far.

Questions to Consider

In suggesting U.S. motives for using the atomic bomb against Japan, how does this document compare with selections A, B, and C? What is the major concern expressed by Stimson in the document? _____

_____

_____

_____

_____

_____

_____

E The following selection is from President Truman's diary, which he kept intermittently during his White House years. He wrote this entry while in Potsdam, Germany, negotiating wartime and postwar issues with the Soviets and the British (see Figure 6.5) shortly after he had received a preliminary report of the successful test of an atomic device in the New Mexico desert.

July 17, 1945

Just spent a couple of hours with Stalin. [My adviser] Joe Davies called [Soviet diplomat Ivan] Maisky and made the date last night for noon today. Promptly a few minutes before twelve I looked up from the desk and there stood Stalin in the doorway. I got to my feet and advanced to meet him. He put out his hand and smiled. I did the same, we shook, I greeted [Soviet Foreign Minister] Molotov and the interpreter, and we sat down. After the usual polite remarks we got down to business. I told Stalin that I am no diplomat but usually said yes & no to questions after hearing all the argument. It pleased him. I asked him if he had the agenda for the meeting. He said he had and that he had some more questions to present. I told him to fire away. He did and it is dynamite — but I have some dynamite too which I'm not exploding now. He wants to fire Franco, to which I wouldn't object, and divide up the Italian colonies and other mandates, some no doubt that the British have. Then he got on the Chinese situation, told us what agreements had been reached and what was in abeyance. Most of the big points are settled. He'll be in the Jap War on August 15th. Fini Japs when that comes about. We had lunch, talked socially, put on a real show drinking toasts to everyone, then had pictures made in the back yard. I can deal with Stalin. He is honest — but smart as hell.[7]

FIGURE 6.5 *Photograph of Churchill, Truman, and Stalin at the Potsdam Conference*

Questions to Consider

Does Truman hope to influence Stalin through his possession of the atomic bomb? Does Truman want the Soviets to enter the war against Japan? Why? Does the document suggest a single reason for using the bomb against Japan, or more than one reason? _____

_____

_____

_____

_____

F The next selection is from Stimson's diary of July 22, the day after top American officials in Potsdam received a detailed report of the successful test of an atomic device five days earlier. On July 21, Stimson described the report in his diary as follows: "It was an immensely powerful document . . . and revealed far greater destructive power than we expected in S-1." General Leslie Groves, the author of the report, was the director of the Manhattan Project.

> At ten-forty [American delegate Harvey] Bundy and I again went to the British headquarters and talked to the Prime Minister and Lord Cherwell for over an hour. Churchill read Groves' report in full. He told me that he had noticed at the meeting of

the Three yesterday that Truman was evidently much fortified by something that had happened and that he stood up to the Russians in a most emphatic manner, telling them as to certain demands that they absolutely could not have and that the United States was entirely against them. He said "Now I know what happened to Truman yesterday. I couldn't understand it. When he got to the meeting after having read this report he was a changed man. He told the Russians just where they got on and off and generally bossed the whole meeting." Churchill said he now understood how this pepping up had taken place and that he felt the same way.

Question to Consider

How does the report on the A-bomb test seem to have influenced Truman's behavior?

_____

_____

_____

_____

_____

G The following excerpt is from Stimson's diary on July 23. The setting was still Potsdam. General George Marshall was the U.S. Army chief of staff.

At eleven o'clock I went down to the "Little White House" . . . and I asked for the President who saw me at once. . . . He told me that he had the warning message which we prepared on his desk . . . and that he proposed to shoot it out as soon as he heard the definite day of the operation. We had a brief discussion about Stalin's recent expansions and he confirmed what I have heard. But he told me that the United States was standing firm and he was apparently relying greatly upon the information as to S-1. He evidently thinks a good deal of the new claims of the Russians are bluff. . . .

After lunch and a short rest I received Generals Marshall and [Hap] Arnold, and had in McCloy and Bundy at the conference. The President had told me at a meeting in the morning that he was very anxious to know whether Marshall felt that we needed the Russians in the war or whether we could get along without them, and that was one of the subjects we talked over. Of course Marshall could not answer directly or explicitly. We had desired the Russians to come into the war originally for the sake of holding up in Manchuria the Japanese Manchurian Army. That now was being accomplished as the Russians have amassed their forces on that border, Marshall said, and were poised, and the Japanese were moving up positions in their Army. But he pointed out that even if we went ahead in the war without the Russians, and compelled the Japanese to surrender to our terms, that would not prevent the Russians from marching into Manchuria anyhow and striking, thus permitting them to get virtually what they wanted in the surrender terms.

Questions to Consider

What appears to be Truman's primary concern in his discussion with Stimson? In the later discussion, does Marshall seem to conclude that the Soviets are needed in the war

against Japan or that they can be kept out through U.S. action? _____

_____

_____

_____

_____

H The following excerpt is from Stimson's diary on July 24.

At nine-twenty I went to "The Little White House" and was at once shown into the President's room. . . . He told me about the events of yesterday's meeting with which he seemed to be very well satisfied. I then told him of my conference with Marshall and the implication that could be inferred as to his feeling that the Russians were not needed. . . .

I then spoke of the importance which I attributed to the reassurance of the Japanese on the continuance of their dynasty, and I had felt that the insertion of that in the formal warning was important and might be just the thing that would make or mar their acceptance, but that I had heard from Byrnes that they preferred not to put it in.

Question to Consider

If the top priority of U.S. leaders was to keep the Soviets out of the war against Japan, should they have assured the Japanese that surrender would not require them to give up

their emperor? _____

_____

_____

_____

_____

I This excerpt is from Truman's diary on July 25. The president was still in Potsdam.

This weapon is to be used against Japan between now and August 10th. I have told the Sec. of War, Mr. Stimson. . . . He & I are in accord. The target will be a purely military one and we will issue a warning statement asking the Japs to surrender and save lives. I'm sure they will not do that, but we will have given them the chance. It is certainly a good thing for the world that Hitler's crowd or Stalin's did not discover this atomic bomb. It seems to be the most terrible thing ever discovered, but it can be made the most useful.[8]

Questions to Consider

What attitude does Truman express toward the Japanese? toward the Soviet Union? Does Truman reveal anything regarding his motives for using the bomb? _____

_____

_____

_____

_____

J This excerpt is from Stimson's diary on August 9. The secretary of war was now back in Washington.

> . . . I could see in my recent trip to Europe what a difficult task at best it will be to keep in existence a contented army of occupation and, if mingled with the inevitable difficulties there is a sense of [the army's] grievance against the unfairness of the government, the situation may become bad. Consequently the paper that we drew last night and continued today was a ticklish one. The bomb and the entrance of the Russians into the war will certainly have an effect on hastening the victory. But just how much that effect is or how long and how many men we will have to keep to accomplish that victory, it is impossible yet to determine. There is a great tendency in the press and among other critics to think that the Army leaders have no feeling for these things and are simply determined to keep a big army in existence because they like it, and therefore it is ticklish to run head on into this feeling with direct counter criticism. Therefore we tried to draft a paper which would make the people [public] feel that we appreciated their views as well as ours, and their difficulties as well as ours, and which would give us the confidence which we will have to have while we are solving these difficult problems.

Question to Consider

This document was written after the A-bombs were dropped on Japan and does not discuss a motive for that action. Do these facts eliminate the document's usefulness in determining U.S. motives? _____

_____

_____

_____

_____

K The following excerpt is from a telegram sent to President Truman on the evening of August 7 from Winder, Georgia. Its author, Senator Richard B. Russell (D, Ga.), is responding to press reports that Under Secretary of State Grew was pushing for a U.S. offer of surrender terms to the Japanese that would permit them to keep their emperor.

> PERMIT ME TO RESPECTFULLY SUGGEST THAT WE CEASE OUR EFFORTS TO CAJOLE JAPAN INTO SURRENDERING IN ACCORDANCE WITH THE POTSDAM DECLARATION. LET US CARRY THE WAR TO THEM UNTIL THEY BEG US TO ACCEPT THE UNCONDITIONAL SURRENDER. THE FOUL ATTACK ON PEARL HARBOR BROUGHT US INTO WAR AND I AM UNABLE TO SEE ANY VALID REASON WHY WE SHOULD BE SO MUCH MORE CONSIDERATE AND LENIENT IN DEALING WITH JAPAN THAN WITH GERMANY. I EARNESTLY INSIST JAPAN SHOULD BE DEALT WITH AS HARSHLY AS GERMANY AND THAT SHE SHOULD NOT BE THE BENEFICIARY OF A SOFT PEACE. THE VAST MAJORITY OF THE AMERICAN PEOPLE, INCLUDING MANY SOUND THINKERS WHO HAVE INTIMATE KNOWLEDGE OF THE ORIENT, DO NOT AGREE WITH MR. GREW IN HIS ATTITUDE THAT THERE IS ANY THING SACROSANCT ABOUT HIROHITO. HE SHOULD GO. WE HAVE NO OBLIGATION TO SHINTOLISM [Shintoism]. THE CONTEMPTUOUS ANSWER OF THE JAPS TO THE POTSDAM ULTIMATUM JUSTIFIES A REVISION OF THAT DOCUMENT AND STERNER PEACE TERMS.

IF WE DO NOT HAVE AVAILABLE A SUFFICIENT NUMBER OF ATOMIC BOMBS WITH WHICH TO FINISH THE JOB IMMEDIATELY, LET US CARRY ON WITH TNT AND FIRE BOMBS UNTIL WE CAN PRODUCE THEM.[9]

Questions to Consider

Does Russell reveal an emotion in the telegram that could have been a factor in the decision to use the bomb against Japan (even though Russell himself did not have a direct role in the decision)? If so, what is that emotion? Is it likely that Russell's views were his

own alone or representative of the views of many Americans at the time? _____

_____

_____

_____

_____

L The final document is Truman's reply on August 9 to the telegram above. Before Truman became vice president in March 1945, he had been a colleague of Russell's in the Senate.

Dear Dick:

I read your telegram of August seventh with a lot of interest.

I know that Japan is a terribly cruel and uncivilized nation in warfare but I can't bring myself to believe that, because they are beasts, we should ourselves act in the same manner.

For myself, I certainly regret the necessity of wiping out whole populations because of the "pigheadedness" of the leaders of a nation and, for your information, I am not going to do it unless it is absolutely necessary. It is my opinion that after the Russians enter into the war the Japanese will very shortly fold up.

My object is to save as many American lives as possible but I also have a humane feeling for the women and children of Japan.[10]

Questions to Consider

Does Truman indicate that he was influenced in his decision to use the bomb by considerations mentioned by Russell in his telegram? What reason does Truman give for using

the bomb against Japan? _____

_____

_____

_____

_____

Now that you have finished reading and taking notes on the documents, write a brief essay (no more than three typewritten, double-spaced pages) stating your conclusions about why Truman used the atomic bomb against Japan and outlining the rationale behind your claims. You may quote the documents provided to develop your interpretation. When you use a document to make a particular point, whether you include a direct quotation or not, identify that document's letter in parentheses after the appropriate sentence. You may want to review the essay-writing tips in Exercise 5 of Chapter 5 before you begin your first draft.

The preceding excerpts represent only a small portion of the documentation that historians have used to explain why the United States used the atomic bomb against Japan. Yet the primary materials included in Exercise 4 alone present a complex picture of the factors that went into the American decision during the spring and summer of 1945. This exercise merely hints at some of the challenges of causal analysis.

Causal analysis is difficult in part because it often entails understanding personalities and their interaction with each other. It is people, after all, who make decisions, and it does not take much contact with them to discover that they are not all the same. With the importance of individuals in history in mind, we turn in the next chapter to the subject of biography.

NOTES

1. E. H. Carr, *What Is History?* (New York: Vintage, 1961), 113.
2. John Lewis Gaddis, *The United States and the Origins of the Cold War, 1941–1947* (New York: Columbia University Press, 1972), 355.
3. Arthur M. Schlesinger, Jr., "Origins of the Cold War," *Foreign Affairs* 46 (October 1967), 46–47.
4. William Appleman Williams, *The Tragedy of American Diplomacy,* rev. ed. (New York: Norton, 1972), 229–232.
5. The diary is in the Stimson Papers, Sterling Library, Yale University, New Haven, Conn. This and subsequent excerpts from the diary are from the microfilm edition.
6. Donald Fleming and Bernard Bailyn, eds., *The Intellectual Migration: Europe and America, 1930–1960* (Cambridge, Mass.: Harvard University Press, 1969), 127–128.
7. Box 333, President's Secretary's Files, Harry S Truman Papers, Harry S Truman Library, Independence, Mo.
8. Ibid.
9. Richard B. Russell Papers, Russell Library, University of Georgia, Athens, Ga.
10. Ibid.

7 BIOGRAPHY: THE INDIVIDUAL IN HISTORY

Martin Luther King, Jr.

Historian John A. Garraty traces biography back to ancient Egyptian kings who, in their "search for immortality," had records of their lives and achievements placed in their tombs.[1] Despite the notable contributions of the Roman Plutarch in the first century of the Christian era and authors of lives of the saints after him, it was not until the publication in 1791 of James Boswell's *Life of Samuel Johnson* that such a work exhibited all the characteristics of what we call modern biography. Boswell's passion for accuracy drove him to do meticulous and exhaustive research. His grasp of biography as an art, his keen eye for the telling anecdote, and his determination to probe the inner life of his subject made his *Life* a model for later scholars. Though Boswell labored before the emergence of psychology as a field of study, with all its sparkling insights into human motivation, some call his masterpiece the greatest biography ever written.

English-language biographies during the next century failed to match Boswell's in quality, but they often served important didactic purposes. For example, some biographies provided moral instruction and cohesion in rapidly changing societies. In the United States, Parson M. L. Weems's *The Life of Washington*, published during the first decade of the nineteenth century, represented an extreme but popular manifestation of biography as moral exhortation. Laced with anecdotes concocted from the author's imagination, including the story of young George and the cherry tree, the book became an integral part of American folklore.

The twentieth-century trend toward professionalism throughout historical writing undermined the old enthusiasm for biography as an instrument of moral instruction but did not dampen the genre's popularity. Biographical or autobiographical works regularly appear on nonfiction bestseller lists. British scholar Alan Shelston offers two reasons for this: people's "curiosity about human personality" and their "interest in factual knowledge."[2]

The purpose of this chapter is to cultivate an appreciation for the aesthetic and functional values of biography. On the one hand, you can derive great pleasure from reading a finely crafted account of another person's life. On the other, you can develop important insights into human motivation that may help you in everyday life, as well as a sense of how individuals mold — and are molded by — the society around them. Finally, the study of biographers' techniques advances your own ability to capture your reader's attention with the written word.

In probing individual motivation and assessing their subjects' place in history, contemporary biographers often use imagination, just as Boswell did. As one historian of biography notes,

> the exact records of a life are, at best, desultory and fragmentary . . . [not to mention] ambiguous. To achieve the leap from the known to the possibly knowable makes imperative some degree of imaginative intervention, and to bring out the ultimate significance of the life thus recreated requires the exercise of personal judgment. Informed speculation . . . is not only permissable but indispensable if a coherent and meaningful story is to be fashioned from the shreds of fact.[3]

In sum, capturing the inner workings of an individual personality presents unique challenges.

At its best, biography tells a good deal not only about an individual, man or woman, but about the events, movements, and institutions of that person's times. Often the biographer's subject made a special contribution to a nation, to a culture, or to human beings in general, or represented a particular time and place or group of people. Biography never ignores the world around the individual. A biography centers on one person, but in tracing that person's interaction with others and penetrating to his or her inner core, it can — indeed it *should* — reveal much about life during a particular time.

The following exercises introduce you to the personality, intellect, and impact of Martin Luther King, Jr. The first two exercises show you how three biographers treated aspects of King's personality. The passages provided demonstrate both the potential appeal of descriptive narrative writing and biography's power to shed light on the times during which the subject lived. The exercises also require you to search passages for hints about the biographer's own values and assumptions.

Next you will examine King's intellectual development, with special attention to his adherence to the strategy of militant nonviolence in advancing the African-American cause. Again, you will see that biography can facilitate the understanding of a period of time as well as of an individual.

The last two exercises address the question of King's place in history. How important was he to the civil-rights movement? Had he not lived or had he made a different career choice in 1954 — for example, taking a job in Detroit, Michigan, rather than Montgomery, Alabama — would the struggle for equality of African-Americans have been significantly affected? How should revelations about his behavior toward women and his plagiarism as a graduate student influence his stature? The exercises provide you with a better appreciation of the purposes of biography and with a deeper understanding of American life during the 1940s, 1950s, and 1960s. At the same time, they give you further practice evaluating secondary and primary sources, which you encountered in earlier chapters.

Personality, the Core of Biography

A major task of any biography is to construct a word portrait of an individual human being. The biographer must describe both a person's physical attributes and his or her behavioral patterns and qualities of mind. By evaluating the ways biographers execute this task, you can learn a good deal about effective writing and about how individuals relate to their environment.

Born on January 15, 1929, Martin Luther King, Jr., grew up in a middle-class African-American neighborhood in Atlanta, Georgia. Racial segregation pervaded the South during those years, in housing, schools, the workplace, and public transportation. African-Americans virtually always found themselves subordinated to whites. Young Martin suffered at the hands of prejudiced white people, whom he resented deeply. Yet he enjoyed a largely happy childhood under the watch of his stern, patriarchal father, a prominent Baptist minister, and his mild-mannered, polished mother, the daughter of a preacher.

EXERCISE 1: *Catching the Reader's Eye and Ear*

The following passages from two biographies of King offer partial portraits of King during his teens. Read the passages, underlining words and phrases that you find particularly effective in creating a mental picture of King's appearance and personality. Circle any words or phrases that you find awkward or confusing.

A. . . . M. L. was a sensuous youth who played a violin, liked opera, and relished soul food — fried chicken, cornbread, and collard greens with ham hocks and bacon drippings. Physically he was small and plump-faced, with almond-shaped eyes, a mahogany complexion, and expressive hands. But the most memorable thing about him was his voice. It had changed into a rich and resonant baritone that commanded attention when he spoke in class or held forth in a nearby drugstore.

He discovered something else about his voice: girls blushed and flirted when he spoke to them in his mellifluent drawl. A natty dresser, nicknamed "Tweed" because of a fondness for tweed suits, he became a connoisseur of lovely young women, many of them from the best Negro families in Atlanta. A. D. could not remember a time when his big brother was not interested in girls, and M. L. himself laughed that women and food were always his main weaknesses. "He kept flitting from chick to chick," A. D. said later, "and I decided I couldn't keep up with him. Especially since he was crazy about dances, and just about the best jitterbug in town."[4]

B. . . . Mike [Martin] developed early the aggressiveness typical of the short male. When he left Morehouse [College in Atlanta], he would be five feet seven inches tall and weigh slightly less than 170 pounds. He was healthy, agile, and solidly built. The young ladies he courted remember his short height only as an after thought. His sartorial fastidiousness and his confident charm and eloquence are the primary legacies of his enterprise among Atlanta's belles. Mike's selection of pretty girls was as careful as the choice of his wardrobe. . . . Lacking aquiline features and long straight hair — near-white attributes upon which black mothers placed a pathetically dogmatic value — Mike charmed with his mellifluent baritone. The genteel damsels of the black aristocracy were told of the Rubicons they caused to be crossed, of the calamitous Waterloos their mere existence created, of the Troys of whose destruction they were the source:

> *On desperate seas, long wont to roam,*
> *Thy hyacinth hair, thy classic face,*
> *Thy Naiad airs have brought me home*
> *To the glory that was Greece and the grandeur that was Rome.*

One catches distinctly the cadences of that earnest, deep voice, the vowels distended three times their normal length. And one pictures the pleasure mirrored in the lovely face of a feminine listener. Mike King played hard, dressed well, and attempted to be a great lover.[5]

Now read the passages a second time. Which one most effectively captures and holds your attention? Use the space provided to explain your conclusion. Identify any principles for good narrative writing that could be drawn from your evaluation of the two passages. _____

_____

_____

_____

_____

_____

_____

_____

_____

Go back and read the passages a third time, this time looking for indications of prevalent values of the society in which King grew up. List those values here. _____

_____

_____

_____

1. Did King fit comfortably into the middle-class African-American community in Atlanta in which he was raised? _____

2. Is there any indication in either passage of the biographer's values? Are there instances in which the biographer goes beyond merely presenting facts and expresses an opinion? _____

_____

Fitting Individuals into Their Times

The year 1952 found King studying for a doctorate in theology at Boston University. He already possessed degrees from Morehouse College and Crozer Theological Seminary in Pennsylvania. King was also searching for a wife. As a minister in the African-American community, he knew that he would be expected to "marry sooner rather than later," that his choice would "affect his career" as well as his personal life, and that "he must look for certain objective qualities in prospective mates."[6]

EXERCISE 2: *Courting in the 1950s*

In the following selections, Pulitzer Prize–winning author Taylor Branch describes King's first encounter with his future wife. Read selection A, keeping in mind that a common purpose of the biographer is to describe his subject in the context of the world around him.

A. King was doing his best to marry. He and Philip Lenud double-dated frequently, and King met other possibilities in the churches where he preached. He had long since invented a coded rating system for eligible women, calling an attractive woman a "doctor" and a stunning one a "constitution," saying that she was "well-established and amply endowed." . . . King's bachelor style fit the postwar fashion. He elbowed his male friends in the ribs if a "constitution" went by, collected phone numbers, and began each contact with a promising new lady by trying out his lines. Early in 1952, he called a woman blindly on the recommendation of a friend. After passing along a few of the friend's compliments as reasons why he had obtained the phone number, King threw out his opening line. "You know every Napoleon has his Waterloo," he said. "I'm like Napoleon. I'm at my Waterloo, and I'm on my knees."

"That's absurd," Coretta Scott replied. "You don't even know me."

Unabashed, King continued with the melodrama and poetry, throwing in some comments about his course work that identified him quickly as a man of substance. His come-on crisscrossed between directness and caricature, authority and humor. When Scott did not hang up on him after his opening flourishes, it was only a matter of minutes until he persuaded her to have lunch with him the next day. He picked her up in his Chevrolet and took her to a cafeteria.[7]

1. Does Branch suggest that King's behavior toward women was commonplace or exceptional for unmarried men during the 1950s? _____

2. How would you describe King's behavior? _____

_____

3. What is implied in King's behavior about his attitude toward women (their likes, their dislikes, and their role in society, for example)? _____

_____

Coretta Scott was the daughter of an Alabama farmer who owned several hundred acres of land. Although a member of the local African-American elite, Obadiah Scott was far from wealthy. As a child, his daughter "had picked cotton in the fields and scrubbed clothes in a washtub," but she received enough education in a local church school to qualify for a partial scholarship at Ohio's recently integrated Antioch College. Graduating from Antioch in 1951, Coretta went to the New England Conservatory of Music in Boston, aspiring "to become a classical singer." She received only a small scholarship, hardly enough to support herself. So she worked "at a fashionable Beacon Hill boarding-house in exchange for room and board."[8] Selection B, again from Branch's study, conveys her state of mind when she first met King and goes on to show how the two reacted to one another. See Figure 7.1.

B. Suffering from the compounded insecurities of race, poverty, and the competitive world of music, Scott struggled to keep her dignity and her optimism above her acute sense of realism. "The next man I give my photograph to is going to be my husband," she told herself. Nearly two years older than King, she would turn twenty-five that spring and was already past the prime marrying age of that era. In the absence of a career break or a prosperous suitor, she would soon be obliged to scale back her ambitions.

King knew all this. It would become one of his stinging jokes to tease her with the remark that she would have wound up picking cotton back in Alabama had he not come along. At their first lunch, however, he praised her looks, especially her long bangs, and launched into discussion of topics from soul food to [Walter] Rauschenbusch [a prominent American theologian]. To Coretta Scott, who had been put off at first sight by King's lack of height, he seemed to grow as he talked. As he drove her back to the Conservatory, he shocked her again by declaring that she would make him a good wife. "The four things that I look for in a wife are character, intelligence, personality, and beauty," he told her. "And you have them all. I want to see you again." She replied unsteadily that she would have to check her schedule.[9]

Read over the first paragraph in the passage above. In explaining Coretta's feelings of insecurity, Branch mentions her race, her poverty, and the competitive nature of her chosen field.

1. What else might he have mentioned? _____

2. What does this omission say about the author? _____

_____

Now look again at passage B as a whole. What does it say about the values of young Martin and Coretta and the society around them? Were they conforming to or rebelling

against their society? _____

FIGURE 7.1 *Coretta Scott King and Martin Luther King Shortly After Their Marriage*

_____

_____

_____

_____

_____

_____

_____

_____

Connecting Personality and Ideas

Martin Luther King, Jr., was a complex man with a sharp, well-trained intellect. In the course of his academic preparation at Morehouse, Crozer, and Boston University, he encountered a wide range of ideas about religion, politics, and human society. By examining the connection between King's readings in school and his later activism on social issues, including his strategy of nonviolent resistance, we can evaluate the impact of King's surroundings on his ideas as well as the degree of originality in his thought.

King's academic readings included the work of American theologians Walter Rauschenbusch (1861–1918) and Reinhold Niebuhr (1892–1971) and of the Indian independence leader Mohandas Gandhi (1869–1948). The following paragraphs provide some background on the three men, followed by passages by each of them. Each passage addresses either the social activism of clergy or nonviolent resistance as a strategy for combating injustice.

A Baptist clergyman, Rauschenbusch had been a leader of the turn-of-the-century social gospel movement, which sought to liberate Protestant churches from a narrow focus on saving individual souls. According to Rauschenbusch and his allies, the clergy should become directly involved in ameliorating the ills of city and factory. Social gospelers believed that humankind had the capacity to Christianize society and to create a Kingdom of God on earth, but only through broad reforms, and Rauschenbusch inclined toward a radical conception of the changes required. He attacked capitalism for dividing "industrial society into two classes, — those who own the instruments and materials of production, and those who furnish the labor for it." In the inevitable struggle between the two classes, labor always held the weaker hand. Only a socialist system, he insisted, would eliminate this class division, restoring "the independence of workingmen by making him once more the owner of his tools and the [recipient]. . . of the full proceeds of his production."[10]

Although Niebuhr criticized capitalism, he also rejected the social gospel's faith in the essential goodness of humankind. An activist in reform causes, he eventually became a prominent writer on Christian doctrine and its application to society's problems. With the publication in 1932 of his *Moral Man and Immoral Society,* he emerged as the key spokesman for what became known as neo-orthodoxy. According to this view, people were born in original sin and could never fully escape that fact. Because people were inherently selfish, they could not expect the coming of a Kingdom of God on earth. Nevertheless, they could (and should) seek changes in an unjust system, often by shifting power away from dominant groups.

American society in the early twentieth century may have been unjust, but at least it was not part of a foreign empire, as was Mohandas Gandhi's native land. Despite

FIGURE 7.2 *Gandhi and His Followers in India*

British oppression in India, Gandhi first became involved in reform causes while practicing law in South Africa's rigidly segregated society. After spending two decades there organizing Indians to resist discrimination, he returned to his homeland and soon became an agitator for change, including independence from British rule. Already an advocate of nonviolent resistance to injustice, which he called *Satyagraha*, he worked diligently to train his countrymen in the technique (see Figure 7.2). In 1930 he organized a march of some 200 miles in protest of the British Salt Acts, which were a particular burden on poor Indians. During World War II he used British desperation for assistance against Japan and Germany to campaign for independence. When the British finally granted India its independence in 1947, Gandhi turned all his efforts to the containment of strife between Hindus and Muslims in India. In January 1948 a Hindu extremist assassinated him in New Delhi.

EXERCISE 3: *The Origins of King's Social Activism and Strategy of Nonviolent Resistance*

Read the following passages from the works of Rauschenbusch, Gandhi, and Niebuhr. All three may be used to explain King's development of a strategy for advancing the African-American cause in the United States. Answer the questions following each passage.

A. [Rauschenbusch] The social gospel is the old message of salvation, but enlarged and intensified. The individualistic gospel has taught us to see the sinfulness of every human heart and has inspired us with faith in the willingness and power of God to save every soul that comes to him. But it has not given us an adequate understanding of the sinfulness of the social order and its share in the sins of all individuals within it. It has not evoked faith in the will and power of God to redeem the permanent institutions of human society from their inherited guilt of oppression and extortion.... The social gospel seeks to bring men under repentance for their collective sins and to create a more sensitive and more modern conscience.[11]

1. What is the difference between the "social gospel" and the "individualistic gospel"?

   _____

   _____

2. How would clergy who subscribe to the social gospel differ in their professional activities from clergy who subscribe to the individual gospel? _____

   _____

3. As an African-American and an aspiring clergyman, how might Martin Luther King, Jr., have used the passage above to define his mission in life? _____

   _____

B. [Gandhi] Satyagraha differs from Passive Resistance as the North Pole from the South. The latter ... does not exclude the use of ... violence for the purpose of gaining one's end, whereas the former ... excludes the use of violence in any shape or form. ...

   Its root meaning is holding on to truth, hence truth-force. ... In the application of Satyagraha I discovered in the earliest stages that pursuit of truth did not admit of violence being inflicted on one's opponent but that he must be weaned from error by patience and sympathy. For what appears to be truth to the one may appear to be error to the other. And patience means self-suffering. So the doctrine came to mean vindication of truth not by infliction of suffering on the opponent but on one's self.

   But on the political field the struggle on behalf of the people mostly consists in opposing error in the shape of unjust laws. When you have failed to bring the error home to the lawgiver by way of petitions and the like, the only remedy open to you, if you do not wish to submit to error, is to compel him by physical force to yield to you or by suffering in your own person by inviting the penalty for the breach of the law. Hence Satyagraha largely appears to the public as Civil Disobedience or Civil Resistance. It is civil in the sense that it is not criminal.

   The lawbreaker breaks the law surreptitiously and tries to avoid the penalty, not so the civil resister. He ever obeys the laws of the State to which he belongs, not out of fear of the sanctions but because he considers them to be good for the welfare of society. But there come occasions, generally rare, when he considers certain laws to be so unjust as to render obedience to them a dishonour. He then openly and civilly breaks them and quietly suffers the penalty for their breach. ...

   The beauty and efficacy of Satyagraha are so great and the doctrine so simple that it can be preached even to children. It was preached by me to thousands of men, women and children commonly called indentured Indians with excellent results.[12]

1. According to Gandhi, what is the difference between Passive Resistance and Satyagraha? _____

   _____

2. Why, under Satyagraha, may personal suffering prove essential? _____

_____

3. How does the practice of Satyagraha differ from the actions of the average lawbreaker?

_____

_____

4. In the American South during the 1950s, to which laws might an African-American

apply Satyagraha? _____

_____

C. [Niebuhr] However large the number of individual white men who . . . identify themselves completely with the Negro cause, the white race in America will not admit the
Negro to equal rights if it is not forced to do so. . . .

On the other hand, any effort at violent revolution on the part of the Negro will ac-
centuate the animosities and prejudices of his oppressors. Since they outnumber him
hopelessly, any appeal to arms must inevitably result in a terrible social catastrophe.
Social ignorance and economic interest are arrayed against him. If the social ignorance
is challenged by ordinary coercive weapons it will bring forth the most violent pas-
sions of which ignorant men are capable. Even if there were more social intelligence,
economic interest would offer stubborn resistance to his claims.

The technique of non-violence will not eliminate all these perils. But it will reduce
them. It will, if persisted in with the same patience and discipline attained by Mr.
Gandhi and his followers, achieve a degree of justice which neither pure moral sua-
sion nor violence could gain. Boycotts against banks which discriminate against
Negroes in granting credit, against stores which refuse to employ Negroes while
serving Negro trade, and against public service corporations which practice racial
discrimination, would undoubtedly be crowned with some measure of success. Non-
payment of taxes against states which spend on education of Negro children only a
fraction of the amount spent on white children, might be an equally efficacious
weapon. . . .

There is no problem of political life to which religious imagination can make a
larger contribution than this problem of developing non-violent resistance. The discovery of elements of common human frailty in the foe and . . . the appreciation of all
human life as possessing transcendent worth . . . creates attitudes which transcend social conflict and thus mitigate its cruelties. . . . These attitudes of repentance which recognize that the evil in the foe is also in the self, and these impulses of love which claim
kinship with all men in spite of social conflict, are the peculiar gifts of religion to the
human spirit. . . . It is no accident of history that the spirit of non-violence has been introduced into contemporary politics by a religious leader of the orient.[13]

1. When Niebuhr says that "the white race in America will not admit the Negro to equal
rights if it is not forced to do so," is he advocating violence by African-Americans to

achieve their rights? _____ Explain. _____

_____

_____

_____

2. Why does Niebuhr believe that Gandhi's ideas are especially applicable to the American South? _____

_____

3. Is Niebuhr's judgment on the applicability of Gandhi's ideas in the American South primarily moral or practical? _____ Explain. _____

_____

Passage D is from King's first book, *Stride Toward Freedom*, written during the year following his triumphant role in the Montgomery bus boycott of 1955–1956. This event began less than two years after King moved to that city to assume the pastorate at Dexter Avenue Baptist Church. Although King played no part in the incident leading to the boycott, he soon emerged as leader of the civil-rights campaign in Montgomery, largely because he had not lived there long enough to become associated with one of the many factions that divided the African-American community. The segregation of Montgomery buses provided ideal circumstances for the application of nonviolent resistance (see Figure 7.3), and King's success elevated him to national prominence. *Stride Toward Freedom* centered on the boycott itself but also included much information about King's life before moving to Montgomery. Read the following selection, from his chapter "Pilgrimage to Nonviolence."

D. [King] Not until I entered Crozer Theological Seminary in 1948 . . . did I begin a serious intellectual quest for a method to eliminate social evil. . . . I spent a great deal of time reading the works of the great social philosophers. . . . Walter Rauschenbusch's *Christianity and the Social Crisis* . . . left an indelible imprint . . . by giving me a theological basis for the social concern which had already grown up in me as a result of my early experiences. . . . I felt that he had fallen victim to the nineteenth century "cult of inevitable progress" which led him to a superficial optimism concerning man's nature. Moreover, he came perilously close to identifying the Kingdom of God with a particular social and economic system — a tendency which should never befall the Church. But . . . Rauschenbusch had done a great service for the Christian Church by insisting that the gospel deals with the whole man, not only his soul but his body; not only his spiritual well-being but his material well-being. . . .

I was also exposed for the first time to the pacifist position in a lecture by Dr. A. J. Muste. I was deeply moved by Dr. Muste's talk, but far from convinced of the practicability of his position. . . . I felt that while war could never be a positive or absolute good, it could serve as a negative good in the sense of preventing the spread and growth of an evil force. War, horrible as it is, might be preferable to surrender to a totalitarian system — Nazi, Fascist, or Communist. . . .

. . . one Sunday afternoon I traveled to Philadelphia to hear a sermon by Dr. Mordecai Johnson, president of Howard University. . . . Dr. Johnson had just returned from a trip to India, and . . . he spoke of the life and teachings of Mahatma Gandhi. . . . I left the meeting and bought a half-dozen books on Gandhi's life and works.

. . . As I read I became deeply fascinated by his campaigns of nonviolent resistance. . . . The whole concept of "Satyagraha" . . . was profoundly significant to me. . . . Prior to reading Gandhi, I had about concluded that the ethics of Jesus were only effective in individual relationships. The "turn the other cheek" philosophy and the "love your enemies" philosophy were only valid, I felt, when individuals were in conflict with other individuals; when racial groups and nations were in conflict a more realistic approach seemed necessary. But after reading Gandhi, I saw how utterly mistaken I was. . . . It was in this Gandhian emphasis on love and nonviolence that I discovered the method for social reform that I had been seeking for so many months. . . .

But my intellectual odyssey to nonviolence did not end here. During my last year in theological school, I began to read the works of Reinhold Niebuhr. The prophetic and realistic elements in Niebuhr's passionate style and profound thought were appealing to me, and I became so enamored of his social ethics that I almost fell into the trap of accepting uncritically everything he wrote.

. . . in *Moral Man and Immoral Society* . . . he argued that there was no intrinsic moral difference between violent and nonviolent resistance. The social consequences of the two methods were different, he contended, but the differences were all in degree rather than kind. Later Niebuhr began emphasizing the irresponsibility of relying on nonviolent resistance when there was no ground for believing that it would be successful in preventing the spread of totalitarian tyranny. It could only be successful, he argued, if the groups against whom the resistance was taking place had some degree of moral conscience, as was the case in Gandhi's struggle against the British. . . .

. . . As I continued to read . . . I came to see more and more the shortcomings of his position. For instance, many of his statements revealed that he interpreted pacifism as a sort of passive nonresistance to evil expressing naive trust in the power of love. But this was a serious distortion. My study of Gandhi convinced me that true pacifism is not nonresistance to evil, but nonviolent resistance to evil. Between the two positions, there is a world of difference. Gandhi resisted evil with as much vigor and power as the violent resister, but he resisted with love instead of hate. True pacifism is . . . a courageous confrontation of evil by the power of love, in the faith that it is better to be the recipient of violence than the inflicter of it, since the latter only multiplies the existence of violence and bitterness in the universe, while the former may develop a sense of shame in the opponent, and thereby bring about a transformation and change of heart.[14]

Complete the following multiple-choice questions by circling the appropriate answer.

1. According to King, Rauschenbusch's primary influence on him was in providing a theological basis for looking at human beings as
   a. individuals rather than as part of a group.
   b. possessing a material as well as a spiritual side to which the clergy must devote attention.
   c. essentially spiritual creatures.
   d. capable of producing a "Heaven on Earth."

2. King criticizes Rauschenbusch on which *two* of the following points? Rauschenbusch was
   a. too pessimistic about human nature.
   b. too optimistic about human nature.
   c. insensitive to the negative impact of capitalism on human society.
   d. too inclined to associate a specific social and economic system with the perfection of human society.

3. Why was King initially dubious about pacifism?
   a. It was impractical.
   b. It was too aggressive in outlook.
   c. He did not like the people espousing it.
   d. It was only useful against totalitarian systems.

4. According to King, Niebuhr distorted pacifism by equating it with
   a. hatred of one's enemies.
   b. violent nonresistance to evil.

FIGURE 7.3 *Montgomery Bus Boycott*

    c. a naive acceptance of democracy.

    d. nonresistance to evil.

5. According to King, Gandhi's Satyagraha could be effective by

    a. forcing opponents to change because of economic pressures.

    b. forcing the state to intervene to protect civil rights.

    c. persuading opponents to change by making them feel ashamed.

    d. persuading opponents to change for fear of violence.

6. According to Niebuhr in passage C, which of the choices in question 5 would make nonviolent resistance potentially successful for African-Americans in the South?

    a.

    b.

    c.

    d.

    In the space following, write a paragraph summarizing the roots of King's nonviolent social activism. In developing your paragraph, you may use documents A through D as well as the background material provided on each selection. Be sure to begin your paragraph with an appropriate topic sentence.

_____

_____

_____

_____

_____

_____

_____

_____

_____

_____

_____

_____

_____

_____

_____

Why Some Are Called

James Thomas Flexner, a biographer of George Washington, calls the first president "the indispensable man." No other person in America during the revolt against Great Britain and the first years of the republic, Flexner asserts, possessed the combination of qualities necessary to bring to a successful conclusion the struggle for independence and to hold the new nation together once that struggle had ended.[15]

Did Martin Luther King, Jr., play an indispensable role in the civil-rights movement for African-Americans between 1955 and his assassination in 1968? Or had the movement already achieved momentum by the time King was thrust upon the national scene in 1955–1956 through the Montgomery bus boycott, thus making his role significant but hardly indispensable? Were the efforts of the National Association for the Advancement of Colored People (NAACP) through the courts and in the U.S. Congress actually more central to the cause of African-Americans than the highly visible activities of King? How important were efforts at grassroots organization in the Deep South, often spurred by the Student Nonviolent Coordinating Committee (SNCC) and peopled by courageous if relatively obscure men and women, both white and black? And what about the significance of individuals whose actions provided the spark for a single event but who then retreated forever to the background? Such questions address the issue of an individual's place in history.

King clearly combined several qualities of leadership matched by no other African-American of his time. He was polished, well educated, and intellectual enough to appeal to wealthy northern liberals, but he was sufficiently down-to-earth, eloquent, and charismatic to reach poor African-Americans in the South as well. King was able to mobilize southern African-Americans behind a movement for desegregation in public facilities and politics as no one else had done before.

Yet, over time, King failed to unite African-Americans, North and South, behind his strategy of nonviolent resistance. In the mid-1960s, when he increasingly directed his activities toward cities above the Mason-Dixon Line and toward economic rather than civil-rights issues, he ran into considerable difficulty. By some estimates, King's stature was in decline at the time of his death, and only his martyrdom saved — or bolstered — his reputation as the preeminent leader of his people.

Furthermore, even King's role in the civil-rights movement is open to question. Although he led the Montgomery bus boycott, for example, the event grew out of the spontaneous refusal late one afternoon of a tired but dignified and determined seamstress, Rosa Parks, to give up her seat in the white section of a public bus. The boycott's success was very much in doubt until the U.S. Supreme Court ruled on November 13, 1956, in a case argued by NAACP lawyers, that segregation on public buses was unconstitutional. Two years earlier, lawyers for the same organization had persuaded the high court to declare racial segregation in public schools unconstitutional.

FIGURE 7.4 *Martin Luther King at the March on Washington, August 1963*

In the aftermath of the March on Washington of August 1963 and King's famous "I Have A Dream" speech (see Figure 7.4), *Time* magazine placed a portrait of the NAACP's executive secretary on its cover, declaring that "if there is one Negro who can lay claim to the position of spokesman and worker for a Negro consensus, it is a slender, stoop-shouldered, sickly, dedicated, rebellious man named Roy Wilkins"[16] (see Figure 7.5). Although King led demonstrations in Birmingham, Alabama, that proved crucial to President John F. Kennedy's submittal of a civil-rights bill to Congress during the summer of 1963, the lobbying efforts of the NAACP's Clarence Mitchell, Jr., arguably produced the bill's enactment early the following year and created the momentum necessary in the legislative branch for passage of the Voting Rights Act in 1965. SNCC's grassroots organizing and protests in the South over the previous three years were also critical.

Even King's detractors concede that, as former NAACP official Denton L. Watson has written, he was "a catalyst and will always remain a monumental figure in civil-rights history." "His greatest contributions," Watson asserts, "were his ability to arouse the human spirit to unparalleled heights and to burden the consciences of white liberals."[17] But Watson and others dispute the almost godlike stature that King attained in the first generation after his death.

How should we contend with this controversy over King's place in history? Certainly we have too little information before us here to render a judgment. In fact, a careful and comprehensive study of the matter would take years to complete, and even then our conclusions would be challenged by others. This is true partly because advocates of different positions on how best to advance the cause of African-Americans have an important stake in resolution of the issue. King espoused a distinct strategy that some rejected, both during his lifetime and later on. To these people, King's nonviolent tactics could never lead to full equality in America.

Another factor, however, rests in the inherently imprecise nature of the enterprise. To address the issue of King's place in history, we at some point must ask what America in

FIGURE 7.5 *NAACP Executive Secretary Roy Wilkins*

the 1950s and 1960s would have been like without him, or at least without his leadership of the civil-rights movement, and that involves asking what would have happened had a situation been different from what it was. Such questions often are interesting and even essential in grappling with important issues, but they can never be answered definitively. Nevertheless, we can frame precise questions to focus our research and to ensure a coherent addressing of the issue. Indeed, framing appropriate questions is an essential skill in doing history.

EXERCISE 4: *King's Place in History (Part I)*

In the space provided, write three specific questions you would want answered in addressing the role of King in the Montgomery bus boycott of 1955–1956. Think about the needs of the African-American community in Montgomery as it confronted a largely hostile white majority, about the organization of the African-American community in Montgomery before King's arrival in 1954, and about the significance of outside forces in influencing the outcome of the bus boycott. In preparing your questions, do not hesitate to refer to earlier sections of this chapter or to your textbook.

1. _____

_____

2. _____

_____

3. _____

_____

King — Warts and All

Other sources of controversy over King's place in history are his marital infidelities and his plagiarizing portions of his writings while in graduate school. After he became a national figure in the Montgomery bus boycott, King was away from home more often than not and was constantly the object of sexual overtures from attractive women. King often accepted their offers — a fact not made public until the mid-1980s. In his Pulitzer Prize–winning biography, David J. Garrow reports that some friends of King saw his behavior "as 'a natural concomitant' of the tense, fast-paced life" he led, while others viewed "it as standard ministerial practice in a context where intimate pastor-parishioner relationships long had been winked at." Still others regarded King's conduct as "typical of the overall movement" — that is, married men in the civil-rights movement frequently engaged in sexual relationships with women other than their wives. Garrow also notes that King insisted that his wife play the role of traditional housewife and mother, rather than taking on a highly visible role in the movement.[18]

King's plagiarism while at Crozer Theological Seminary (1948–1951) and at Boston University (1951–1954) became public knowledge in 1990 and was the subject the following year of a roundtable discussion in the *Journal of American History*. The publication offered a standard definition of *plagiarism* as "*any* unacknowledged appropriation of words or ideas," and it judged King guilty of the practice in a large number of "his academic papers, including the dissertation."[19] In commenting on the findings, King biographers Garrow and David L. Lewis agreed that King had to have been aware that he was engaging in behavior unacceptable in the academic world. But they and others also pointed out that, as David Thelen writes, King often "grounded his activities on the borders between cultures [, most notably]. . . between expectations bred of evangelical, southern, African American folk cultures [, where the borrowing of words and ideas without acknowledgment was widespread and acceptable,] and those bred of northern, white, university scholarship," where such borrowing in written work was generally forbidden.[20]

Cornish Rogers, a fellow African-American student with King at Boston University, suggested to David Thelen that King expected Professor L. Harold DeWolf, his adviser there, to examine his work "with a fine-tooth comb," and that when DeWolf passed it, King simply assumed it was all right.[21] David L. Lewis speculated that DeWolf and other professors applied a lower standard to King because he was African-American. DeWolf in particular among his professors was known as a stickler for detail, so it is hard to believe, according to Lewis, that he was unaware of King's practice.

Whatever the precise details, King's sexual conduct and his plagiarism have stirred a lively discussion among scholars and editorialists in the popular press. Historians generally regard discovering what happened and then explaining why it happened as their two primary tasks. In contrast, editorialists preoccupy themselves with assessing the meaning of what happened. Many historians engage in this enterprise as well, even if only as a secondary activity. The final exercise of this chapter asks you to examine the behavior of King in relation to the question of his position as a historic figure.

EXERCISE 5: *King's Place in History (Part II)*

On separate sheets of paper, write a short essay on King's place in history in the context of his overall record. In completing this assignment, ask yourself how important his illicit sexual relations and plagiarism are in comparison to his efforts to promote civil rights for African Americans. Think of what we now know of the philandering of former president John F. Kennedy and of the suspected philandering of current president Bill Clinton. Think of the fact that much of Kennedy's Pulitzer Prize–winning book *Profiles of Courage* was ghostwritten. Should these embarrassing facts in the historical record influence the judgments we make of individuals who have held — or hold — positions of leadership in our society? If so, how? Do these facts diminish their accomplishments in other areas? For example, is King's record on civil rights for African-Americans diminished by his traditional conception of the role of women — at least of the woman he chose as his wife?

This chapter has concentrated on written evidence and on examining the individual in the context of history and society. In the next chapter, we shift the focus to two elements of the modern media — motion pictures and television — and to the ways in which they reflect popular tastes and attitudes.

NOTES

1. John A. Garraty, *The Nature of Biography* (New York: Knopf, 1957), 31.
2. Alan Shelston, *Biography* (London: Methuen, 1977), 3.
3. Ibid., 348.

4. Stephen Oates, *Let the Trumpet Sound: The Life of Martin Luther King, Jr.* (New York: Harper & Row, 1982), 15–16.

5. David L. Lewis, *King: A Critical Biography* (Baltimore: Penguin Books, 1970), 22.

6. Reprinted with the permission of Simon & Schuster from *Parting the Waters: America in the King Years, 1954–63* by Taylor Branch. Copyright © 1988 by Taylor Branch.

7. Ibid., 94–95.

8. Ibid., 95.

9. Ibid., 95–96.

10. Walter Rauschenbusch, *Christianity and the Social Crisis* (New York: Macmillan, 1907), 406–407.

11. Walter Rauschenbusch, *A Theology for the Social Gospel* (New York: Macmillan, 1918), 4–6.

12. Excerpted with permission from M. K. Gandhi, *Satyagraha,* (Ahmedabad: Navajivan Publishing, 1951), pp. 6–7.

13. Reprinted with the permission of Scribner, a division of Simon & Schuster, from *Moral Man and Immoral Society* by Reinhold Niebuhr. Copyright 1932 by Charles Scribner's Sons; copyright renewed © 1960 by Reinhold Niebuhr.

14. Reprinted by arrangement with the Heirs to the Estate of Martin Luther King, Jr., c/o Writers House, Inc. as agent for the proprietor. Copyright © 1958 by Martin Luther King, Jr., copyright renewed 1986 by Coretta Scott King, Dexter King, Martin Luther King III, Yolanda King, and Bernice King.

15. James Thomas Flexner, *Washington: The Indispensable Man* (Boston: Little, Brown, 1974).

16. *Time,* August 30 1963, 9.

17. Denton L. Watson, "Scholars' Focus on Martin Luther King Has Skewed Our Understanding of the Civil-Rights Struggle," *Chronicle of Higher Education,* January 23, 1991, A44.

18. David J. Garrow, *Bearing the Cross: Martin Luther King, Jr., and the Southern Christian Leadership Movement* (New York: Morrow, 1986), 374–376.

19. Martin Luther King, Jr., Papers Project, "The Student Papers of Martin Luther King, Jr.: A Summary Statement on Research," *Journal of American History* (June 1991), 31.

20. David Thelen, "Becoming Martin Luther King, Jr.: An Introduction," ibid., 11.

21. "Conversation Between David Thelen and Cornish Rogers," ibid., 54.

8 ANALYZING VISUAL MEDIA: MOVIES AND TELEVISION

Mass Culture in America, 1950–1990

In 1956 American culture critic Bernard Rosenberg sadly warned that "contemporary man . . . finds that his life has been emptied of meaning, that it has been trivialized. He is alienated from his past, from his work, from his community, and possibly from himself . . . [at a moment when] he has an unprecedented amount of time on his hands which . . . he must kill lest it kill him." Rosenberg accused television of vulgarizing art and literature. "Never before," he lamented, "have the sacred and the profane, the genuine and the specious, the exalted and the debased, been so thoroughly mixed that they are all but indistinguishable." "Mass culture" threatened simultaneously "to cretinize our taste," "brutalize our senses," and "pave the way to totalitarianism."[1]

Although many analysts of American culture agreed with Rosenberg, his view did not go unchallenged. Fellow critic David Manning White questioned Rosenberg's and his allies' view of contemporary American society, contending that the highbrow critics of mass culture lacked a true sense of history. As White suggested, those who worked themselves into "such a frenzy over the stereotyped activity of the Lone Ranger as he shoots a couple of bad hombres [on television] on a Sunday's afternoon" should consider that, for nearly seven hundred years leading up to the twentieth century, bearbaiting, in which crowds watched dogs rip apart a chained bear, had been among the most popular recreations in England. Furthermore, whatever the quality of most offerings of the modern mass media, White pointed out that it made available a substantial menu of high culture to a larger audience than ever before. In 1956, for example, network television presented William Shakespeare's *Richard III,* starring Sir Laurence Olivier, and more than 50 million people tuned in to at least some portion of it. White found the United States in the 1950s to be far from the "cultural wasteland" that its critics lamented.[2]

Commentators of the 1950s disputed the quality of mass culture in the United States, just as they do today, but no one denied that television was playing an ever-increasing role in the lives of Americans. In 1950 only 12 percent of American homes possessed this ultimate dispenser of mass culture; five years later the figure was up to 67 percent. By 1960 nearly 46 million American homes — 88 percent of the total — included at least one television set. A decade later, nearly one in three households had *more* than one set. In

1956 the average hours of daily television watching topped five hours. Fifteen years later, the average daily usage per household was up to six hours.

Television provided tough competition for its predecessor in the mass visual arts, the movies. Financing for television came from on-the-air advertising, a system that allowed viewers to watch programs for nothing more than a small addition to their monthly electricity bills. Going to the movies meant leaving home and paying an admission fee. On any given evening, the average American family could enjoy several hours of entertainment at home for a few pennies, whereas two hours of movie entertainment would cost several dollars and require miles of travel. More and more Americans chose home and television. Weekly attendance at cinemas in the United States stood at 90 million for the first three years after World War II; by the mid-1950s the figure was half that, and it continued to drop. In 1987 only 25 million people a week went to the cinema. Yet movies still played a significant role in American culture. The emergence of home videos in the 1980s ensured their popularity well into the future.

The Mass Media and Cultural Change

Because television and movies occupy a substantial portion of our leisure time, our skill in interpreting their offerings plays an important part in our effort to understand the world around us. This chapter seeks to develop that skill by introducing you to movies and television as representations of American culture and as instruments for comprehending change over time.

Movie and television companies operate to make a profit. Most of the time, major production companies present what they think at least a substantial portion of us want to hear and see. Thus their productions say a good deal about mainstream American values, tastes, and ways of doing things. Companies sometimes try to mold our tastes and attitudes as well, but if they do so with a heavy hand or without a sense of the boundaries of public tolerance, they risk financial disaster.

The following exercises take you through a series of the most successful television programs of the last four decades. Then you will compare two well-known movies, one from the 1950s, the other from the 1980s. By analyzing these popular examples of the mass media, you should grasp some of the changes and continuities in American life during the last two generations and develop some skill in evaluating television and film offerings as historical evidence.

EXERCISE 1: *Situation Comedy During the 1950s*

This exercise focuses on a significant element of the emerging television culture of the 1950s, the situation comedy. During those years, six sitcoms made the top 25 in the Nielsen ratings for at least three years. (The number of television-equipped homes tuned to a particular program on an average evening determines these ratings.) Most popular of all was "I Love Lucy," which in its six years of original shows finished first four times and never ranked lower than third. No other situation comedy approached that record, yet many were staples of American viewers. Each of the following three paragraphs provides a brief description of one of the highest-rated situation comedies from the 1950s. Exercise 1 tests your skill in making connections among the shows and encourages you to examine the significance of these connections in the context of American society and culture of the period.[3]

A The lead characters in "I Love Lucy" were Lucy (Lucille Ball) and Ricky Ricardo (Desi Arnaz). Of Scottish ancestry, Lucy was a housewife. Her Cuban husband Ricky, the leader of a band that performed in a New York nightclub, wanted to keep her that way. Lucy had different ideas. She wanted to be in show business, just like her husband, and her plots to get on stage often produced hilarious situations for the audience, maddening and embarrassing ones for her husband. The Ricardos lived in a middle-class apartment building in Manhattan (see Figure 8.1). Their landlords, Ethel (Vivian Vance) and Fred Mertz (William Frawley), were the leading secondary characters. Ethel often joined Lucy in her misguided adventures, much to Fred's dismay. In the episode of January 19, 1953, after a considerable publicity campaign, Lucy gave birth to Little Ricky. During the program's last season of weekly production (1956–1957), Little Ricky (Richard Keith) became a regular character. In early 1957, the Ricardo family, blessed by Ricky's steady advancement in the entertainment business, moved into a country home in Connecticut.

B "Father Knows Best" has been described as "the classic wholesome family situation comedy." The series took four years to reach the top 25, but it then rose all the way to

FIGURE 8.1 *The Ricardos at Home*

FIGURE 8.2 *The Andersons of "Father Knows Best"*

sixth place in the 1959–1960 season. The setting was Springfield, a typical midwestern town, where Jim Anderson (Robert Young) resided with his wife Margaret (Jane Wyatt) and their three children, Betty (Elinor Donahue), Bud (Billy Gray), and Kathy (Lauren Chapin) (see Figure 8.2). After a day on the job with the General Insurance Company, Jim came home to face the problems of a suburban family. Margaret was a sensitive, concerned homemaker, but, in the midst of a crisis, it was usually father who, "with a warm smile and some sensible advice," resolved the issue. Conflicts occasionally arose among the three children, but they were always mild in nature and they rarely carried over to the next episode.

C "The Danny Thomas Show" was the top-ranked situation comedy for the last three seasons of the 1950s. The series began in 1953 as "Make Room for Daddy" and changed in the fall of 1956 to its better-known title after actress Jean Hagen quit her role as wife of Danny Williams. Danny was "a sometimes loud but ultimately soft-hearted lord of household," whose job as a nightclub entertainer frequently took him away from home. The show focused on problems created by his absence from his two children, Terry (Sherry Jackson) and Rusty (Rusty Thomas). When Hagen left the show, Mrs. Williams was written out as having died, and the next season featured Danny — with the determined assistance of his children — exploring his new options for matrimony. By the beginning of the fall 1957 season, Danny had married Kathy (Marjorie Lord), who also added Linda (Angela Cartwright), a child from a previous marriage, to the household. The series continued in original episodes until 1964, with occasional changes in the cast of young people.

Go back over the descriptions of the three sitcoms, looking for patterns that reflect the values and ways of doing things in America during the 1950s. (*Hint:* Your may find your textbook and the first two exercises in Chapter 7 in this book helpful.) Identify three patterns that fit all three popular programs.

1. _____

2. _____

3. _____

EXERCISE 2: *Identifying Changes in Cultural Values*

A common technique for examining cultural change is to compare evidence from different time periods. This exercise turns to leading sitcoms of the 1970s and offers you a chance to further develop your skill in detecting patterns of change over time.

The 1970s were great years for sitcoms. Sixteen of the genre finished in the top 25 of the Nielsen ratings for at least three years. During eight of the ten years, a sitcom finished first in those ratings. Five times, sitcoms controlled the top two positions and, in the 1974–1975 season, sitcoms held eight of the first ten slots, including numbers one through seven.

We have singled out four top shows to provide you with a source for comparison with the earlier decade. When you compare these descriptions with those in Exercise 1, some differences should become readily apparent. In addition, as you contemplate these differences, you will readily recognize some of the changes that had occurred in the United States between the two decades.

Read the following descriptions and complete the writing exercises that follow.

A "All in the Family" finished at the top of the Nielsen ratings for five seasons. As two broadcast historians have remarked, the program "changed the course of television comedy" by injecting "a sense of harsh reality to a TV world . . . previously . . . populated largely by homogenized, inoffensive characters and stories that seemed to have been laundered before [reaching the airwaves]. . . ." Lead character Archie Bunker (Carroll O'Connor) certainly was offensive to large numbers of potential viewers. A foreman for a tool and die company in New York City, Archie possessed a variety of prejudices often associated with poorly educated, working-class Americans of white, Anglo-Saxon Protestant lineage. As a resident of a city with representatives of virtually every racial and ethnic group imaginable, Archie came into frequent contact with people not to his liking. To him, African-Americans were "jungle bunnies" or "spades"; Chinese "chinks"; Jews "hebes"; Poles "Polacks"; and Puerto Ricans "spics." In his own home in the borough of Queens, he had to put up with his Polish son-in-law Mike Stivic (Rob Reiner). Mike, or "Meat Head" as Archie called him, did not hold a job because he was studying for a degree in sociology, and he was every bit as liberal as his father-in-law was conservative. The family next door, the Jeffersons, was black. Its head, George (Sherman Hemsley), owned a cleaning business, and his own feelings toward whites rivaled Archie's prejudice toward blacks. Archie's wife, Edith (Jean Stapleton), a homemaker, was best friends with George's wife, Louise (Isabel Sanford), also a homemaker, and "Meat Head" was a buddy of the Jeffersons' son, Lionel (Mike Evans), which ensured that Archie constantly had to contend with people of different races and ethnicity. The more tolerant women — Louise, Edith, and Archie's daughter Gloria (Sally Struthers) — often played peacemakers when the men grew raucous.

When "All in the Family" first aired in early 1971, it stirred so much controversy that it was nearly canceled. After a few months, however, it hit the top of the ratings. Crucial to its appeal was the fact that different groups reacted to it in different ways. Liberals saw Archie's lines, which among other things were laced with incorrect word usages, as a satire on bigotry, whereas many others sympathized with his prejudices and applauded him as one of their own.

B "Sanford and Son" finished in the top five of the Nielson ratings four times during the 1970s. The show starred Fred Sanford (Redd Foxx), a sixty-five-year-old African-American junkyard owner in Los Angeles, and his live-in son and business partner, Lamont (Demond Wilson). A widower, Fred was perfectly content with his small business but was always under pressure from his more ambitious son to pursue it more vigorously. Lamont, in turn, frequently threatened to leave the business for something more profitable. Invariably, the threats would lead Fred to feign a heart attack and declare, with his head turned skyward, "I'm comin', Elizabeth [his deceased wife], I'm comin' to join you." Secondary characters included Donna Harris (Lynn **Hamilton**), a nurse and Fred's girlfriend, and Aunt Esther Anderson (LaWanda Page), who operated a rooming house next to the Sanfords' junkyard and home. The setting for most of the episodes was the Sanfords' living room.

C "Happy Days" began slowly in the 1974–1975 season, but, as a result of a shift in billing among the main characters, it rose in its third year to the top of the ratings. The series exploited nostalgia for the 1950s and its supposedly simpler, more wholesome lifestyle. The setting was Milwaukee, Wisconsin, and initially the two main characters were high school students Richie Cunningham (Ron Howard) and Potsie Weber (Anson Williams). Secondary characters included Richie's father Howard (Tom Bosley), owner of a hardware store; his mother Marion (Marion Ross), a housewife; and Arthur "Fonzie" Fonzarelli (Henry Winkler), a stereotypical "greasy-haired motorcycle kid." What pushed the show up the charts was its shift in emphasis from the relationship between the naive Richie and his more experienced pal Potsy to that between the "cool" dropout Fonz and the "straight" kids represented by Richie. Fonzie's mannerisms, especially his thumbs-up gesture, were often imitated by American teenagers. For the most part, scenes alternated among Richie's home, Arnold's malt shop — a teenage hangout — and Jefferson High School.

D "Three's Company," set in Santa Monica, California, centered on the relationship of three roommates (see Figure 8.3) — Jack Tripper (John Ritter), Janet Wood (Joyce De-Witt), and Chrissy Snow (Suzanne Somers) — and their persistent efforts to persuade their landlords and others that nothing inappropriate was going on among them. Given the obvious sex appeal of the two women, doing so was not easy. Jack sometimes implied that he was a homosexual, and his adeptness in the kitchen added plausibility to the idea in the minds of his traditional landlords, the Ropers (Audra Lindley and Norman Fell). Janet, who worked in a florist shop, and Chrissy, a typist, totally lacked culinary skills, while Jack was training to become a chef. The sexual innuendos that abounded in the script led to complaints from religious groups, but the show finished twice in the second slot in the Nielson ratings.

If you compare the preceding descriptions with those from the 1950s, you will find that there was much greater diversity in leading sitcoms during the 1970s. Indeed, for

FIGURE 8.3 *"Three's Company"*

the later period, it is difficult to think of three patterns that fit all or almost all of the programs covered as Exercise 1 asked you to do for the 1950s. Instead, list five elements that you found in any of the sitcoms of the 1970s that you did *not* find in the series from the 1950s.

1. _____

   _____

2. _____

   _____

3. _____

   _____

4. _____

   _____

5. _____

   _____

EXERCISE 3: *Change and Continuity in American Culture from the 1950s to the 1980s*

Now let us turn to an examination of a situation comedy that dominated the Nielsen ratings during the second half of the 1980s — "The Cosby Show," which began telecasting on September 20, 1984. The show featured the Huxtables, an upper-middle-class African-American family. Most of the episodes took place in their residence (see Figure 8.4), a New York City brownstone. The father, Cliff Huxtable (Bill Cosby), was an obstetrician whose office was attached to his home. The mother, Claire (Phylicia Rashad), was a lawyer. The parents did their best to juggle their careers with the task of raising four children. "I just hope they get out of the house before we die," Cliff gasped as he collapsed into bed at the end of the first episode. Yet the parents constantly showed warmth and affection toward their children, and toward each other, even when disciplining them for a variety of infractions.

Bill Cosby, who controlled the scripts, used the show to promote "child-rearing theories he had developed while pursuing his doctorate in education in the 1970s," as well as to celebrate aspects of African-American culture. Some critics attacked his approach for portraying African-Americans unrealistically and for ignoring the issue of race relations, but the show touched a responsive chord for American viewers. In the 1986–1987 season,

FIGURE 8.4 *"The Cosby Show"*

35 percent of homes with televisions on during its time-slot tuned into "The Cosby Show," a remarkable figure when one considers the steady decline of network viewing during the 1980s with the expansion of cable TV. One would have to go all the way back to the 1964–1965 season to find a program, the western "Bonanza," with a higher rating.

Write a paragraph on a separate sheet of paper outlining *at least* one aspect of "The Cosby Show" that is different from the sitcoms from the 1950s and 1970s discussed above and *at least* one aspect that appears in two or more of those sitcoms. Do the similarities and differences suggest anything about change and continuity in American life between the 1950s and 1980s?

EXERCISE 4: *Patterns in Sitcoms of the 1990s*

In comparing sitcoms of the 1950s and 1970s, we saw that by the latter decade much greater diversity existed in the types of people featured and the issues addressed. That pattern has continued right to the present, and it reflects the access to a larger number of channels enjoyed by a growing portion of the population. In class, region, race, and ethnicity, the viewing audience has become increasingly diverse, and entrepreneurs, whether people seeking to expand their markets through television advertising or producers of television programs trying to attract advertising, must find ways to appeal to segments of that audience.

"Seinfeld" is the most successful sitcom of the mid-1990s. It first aired in May 1990, when "Cheers" was at the top of the Nielson charts, followed closely by "Roseanne," "A Different World" (a spinoff of "The Cosby Show"), "The Cosby Show," and "Murphy Brown." "Seinfield" did not make the top 25 in the Nielson chart until the 1992–1993 season, but in the season after that it ranked third, and over the next two seasons it finished at the very top. Just as significant, it generated successful "clones," programs that use different characters but essentially the same formula. We describe "Seinfeld" and the most obvious clone, "Friends," below and then pose questions, first about what they have in common with each other, then about how they compare with other sitcoms discussed in this chapter.

Although significant generalizations are possible from examining two programs that are similar and popular at the same time, "Seinfeld" and "Friends" represent only a portion of the popular sitcoms of the 1990s. Successful sitcoms "Roseanne" and "Home Improvement," for example, employ very different formulas. Thus tastes vary, not just across time, but from group to group and even person to person, at the same time.

A "Seinfeld" is set on the Upper West Side of New York City and includes four main characters, all in their thirties, all white, and all single. Jerry Seinfeld (himself) is a standup comic "coping with dating, nutty friends, and the indignities of city life." His former lover, Elaine Benes (Julia Louis-Dreyfus), is now his close but platonic friend. George Costanza (Jason Alexander), balding, stocky, and short, is a classic "worrywart" and Jerry's best friend. Cosmo Kramer (Michael Richards), Jerry's "next-door neighbor," is an "eccentric entrepreneur" who, despite his clumsiness, tends to emerge upright from his many scrapes. Often referred to as the "show about nothing," "Seinfeld" displays its characters during leisure time, either in Jerry's apartment or in a nearby diner, dealing with "life's trivia," but also in romantic relationships. Treatment of issues of human sexuality are sometimes quite explicit.

B "Friends" began broadcasting in September 1994 and tied for eighth place on the Nielson chart during its first season. The program is set in New York City and features six intelligent, attractive, white men and women in their twenties. All of them are single.

They are shown "hanging out" either at the apartment of Monica Geller (Courteney Cox) or at a nearby coffeehouse discussing "love, sex, feelings, dates, lack of dates, the prospect of dates, and other matters of importance in their lives."

1. Identify six similarities between "Seinfeld" and "Friends."

   a. _____

   b. _____

   c. _____

   d. _____

   e. _____

   f. _____

2. How many of those similarities fit "The Cosby Show"? Which ones? _____

   _____

   _____

   _____

   _____

3. Which program from the 1970s of those described in Exercise 2 has the most in common with "Seinfeld" and "Friends"? Explain. _____

   _____

   _____

   _____

4. Identify at least four differences between "Seinfeld" and "Friends" on the one hand and the programs from the 1950s discussed in Exercise 1 on the other. _____

   _____

   _____

   _____

   _____

   _____

   _____

   _____

   _____

EXERCISE 5: *Change and Continuity in American Culture from the 1950s to the Present*

Some cultural values persist and others change. Now that you have examined some of the leading sitcoms of the last two generations, you are prepared to comment on change and continuity in American culture since 1950.

On a separate sheet of paper, write a short (500-word) essay comparing leading sitcoms from the 1950s to the present (their settings, their characters, their characters' relationships and values, and so forth). The key question you should address is, What does your comparison tell you about change and continuity in America during the last two generations? Use your responses to Exercises 1 through 4, as well as your textbook, to complete this assignment. You may also want to consult the sixth edition of Tim Brooks and Earl Marsh's *The Complete Dictionary to Prime Time and Cable TV Shows 1946–Present* (New York: Ballantine Books, 1995). In thinking about continuities, or aspects that stay the same, do not ignore the obvious. Changes often stand out in comparisons over time simply because they represent differences. Similarities are taken for granted because they are so common.

Once you have collected your thoughts, follow the same procedures you used in preparing essays in Chapters 5 and 6: construct a thesis; develop an outline, including sections for an introduction, a body, and a conclusion; write a first draft; and then revise it to produce a final draft.

EXERCISE 6: *Movies and Culture*

Now that you have some experience evaluating television programs as reflections of American culture, let us move on to a more challenging exercise on movies. This time you will go to the sources themselves — two movies, one from the 1950s and one from the 1980s — and use them to understand change and continuity in American life. This exercise will also ask you to find reviews or commentaries on these movies, which will reinforce the library skills you acquired in Chapter 4 and enhance your understanding of how each film fits into its time period.

The movies are *The Man in the Gray Flannel Suit* (1956), the story of a man trying to juggle the demands of career and family, and *Working Girl* (1986), which depicts a young woman's struggle to succeed on Wall Street. The movies have some obvious differences: for example, the first is a drama, the second a romantic comedy. Yet they reveal much about the times in which they appeared, and some of the differences between them reflect changes in American culture over a thirty-year period. The same is true of the reviews and commentaries. What critics said, and who said it where can be every bit as important in identifying contemporary values and concerns as the movies themselves.

Two reasons for including these particular films are (1) they should be readily available to you (either in your university film library or in a local video outlet) and (2) they were widely commented on at the time of their release. Your instructor will help you make arrangements to view the films as a group.

As your final assignment in this chapter, write a three-to-five-page essay analyzing the movies and the reactions to them as reflections of change and continuity in recent American history. In preparing your essay, take the following steps:

1. Watch each movie. Take careful notes throughout, especially on the parts that convey a message or portray something striking about the time period in which the movies were produced. Try to answer these questions:
   a. How are gender roles portrayed in the films?
   b. How is success defined?
   c. What produces the main conflicts in the two movies?
   d. How does the use of language compare in the films?
   e. How is human sexuality treated?
   f. What is the pace of the action?

2. Look up these commentaries, and take extensive notes. Then try to answer the questions that follow.

The Man in the Gray Flannel Suit: See the *New York Times,* April 13, 1956, p. 21, and April 22, 1956, section II, p. 1; and *The New Yorker* 32 (April 21, 1956), 75–76.

Working Girl: See the *New York Times,* December 21, 1988, p. C22; January 15, 1989, p. E27; and February 3, 1989, p. 30.

   a. How do you think commentators might have reacted to each movie if the time frame of each release were reversed?
   b. What do your conclusions tell you about change and continuity in America from the mid-1950s to the late 1980s?

3. Think back to what you learned in the exercises on television sitcoms about cultural change from the 1950s to the 1980s. Do the films confirm your conclusions?

4. Review the steps on essay writing in Exercise 5 of Chapter 5. Use them as guides in writing your essay.

This chapter has introduced you to the challenge of examining television programs and movies in different time periods. You should now have a greater understanding of change and continuity in American life, and of the attitudes and behavior of individuals or generations other than your own. Comparisons across time can also prove useful to people faced with important decisions in their personal lives or work. With this point in mind, we turn to the concept of historical analogy in Chapter 9.

NOTES

1. Bernard Rosenberg and David Manning White, eds., *Mass Culture* (Glencoe, Ill.: Free Press, 1957), 4, 5, 9.

2. Ibid., 14, 16.

3. The descriptions in Exercises 1, 2, and 3, with occasional direct quotations, are based on Tim Brooks and Earle Marsh, *The Complete Dictionary to Prime Time Network and Cable TV Shows, 1946–Present,* 6th ed. (New York: Ballantine Books, 1995), 26–28, 168–169, 184–185, 257–258, 322–324, 365–366, 377–378, 687–688, 792–793, 917.

9 HISTORICAL ANALOGY: USING THE PAST IN THE PRESENT

Korea, Vietnam, and the Persian Gulf

In making decisions, people often compare a present situation to a past occurrence, using a similarity between two events for guidance. The course chosen in that past occurrence may have had negative consequences, for example, so the person in the present situation avoids a similar approach. However, such a procedure can sometimes prove costly. As discussed at the beginning of this volume, all human events possess unique qualities, thus making reasoning by historical analogy a precarious enterprise.

Yet as scholars Richard E. Neustadt and Ernest R. May observe, "The future has no place to come from but the past, hence the past has predictive value."[1] The challenge is not to resist using history to guide us; rather, it is to gauge *when* to use history and *how*. This chapter shows you how some American leaders have used the past to make important foreign policy decisions and offers you the opportunity to decide whether they used it well. In the process, you will develop insights about the limits that history holds for policymakers as well as its potential. These insights, in turn, should advance your skill in using historical analogy in your own life.

The Lessons of World War II

Since 1945 the lessons of World War II have served a fundamental purpose for the makers of U.S. foreign policy. The idea emerged during the war that if only the United States had acted differently between 1931 and 1939 the conflict could have been averted. The United States should have halted the aggressions of Japan, Italy, and Germany before those powers became so strong that only a major war could stop them. With the defeat of those nations, American leaders determined to thrust their country into the international arena as never before in peacetime. Only such involvement, they believed, could avert another global conflict. Thus the postwar era became one of expanding U.S. intervention abroad — politically, economically, and militarily.

The following exercises center on decisions leading to the three largest U.S. military interventions since 1945 — Korea in 1950, Vietnam in 1965, and the Persian Gulf in 1990. In each case, American leaders used historical analogies to make their decisions. We ask you to examine those analogies and to reach your own conclusions about their applicability.

EXERCISE 1: *Korea and the Lessons of the 1930s*

In the wee hours of the morning of June 25, 1950 (Korean time), communist North Korea launched an all-out military attack on its American-sponsored neighbor to the south, the Republic of Korea (ROK). Over the next several days, North Korean forces advanced rapidly, capturing Seoul, the South Korean capital, and routing ROK troops all along the front. Only a quick movement of American troops to the peninsula from Japan could prevent the North Koreans from overrunning the entire country. See Figure 9.1.

U.S. President Harry S Truman received word of the North Korean attack late on a Saturday evening while relaxing at his home in Independence, Missouri. He rushed back to Washington the next day and convened a series of meetings of his top advisers to discuss the evolving crisis. On the three-hour flight to the nation's capital, Truman later wrote in his memoirs, he reflected on events of the last two days:

> I recalled some earlier instances: Manchuria, Ethiopia, Austria. I remembered how each time that the democracies failed to act it had encouraged the aggressors to keep going ahead. Communism was acting in Korea just as Hitler, Mussolini, and the Japanese had acted ten, fifteen, and twenty years earlier. I felt certain that if South Korea was allowed to fall, Communist leaders would be emboldened to override nations closer to our own shores. If the Communists were permitted to force their way into the

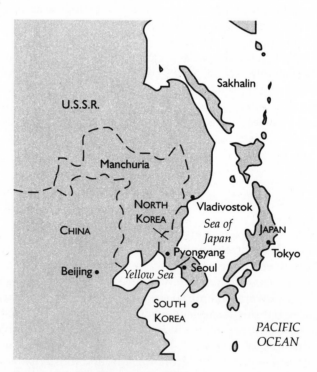

FIGURE 9.1 *Northeast Asia, 1950*

Republic of Korea without opposition from the free world, no small nation would have the courage to resist threats and aggression by stronger Communist neighbors. If this was allowed to go unchallenged, it would mean a third world war, just as similar incidents had brought on the second world war.[2]

By the time Truman's plane landed in Washington, the United Nations Security Council had convened in New York at American behest and voted unanimously to call for a cease-fire in Korea and a withdrawal of North Korean forces from South Korea. (The Soviet Union was boycotting the United Nations at the time.) Two days later, again at American beckoning, the U.N. Security Council recommended that member nations "furnish such assistance to the Republic of Korea (South Korea) as may be necessary to repel the armed attack and to restore international security to the area."[3] Finally, on June 30, with a plea before him from field commander General Douglas MacArthur for the commitment of American troops to the fighting, Truman approved the dispatch of U.S. army units from Japan. The president's actions received widespread support in the United States and from America's allies in Europe, Asia, and Latin America. Even neutral India expressed approval.

Your task here is to evaluate the appropriateness of Truman's historical analogy. First we provide you with background on the three cases from the 1930s cited by Truman: Japan's attack on Manchuria, Italy's invasion of Ethiopia, and Germany's occupation of Austria. We also provide background on Korea. Then we ask you to examine Truman's use of history.

As you read the following material, keep comparing the cases to Korea.

Case Study 1: Manchuria

Japan had been expanding its influence in Manchuria, the rich, northeastern region of China, since the turn of the century. During the 1920s, however, the rising tide of nationalism in China jeopardized Japan's position. The Nationalist government of China frequently encouraged boycotts of Japanese goods. With the onset of the worldwide depression in 1930, this policy increasingly threatened Japan's interests.

On September 18, 1931, Japanese troops, guarding a railway that Japan had controlled in Manchuria since 1906, used an explosion outside Mukden as a pretext to seize key cities and towns throughout the region. During the following months, Japan's Kwantung army occupied all of Manchuria and set up a puppet regime. Japan's action violated three treaties to which Japan was a signatory: the Kellogg-Briand Pact of 1928, which outlawed war, the Nine-Power Treaty of 1922, which recognized the territorial integrity of China, and the covenant of the League of Nations, which prohibited members from resorting to war before exhausting its mechanisms for the peaceful resolution of conflicts.

The League of Nations moved sluggishly in response to Japan's action. It gave little consideration to applying economic sanctions, which, in any event, would have been useless without cooperation from the United States (not a member of the League). In March 1932, the League finally voted not to recognize Japan's conquest of Manchuria, a stance that the United States had adopted two months earlier. Later in the year, the League assigned blame for the entire incident to Japan. Japan responded by withdrawing from the organization but not from Manchuria.

Japan's expansion in Asia did not end with Manchuria. In 1937 Japan moved southward along the China coast. Three years later, it occupied northern Indochina and during the following summer it advanced into the southern portion of that French colony. With the last action, the United States instituted an economic embargo on Japan, thus setting the two nations on a collision course that culminated at Pearl Harbor on December 7, 1941.

Case Study 2: Ethiopia

Italy's attack on Ethiopia was the first act of aggression by a European power during the 1930s. Italy had attempted to conquer that East African nation in the late nineteenth century, only to suffer a humiliating defeat. In October 1935, Benito Mussolini, Italy's fascist dictator, sought to avenge that defeat and expand his African empire. Although the weakest of Europe's great powers, Italy possessed a modern, mechanized army against which Ethiopia's troops, often armed with knives and spears, were clearly overmatched.

In this case, the League of Nations acted immediately. It condemned Italy for violating its covenant and called for economic sanctions against the aggressor. These sanctions did not include an embargo on petroleum, however, which was Italy's paramount need. Great Britain and France refused to support a petroleum embargo, fearing that Italy would retaliate in the Mediterranean and that the United States, which at the time was a major oil exporter, would refuse to comply. Many in Great Britain and France also feared that extreme action would lead Mussolini to turn to Germany, which, under the rule of Nazi Adolf Hitler, already was making noises about altering the European balance of power.

Because of these nations' fears, an effective system of collective security never emerged against Italy, and it conquered and annexed Ethiopia in May 1936. The League rescinded its economic sanctions two months later.

Emboldened by his Ethiopian success, Mussolini soon sent large quantities of men and materiel to Spain to support a fascist rebellion against the republic there. France and Great Britain sponsored a Non-Intervention Committee to discourage outside involvement in the Spanish civil war, but despite Italian and German membership in that group, Mussolini and Hitler openly flouted its purpose. The United States Congress passed a neutrality act prohibiting shipments to either side. Given the magnitude of assistance provided to the Spanish rebels by Italy and Germany, U.S. policy clearly helped the fascists to emerge victorious in Spain in the spring of 1939.

Meanwhile, Italy withdrew from the League of Nations, formed a close alliance with Germany, and swallowed Albania. In June 1940, Italy joined Germany in war against France and Great Britain.

Case Study 3: Austria

Germany's annexation of Austria in March 1938 was only the first step in Hitler's expansion in Europe. He already had flouted the terms of the Treaty of Versailles ending World War I by rearming and by reoccupying the Rhineland on Germany's western frontier. Now he turned to annexing new territory. See Figure 9.2.

Austria was a small, ethnically German nation, but the Treaty of Versailles forbade *Anschluss* (union) between Germany and Austria. In the early 1930s France moved to prevent even a customs union between the two nations. Yet Hitler acted with a boldness that kept both France and Great Britain off balance.

In February 1938, Hitler declared it Germany's responsibility to promote the rights of Germans no matter where they resided. Those rights included self-determination, he announced, and the 7 million Austrian Germans were being denied that right. In the face of this external pressure and considerable agitation by Nazis within his own realm, Austrian chancellor Kurt von Schuschnigg called a plebiscite for March 9 to determine whether the people desired union with Germany. Hitler mobilized his troops along Austria's border, insisting that the plebiscite be called off. Schuschnigg complied, but now Hitler demanded his resignation and replacement by Nazi leader Arthur Seyss-Inquart. Austrian president Wilhelm Miklas resisted this demand, however, and on March 11 troops from Germany crossed the border into Austria. Four days later, Hitler's armies seized Vienna. Great Britain and France did nothing beyond issuing verbal protests.

FIGURE 9.2 *Europe, 1935*

Soon Hitler began pressuring Czechoslovakia for the liberation of its Sudeten Germans. Czechoslovakia was a multiethnic nation carved out of the Habsburg empire after World War I. On its western border with Germany lay the Sudetenland, which possessed a German majority. When Hitler's harassment of Czechoslovakia reached a climax in September 1938, British and French leaders supported his demand for annexation of the Sudetenland rather than risk early war. Completely isolated politically, its country virtually surrounded by German forces and its ethnic Germans agitating in the Sudetenland, the Czechoslovakian government complied. To cheering crowds in London, British prime minister Neville Chamberlain declared, "I believe that this is peace in our time." Hitler promised that the Sudetenland was his last territorial demand in Europe. In March 1939, however, he took the remainder of Czechoslovakia.

Great Britain and France finally balked, and when Hitler turned on Poland they guaranteed its borders. Poland had been divided among Russia, Prussia (later Germany), and Austria late in the eighteenth century only to be pieced back together in the aftermath of World War I. In the west, it received territory inhabited by a German-speaking majority, and this land — the Polish corridor — separated Germany proper from its easternmost province, East Prussia.

Poland's resistance to Hitler, unlike Czechoslovakia's, failed to collapse. Thus on September 1, 1939, Hitler moved his armies into Poland to take what he wanted by force. In response, Great Britain and France declared war on Germany.

By this time, Germany controlled central Europe, had fortified its western frontiers, and had protected its eastern flank through a nonaggression pact with the Soviet Union. With the United States adhering to a strict policy of neutrality regarding European conflicts, the British and French stood alone against Germany. The only recourse for Great

Britain and France was to fight a long war, which eventually drew in the Soviet Union and the United States and became the most destructive conflict in human history.

Case Study 4: Korea

Annexed by Japan in 1910, Korea gained an opportunity for independence with its oppressor's defeat in World War II. During that conflict, the three major nations of the Allied camp — the Soviet Union, the United States, and Great Britain — agreed that Japan should lose its vast empire. "In due course," Korea should become "free and independent."[4] Detailed agreements were not made about Korea's postwar fate, however; the Allies merely committed themselves verbally to a four-power (the three Allies plus China) trusteeship over Korea as a means of guiding its people toward self-government. As World War II came to a close in August 1945, the United States proposed to the Soviet Union that Soviet and American troops alone occupy the Korean peninsula, with the thirty-eighth parallel providing the dividing line between them. The Soviets immediately accepted.

The Americans considered the division temporary, but the Soviets moved quickly to close off their zone to outside influence. Over the next two years, the two sides failed to agree on methods for reuniting the country. Finally, in September 1947, the Truman administration decided to present the Korean issue to the U.N. General Assembly.

In November, the General Assembly overwhelmingly passed a resolution sponsored by the United States recommending that the United Nations supervise elections throughout Korea as a first step toward creating a united, independent nation. The Soviet Union, which earlier had proposed a withdrawal of foreign forces from the peninsula to permit Koreans themselves to determine their own fate, refused to cooperate with the United Nations in conducting elections. Under U.S. urging, the international organization set up elections below the thirty-eighth parallel. In August 1948, again under joint sponsorship by the United States and United Nations, the Republic of Korea (ROK) was established under the right-wing leadership of President Syngman Rhee. The ROK claimed authority over the entire peninsula, but the United Nations recognized its sovereignty only over territory below the thirty-eighth parallel.

Meanwhile, the Soviet Union supervised elections in its own zone. This process led in September to the declaration of the Democratic People's Republic of Korea (DPRK) under the communist leadership of Kim Il-sung. Like its southern counterpart, the DPRK claimed authority over the whole country. Thus by the fall of 1948, the peninsula was divided between two hostile governments, each denying the legitimacy of its neighbor. Each received sponsorship from a superpower and occupier that, in turn, was engaged in a larger "cold war" with the other.

At the end of 1948, the Soviet Union announced the withdrawal of its troops from North Korea, but the United States kept some eight thousand soldiers in the south. Conditions below the thirty-eighth parallel had been extremely unsettled since the fall of 1946, as a civil war raged between leftist and rightist forces. Washington feared that removing its troops prematurely would lead to a collapse of the ROK and a severe blow to U.S. credibility. Yet in June 1949 the United States followed the Soviet lead, leaving behind only a group of several hundred military advisers.

South and North Korean military forces were of relatively equal strength in mid-1949, but that balance did not last. The North soon acquired a substantial body of heavy equipment from the Soviet Union, including tanks, artillery, and fighter planes. Then, in early 1950, thousands of Korean nationals who had fought with victorious communist armies in China during the civil war there returned home and joined the North Korean armed forces.

In the South, meanwhile, the ROK army virtually destroyed the guerrilla movement below the thirty-eighth parallel. Although the Rhee regime remained unpopular with many people — indeed, it was constantly at loggerheads with the National Assembly — it showed no sign of falling apart. If the North was to take over the entire peninsula in the near future, it clearly would have to resort to conventional military action.

On June 25, 1950, North Korea attacked South Korea. Soviet troops did not participate directly in the North Korean attack, but Soviet equipment and training had played a key role in the development of the DPRK army. American leaders assumed that Moscow was behind the offensive.

Identifying Likenesses and Differences

You are now prepared to evaluate Truman's use of history in the Korean case. Richard E. Neustadt and Ernest R. May, who have written a book on how policymakers can use history for guidance, advocate constructing lists of likenesses and differences to gauge the applicability of past cases to present conditions. The writing down of pertinent information, they argue, ensures a disciplined process of evaluation and guards against rushing into poorly thought-out courses of action based on inadequate or faulty data.[5] The following chart provides you with an instrument for following Neustadt and May's procedure. We have started to fill it out by listing one likeness and one difference between Manchuria and Korea. Complete the rest yourself, and then answer the questions that follow in the space provided.

Korea and Manchuria

Likenesses: A government uses force to take territory from an internationally recognized

government. _____

_____

_____

Differences: No great power was directly involved in Korea, as was the case in Manchuria.

_____

_____

_____

Korea and Ethiopia

Likenesses: _____

_____

_____

Differences: _____

_____

_____

Korea and Austria

Likenesses: _____

_____

_____

Differences: _____

_____

_____

1. To President Truman, incidents of the 1930s such as the Japanese seizure of Manchuria, the Italian conquest of Ethiopia, and Hitler's annexation of Austria suggested the truth of what principle? _____

_____

2. Compare the ethnic makeup of the territory occupied by Germany in March and October 1938 and that of the territories occupied by Japan and Italy during the 1930s. What was the difference? _____

_____

3. In ethnic makeup, was the territory that North Korea attempted to occupy in 1950 more like that occupied by Germany or by Japan and Italy? _____

_____

4. In what way were the methods used by Germany, Italy, and Japan in the 1930s and North Korea in 1950 similar? _____

_____

5. Which do you consider more important in evaluating Truman's analogy — your response to question 3 or to question 4? Explain. _____

_____

6. Which nation would you say was a bigger threat to the United States: Germany, Japan, and Italy during the 1930s, or North Korea in 1950? Explain. _____

_____

7. Did North Korea's relationship with the Soviet Union make its action on June 25, 1950, more or less significant to the United States? _____ Explain. _____

_____

8. Overall, do you find Truman's analogy persuasive or not? Write a paragraph supporting your choice. _____

_____

_____

_____

_____
_____
_____
_____
_____
_____
_____

EXERCISE 2: *Vietnam and the Lessons of World War II and Korea*

In the minds of most Americans, the Vietnam War is the greatest tragedy in U.S. foreign policy since World War II. The United States failed to achieve its fundamental objective — the prevention of a communist victory in South Vietnam. During the secret policy deliberations of 1964 and 1965 leading up to the massive escalation of U.S. military action, American leaders frequently used historical analogies to make their cases, sometimes in favor of and sometimes against deeper involvement. The Korean War often entered the discussions. Once President Johnson had made the decision to escalate, he and Secretary of State Dean Rusk emphasized the lessons of the 1930s in their *public* justifications.

In this exercise, we provide a background section on Vietnam and then portions of two documents, one by Undersecretary of State George Ball, who opposed U.S. escalation in Vietnam, and one by President Johnson, who ultimately rejected Ball's advice. In the former document, Ball, using the analogy of Korea, argued for caution. In the latter document, Johnson defended U.S. escalation in Vietnam, using the older 1930s analogy. Read the material presented, and answer the questions that follow.

Vietnam

As in Korea, Japan's defeat in 1945 led to an end of its occupation of Vietnam.[6] Japan had taken control of that French colony in 1940 and 1941 following France's defeat at the hands of Germany. With Japan's surrender, France tried to regain control not only of Vietnam but also of its two other Indochinese colonies, Laos and Cambodia. Great Britain's assistance and America's acquiescence enabled French troops to return, only to face resistance from a communist-led, nationalist-inspired organization called the Vietminh. In December 1946, after the breakdown of lengthy negotiations between the French and the Vietminh, the first Indochinese war began.

As the Cold War with the Soviet Union intensified and American fears of Asian communism grew with Mao Zedong's victory in the Chinese civil war during 1949, U.S. policy moved decisively into the French camp. In May 1950 the United States began furnishing aid to the French war effort. In the crisis atmosphere fueled by the outbreak of fighting in Korea in June 1950, U.S. assistance to the French grew steadily until 1954. Communist Chinese aid to the Vietminh reinforced America's determination.

In 1954 the French decided to withdraw from Indochina. The Eisenhower administration in Washington flirted with direct intervention but resisted the temptation. The threat of U.S. intervention, however, persuaded the Soviet Union and Communist China to pressure the Vietminh to accept less-than-total victory. At the Geneva Conference during the spring and summer of 1954, Vietnam, Laos, and Cambodia received independence, and Vietnam was divided at the seventeenth parallel into "regrouping" zones, with the communist-controlled Democratic Republic of Vietnam located north of the line and the anticommunist Republic of Vietnam holding territory to the south (see Figure

9.3). The country was to be reunited in 1956 through internationally supervised elections. Although the United States participated in the Geneva Conference, it refused to sign the agreements, saying only that it would not use military force to disrupt the elections.

With the French withdrawing from Vietnam, the United States quickly became the most influential outside force, at least below the seventeenth parallel. Washington strongly backed Ngo Dinh Diem, the prime minister of the Republic of Vietnam, and took the lead in creating the Southeast Asia Treaty Organization (SEATO), which included the United States, New Zealand, Australia, the Philippines, Thailand, Pakistan, Great Britain, and France. Under the Geneva Accords, the Indochinese states were not permitted to join a military alliance, but SEATO members signed a protocol that put Laos, Cambodia, and South Vietnam under their protection. SEATO members agreed to *consult* one another if subversion or insurrection threatened one of the governments, although in the event of external aggression any member *could* react immediately under its own authority. In the mid-1960s, American leaders claimed that SEATO obligations dictated U.S. military intervention to save South Vietnam from communism.

Despite U.S. support, the Republic of Vietnam never prospered. Aware that North Vietnam's Ho Chi Minh would win any national election, Diem and the United States refused to permit such an event in 1956. Diem proved a reclusive leader who made little effort to build popular support in the countryside, where the vast majority of Vietnamese resided. By early 1961, when John F. Kennedy became president of the United States, rebellion was spreading rapidly in rural South Vietnam. That rebellion originated in popu-

FIGURE 9.3 *Indochina After the Geneva Conference, 1954*

lar discontent below the seventeenth parallel. In late 1960, however, North Vietnam helped to found the National Liberation Front (NLF) below the seventeenth parallel. Though dominated by communists, the NLF (also known as the Vietcong) received backing from South Vietnamese of various ideological stripes.

President Kennedy deepened U.S. involvement by increasing American military advisers in South Vietnam from 692 in early 1961 to nearly 16,000 two years later. In the fall of 1963 Kennedy finally gave the green light to a group of South Vietnamese military officers to overthrow Diem. Three weeks after Diem's overthrow and assassination, Kennedy himself was assassinated and succeeded in the White House by Lyndon B. Johnson. Conditions in South Vietnam continued to deteriorate, presenting Johnson with the unenviable choice of an embarrassing retreat or a stepped-up effort.

The choice grew increasingly stark as Diem's successors proved even less capable than he. The Military Revolutionary Council that took over from Diem lasted merely three months before being replaced in a bloodless coup by General Nguyen Khanh. Weakened by corruption and intense internal factionalism, not to mention growing insurrection in the countryside, the Khanh regime staggered along until February 1965, when Generals Nguyen Cao Ky and Nguyen Van Thieu seized power in Saigon.

Through all this, President Johnson refused to make a decisive commitment either to escalate U.S. involvement drastically or to pull out. He knew from his experience as a senator during the late 1940s and early 1950s that events abroad could have a disastrous effect on domestic programs, not to mention the political fate of a sitting president and his party. On the one hand, the communist victory in China, which the United States had tried to prevent without direct military intervention, had produced sharp criticism of the Truman administration at home. On the other hand, so did the U.S. intervention in Korea in the early 1950s, which in its initial stages received widespread public approval. Chinese intervention in response to the movement of U.S. ground forces into North Korea produced an eventual military stalemate near the thirty-eighth parallel, however, and prolonged and indecisive fighting left the American people disgruntled. The ongoing war in Korea was the key issue in the Republican electoral victory of 1952. With that lesson before him, Johnson postponed a decision until after the election in November 1964. Given the hawkish rhetoric of his Republican opponent, Barry Goldwater, Johnson appeared moderate and statesmanlike. He won a landslide victory.

By early 1965 the Republic of Vietnam's fortunes were in such decline that Johnson had to make a choice. In February, he ordered sustained bombing missions above the seventeenth parallel in retaliation for Vietcong (communist) attacks on American bases in the south. By spring the NLF controlled as much as 75 percent of the countryside; soldiers from the South Vietnamese army deserted by the thousands; and infiltration of troops from North Vietnam increased, in part perhaps in response to U.S. bombing. If the United States did not sharply increase its role in the war on the ground in South Vietnam, where some 56,000 American soldiers already had landed, that area soon would be in communist hands. In April, Johnson approved the dispatch of 40,000 additional troops to help protect American bases along the coast and to launch limited attacks against the enemy.

Events continued to conspire against Johnson. By mid-May, American escalation had stirred significant protests at home, on college campuses, in the press, and in Congress, as well as in allied capitals such as London and Ottawa and at the United Nations. To exacerbate LBJ's dilemma, the Vietcong launched a major offensive against the South Vietnamese army, inflicting the heaviest casualties to date. In late July the president decided to commence saturation bombing in South Vietnam and, despite fears of Chinese intervention, a gradual increase in air attacks on North Vietnam. He also dispatched 50,000 more U.S. troops. By the end of the year, he promised General William Westmoreland, the commander of American forces in Vietnam, an additional 50,000. The decision for open-ended escalation had been made, although Johnson's ongoing sensitivity to elements of the Korean analogy kept him from ordering U.S. ground forces to operate north of the seventeenth parallel.

The escalation continued for nearly three years. In the spring of 1966, the United States began using its heaviest bombers against North Vietnam and in late June commenced bombing in the Hanoi and Haiphong areas. Secret bombing of North Vietnamese infiltration routes in Laos had begun two years before, but Johnson continued to restrict U.S. ground operations to South Vietnam. His primary objective was to produce high enemy casualties rather than to occupy new territory. By early 1968 more than 520,000 troops were in South Vietnam.

Escalation ended after the enemy launched a major military operation, the Tet offensive, in early 1968. Although the action produced high casualties for North Vietnamese and Vietcong forces and no significant territorial gains, it catalyzed antiwar protests in the United States. Public support for the war had been declining for some time, and when the Tet offensive showed that no victory for the United States was on the horizon, organized opposition to the war heightened. Thus when American military leaders requested more U.S. troops at the end of February, President Johnson turned them down. At the end of March, he deescalated the bombing campaign in North Vietnam in an effort to begin peace talks. He also announced an end of his bid for reelection in November. The gradual withdrawal of American troops from South Vietnam commenced under President Richard Nixon in 1969 and was completed in 1973. South Vietnam fell to North Vietnam two years later.

Document A is an excerpt from President Johnson's news conference of July 28, 1965.

A. Why must young Americans, born into a land exultant with hope and with golden promise, toil and suffer and sometimes die in such a remote and distant place?

The answer, like the war itself, is not an easy one, but it echoes clearly from the painful lessons of half a century. Three times in my lifetime, in two World Wars and in Korea, Americans have gone to far lands to fight for freedom. We have learned at a terrible and a brutal cost that retreat does not bring safety and weakness does not bring peace.

It is this lesson that has brought us to Viet-Nam. This is a different kind of war. There are no marching armies or solemn declarations. Some citizens of South Viet-Nam at times, with understandable grievances, have joined in the attack on their own government.

But we must not let this mask the central fact that this is really war. It is guided by North Viet-Nam and it is spurred by Communist China. Its goal is to conquer the South, to defeat American power, and to extend the Asiatic dominion of communism.

There are great stakes in the balance.

Most of the non-Communist nations of Asia cannot, by themselves and alone, resist the growing might and the grasping ambition of Asian communism.

Our power, therefore, is a very vital shield. . . . Surrender in Viet-Nam [would not] bring peace, because we learned from Hitler . . . that success only feeds the appetite of aggression. The battle would be renewed in one country and then another country, bringing with it perhaps even larger and crueler conflict, as we have learned from the lessons of history.[7]

Document B is an excerpt from a memorandum that Undersecretary of State George Ball wrote to Secretary of State Dean Rusk, Secretary of Defense Robert McNamara, and White House Chief of Staff McGeorge Bundy on October 5, 1964.

B. . . . There are at least five principal differences between the present position of the United States in South Viet-Nam and our situation in South Korea in 1951:

a. We were in South Korea under a clear UN mandate. Our presence in South Viet-Nam depends upon the continuing request of the GVN [Government of South Vietnam] plus the SEATO [Southeast Asia Treaty Organization] protocol.

b. At their peak, UN forces in South Korea (other than ours and those of the ROK) included 53,000 infantrymen and 1000 other troops provided by fifty-three nations.*

In Viet-Nam we are going it alone with no substantial help from any other country.

c. In 1950 the Korean Government under Syngman Rhee was stable. It had the general support of the principal elements in the country. There was little factional fighting and jockeying for power.

In South Viet-Nam we face governmental chaos.

d. The Korean War started only two years after Korean independence. The Korean people were still excited by their newfound freedom, they were fresh for the war.

In contrast, the people of Indochina have been fighting for almost twenty years. . . . All evidence points to the fact that they are tired of conflict.

e. Finally, the Korean War started with . . . a classical type of invasion across an established border. It was so reported within twelve hours by the UN Commission on the spot. It gave us an unassailable political and legal base for counteraction.

In South Vietnam there has been no invasion — only a slow infiltration. . . . The Viet Cong insurgency does have substantial indigenous support. Americans know that the insurgency is actively directed and supported by Hanoi [capital of North Vietnam], but the rest of the world is not so sure. . . . Many nations remain unpersuaded that Hanoi is the principal source of the revolt. And, as the weakness of the Saigon government becomes more and more evident, an increasing number of governments will be inclined to believe that the Viet Cong insurgency is, in fact, an internal rebellion.[8]

Before answering the questions at the end of this exercise, fill in the chart of likenesses and differences. We have assisted you in getting started by including one likeness and one difference between the 1930s and Vietnam. In completing the chart or answering the questions that follow, do not hesitate to refer to the background material in Exercise 1.

1930s and Vietnam

Likenesses: Attempt by one government to overthrow another. _____

_____

_____

_____

Differences: Legitimacy of government of South Vietnam widely questioned, unlike China (Manchuria), Ethiopia, and Austria. _____

_____

_____

_____

Korea and Vietnam

Likenesses: _____

_____

_____

_____

Author's Note: In fact, only seventeen nations contributed combat forces to Korea.

Differences: _____

_____

_____

_____

1. Document A was a *public* statement immediately accessible to millions of people. Document B was a *private* statement available only to top government officials in the State Department and the White House. How does this fact influence the way you evaluate them? Explain. _____

_____

_____

_____

2. One assertion in George Ball's comparison of Korea and Vietnam clearly conflicts with information in the background material we provide. What is that statement? Does the conflicting background information undermine Ball's overall analysis? Explain.

_____

_____

_____

_____

3. Compare Ball's characterization of the situation in Vietnam with Johnson's. _____

_____

_____

_____

4. What background information on Vietnam do you find most important in evaluating the arguments of Johnson and Ball? Explain. _____

_____

_____

_____

5. Although Johnson rejected Ball's comparison of Korea and Vietnam in his ultimate decision to escalate, there was another analogy involving Korea that the president did take into account in defining the limits of U.S. escalation in Vietnam. Identify that analogy. _____

_____

_____

_____

6. On the basis of the information you have, which man — Johnson or Ball — do you think drew more valid historical comparisons? Why? Write a well-constructed paragraph answering these questions. _____

_____

EXERCISE 3: *The Persian Gulf, Vietnam, and World War II*

We move now to the Persian Gulf crisis and war of 1990–1991. We lack the kind of official documents for this series of events that we have for the 1930s, Korea, or Vietnam, but we do have a large body of public statements from leading U.S. decisionmakers, including President George Bush and Senator John Kerry (D, Mass.). Although such evidence must be used cautiously in explaining decisions, it at least gives us a sense of what American leaders thought would appeal to the public and the world at large, and it often gives real insight into official thinking. Following are some of the analogies that President Bush and Senator Kerry advanced in debating the case for a military response to Iraq's attack on Kuwait. This exercise asks you to evaluate the analogies by examining the background information provided here and in Exercises 1 and 2. Note whether or not this exercise undermines or reinforces the views you now hold on why Bush chose the course he did and whether he chose wisely.

The Persian Gulf Crisis

After weeks of building tension, Iraq invaded Kuwait several hours before dawn on August 2, 1990 (see Figure 9.4). Kuwait's tiny army could not match the well-equipped Iraqi armed forces, which had spent the bulk of the previous decade fighting Iran. Iraq's troops met only brief and scattered resistance in Kuwait and within days occupied the entire country. Mechanized Iraqi units soon perched ominously on Kuwait's border with Saudi Arabia, possessor of the world's largest known oil reserves.

Iraq's action left Arabs deeply divided, but most of the world reacted with horror and outrage. President Bush immediately ordered economic sanctions against Iraq and froze Iraqi assets in the United States. "This [aggression against Kuwait] will not stand," he declared. The Soviet Union joined the United States in condemning the attack and suspended arms shipments to Iraq. The twelve-nation European Community, plus Japan and Canada, joined the United States in imposing trade sanctions. In Cairo, fourteen of the twenty-one members of the Arab League voted to condemn Iraqi aggression. On August 6 the United Nations Security Council passed a resolution by a 13-to-0 vote (Yemen and Cuba abstained) calling on U.N. members to end all economic dealings with Iraq and occupied Kuwait. Fearful of an Iraqi attack on Saudi Arabia, Bush received permission from the Saudi government to station U.S. air and ground forces on its territory. Deployment from the United States began early on August 7. On the same day, Turkey announced the closing of its oil pipeline out of Iraq.

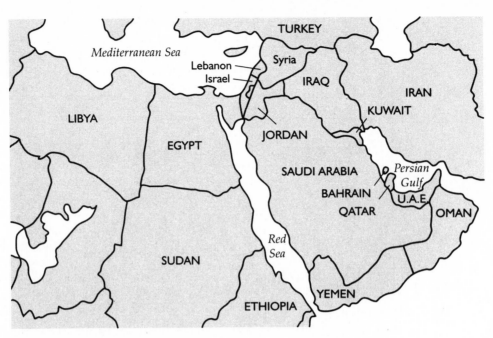

FIGURE 9.4 *The Middle East, 1990*

Iraqi president Saddam Hussein responded by declaring Kuwait's annexation to Iraq. His government had announced on August 5 that Iraq's forces soon would begin withdrawing from Kuwait, but now Hussein claimed that his troops were needed to redraw boundaries established during an earlier era of Western colonialism. Those boundaries, he asserted, had enabled a corrupt Arab minority, the ruling class of Kuwait, to grasp a huge portion of Arab wealth. "Thank God that we are now one people, one state that will be the pride of the Arabs," he exulted.

Iraq had laid claim to Kuwait years before Hussein came to power. In 1961, when Great Britain granted full independence to the small sheikdom, the government in Baghdad asserted that Kuwait was part of Iraq, that it had been separated from Iraq by the British in the aftermath of World War I. Iraq's threat of military action led Great Britain to send troops to Kuwait, and tensions eventually subsided. The Arab League, as well as the United Nations, admitted Kuwait to membership, thus rejecting Iraq's claim. In October 1963 Iraq finally recognized Kuwait's independence. During the Iran-Iraq war from 1980 to 1988, Kuwait supported Iraq with generous loans. The United States did the same with arms aid. Both countries feared the expansion of an Iran governed by Muslim fundamentalists. But in 1990 repayment of the loans became an issue between Kuwait and a financially strapped Iraq, which, in part because of past U.S. assistance, had emerged as the strongest military power between Israel and Pakistan.

In mid-July 1990, Iraq's verbal attacks on Kuwait turned extreme, particularly over the smaller country's production of oil far in excess of OPEC quotas. Kuwait's production levels, along with those of Saudi Arabia and the United Arab Emirates, kept international prices low and impeded Iraq's effort to restore a healthy economy. Yet in late July, Hussein told Egypt and the United States that his intentions were peaceful.

Iraq's action on August 2 belied this claim. If Iraq's seizure of Kuwait held up, Hussein would control 20 percent of the world's known oil reserves. Even if he refrained from occupying all or part of Saudi Arabia, his armed forces of more than a million men would outclass any other in the region. His show of force against Kuwait would give him considerable power to intimidate his oil-rich neighbors. He would be able to push world oil prices steadily upward, which not only would help Iraq's economic recovery but allow him to build up his armed strength to even greater heights. Already he had a substantial arsenal of chemical weapons and was reportedly no more than five years away from possessing nuclear arms. Such concerns brought together a diverse coalition to oppose Iraq.

The United States led that coalition, but it was hardly the only contributor to the economic sanctions or the military buildup in the Saudi desert. The trade embargo was reinforced by U.N. Security Council resolutions authorizing the use of force to prevent the transport of goods by water to and from Iraq and then to extend the blockade to the air. By the end of September, the embargo seemed relatively leakproof, and twenty-one other nations had committed armed forces to the coalition. West Germany and Japan had promised other assistance.

Still, many people worried that if the sanctions, along with coalition military forces in the Saudi desert, stayed in place for an extended period the coalition would split apart. Despite the support of most Arab leaders, the coalition drew much opposition among Arab peoples, especially after Saddam hinted that he might withdraw from Kuwait if Israel were to withdraw from territories it occupied on its borders. Saddam also might divide his adversaries by offering to withdraw from Kuwait on the condition that Iraq receive the disputed Rumaila oil field in northern Kuwait and two strategic islands in the Persian Gulf. Evolving public opinion in the United States was an additional concern. By mid-October, polls showed Bush's favorable rating down to 56 percent from 79 percent at the beginning of the year, and antiwar demonstrators organized marches in twenty cities throughout the country.

Bush decided during the second half of October that the United States needed to build up its ground forces in Saudi Arabia to give him an offensive option. His military advisers believed that to push Iraq out of Kuwait quickly and at a low cost to friendly forces would require a virtual doubling of troops to more than 400,000. Over the next two months, an intense public debate developed over whether the United States should make an early military move to expel Iraq from Kuwait or wait longer to see if the economic sanctions would produce the desired result. The debate took on a real sense of urgency after the U.N. Security Council voted on November 29 to authorize the use of force against Iraq if it did not withdraw from Kuwait by January 15, 1991. Informed observers knew that the best time for military operations in the region would be during January, February, and early March, before the heat and windstorms or Muslim religious holidays. Some analysts in the United States suspected that President Bush wanted early military action to ensure resolution of the conflict prior to his reelection campaign in 1992. The debate culminated between January 10 and 12, 1991, when Congress took up the matter, finally voting by a narrow margin in the Senate and a larger one in the House to authorize the president to use force against Iraq.

Early on the evening of January 16, Eastern Standard Time, as coalition aircraft flooded the skies over Iraq, White House spokesman Marlin Fitzwater announced to the world that "the liberation of Kuwait has begun."

Historical Analogy in the Persian Gulf Crisis

We now turn to excerpts from two speeches by President Bush, the first given less than two weeks after Iraq invaded Kuwait, the second only hours after coalition forces launched Operation Desert Storm, the military campaign to liberate Kuwait. Following these excerpts is a speech by Senator John Kerry during the debate in Congress over whether or not to authorize early offensive action against Iraq. In his first speech (document A), Bush sought to justify his decision to deploy U.S. forces in the Persian Gulf and the Saudi desert; in the second (document B), he sought to justify the decision for war. In one instance, he used the experience of the 1930s to bolster his arguments; in the other, he used Vietnam. Kerry, a Vietnam veteran, centered his speech (document C) on that conflict in pleading for patience in the Persian Gulf.

Document A is excerpts from remarks that President Bush made to the Department of Defense on August 15, 1990.

A. . . . Our action in the Gulf is about fighting aggression and preserving the sovereignty of nations. It is about keeping our word . . . and standing by old friends. It is about our own national security interests and ensuring the peace and stability of the entire world. We are also talking about maintaining access to energy resources that are key, not just to the functioning of this country but to the entire world. Our jobs, our way of life, our own freedom [and that] of friendly countries around the world would all suffer if control of the world's great oil reserves fell into the hands of that one man, Saddam Hussein.

So, we've made our stand not simply to protect resources or real estate but to protect the freedom of nations. We're making good on longstanding assurances to protect and defend our friends. . . . We are striking a blow for the principle that might does not make right. Kuwait is small. But one conquered nation is one too many.

A half century ago our nation and the world paid dearly for appeasing an aggressor who should and could have been stopped. We're not about to make that mistake twice.[9]

Document B is a portion of Bush's January 16, 1991, address to the nation announcing allied military action in the Persian Gulf.

B. Some may ask: Why act now? Why not wait? The answer is clear: . . .

The United States, together with the United Nations, exhausted every means at our disposal to bring this crisis to a peaceful end. However, Saddam clearly felt that by stalling and threatening and defying the United Nations, he could weaken the forces arrayed against him. . . .

Prior to ordering our forces into battle, I instructed our military commanders to take every necessary step to prevail as quickly as possible, and with the greatest degree of protection possible for American and allied service men and women. I've told the American people before that this will not be another Vietnam, and I repeat this here tonight. Our troops will have the possible support of the entire world, and they will not be asked to fight with one hand tied behind their back. I'm hopeful that this fighting will not go on for long and that casualties will be held to an absolute minimum.[10]

Document C is from Senator John Kerry's address to the U.S. Senate on January 11, 1991.

C. . . . I am willing to accept the horror that goes with war — when the interests or stakes warrant it. My belief is, though, that our impatience with sanctions and diplomacy does not yet warrant accepting that horror and my fear is that our beloved country is not yet ready for what it will witness and bear if we go to war.

The question of being ready and certain is important to many of us of the Vietnam generation. We come to this debate with . . . a searing commitment to ask honest questions and with a resolve to get satisfactory answers so that we are not misled again. . . .

Our VA hospitals are already full of several generations of veterans who carry or wear daily reminders of the costs of war. . . . In a country that still struggles with agent orange, outreach centers, post-traumatic stress disorder, homeless veterans — is this country ready for the next wave?

. . . Let me say right up front that the Iraqi crisis is in most ways not like Vietnam. It is very different indeed — different in international implications — different in purposes — different in risks — different in stakes — different in military strategy and opportunities. I am convinced also that it will be different in outcome.

But in one . . . critical facet, it demands that one of the central lessons of the Vietnam experience be applied — do not commit U.S. forces to combat in a potentially prolonged or bloody conflict unless Americans have reached a consensus on the need to do so. That consensus must be broad and openly arrived at with full respect for the constitutional role of the Congress — not by unilateral action by the president. . . . The memory of Vietnam says to all of us that it is far, far better that we risk . . . reining in this rush to war now, rather than trying to get the American people [to] support it at some time down the road after the shooting has started. Nothing, nothing could faster bring us a repetition of the divisions and the torment this nation faced during the 1960s and 1970s. . . .

Some . . . have suggested that sanctions alone cannot force Saddam Hussein to withdraw from Kuwait. They note that sanctions can be evaded; that the alliance could break up, with Iran agreeing to pipe Iraqi oil or the Soviet Union suddenly shifting its support for our policy to opposition. They say now is the time to strike, while the alliance is strong. They suggest that the failure of sanctions is an obvious truth that the rest of us are willfully ignoring. . . .

[Yet] with the sanctions, time is not on Saddam Hussein's side, but ours. Sanctions cost Iraq much, they cost us little. . . .

Some say look at how he survived a 7-year war with Iran. If he can do that, he will survive the sanctions. . . . However, there are major differences. During that war, it was Iran which was, for the most part, cut off from the outside world, not Iraq. And it was during that war that the Soviet Union, France, China, the United States, and other Western nations provided Saddam Hussein the guns and butter to wage the campaign against Iran. . . .

Today, Saddam Hussein does not enjoy any of that luxury.[11]

Rather than answering a series of specific questions about the materials you have read, write a 1,000-word essay on separate sheets of paper analyzing Bush's and Kerry's use of historical analogy in addressing the Persian Gulf crisis. The 1930s and Vietnam taught very different lessons. Identify those lessons and the method by which Bush applied them to the issues at hand. Also explain how Bush's lessons learned from Vietnam differed from those learned by Kerry. Finally, evaluate the persuasiveness with which the two men used history to justify their positions. In doing so, you may go beyond the analogies made by Bush and Kerry to outline analogies of your own. To complete this assignment, create your own likenesses/differences chart along the lines of those in Exercises 1 and 2. Also review the steps for essay writing in Chapter 5, Exercise 5.

You now have a good deal of experience in analyzing historical analogies. This skill should help you both as a citizen in evaluating the uses of the past by political leaders and as a professional attempting to make difficult choices in the workplace. We hope that these exercises have reinforced in your mind the importance of collecting facts and of carefully weighing them before you make judgments. The next chapter will further support that point as well as show you how history can be used to address some of the fundamental issues facing our nation as we move toward the twenty-first century.

NOTES

1. Richard E. Neustadt and Ernest R. May, *Thinking in Time* (New York: Free Press, 1986), 251.

2. Harry S Truman, *Memoirs*, vol. 2 (Garden City, N.Y.: Doubleday, 1956), 334. In writing this exercise, we have made extensive use of "Korea and the Thirties," Case Project, John F. Kennedy School of Government, Harvard University.

3. U.N. document S/1511.

4. Truman, *Memoirs*, 2:316.

5. May and Neustadt, *Thinking in Time*, chs. 3–6.

6. In preparing this background section, we have made extensive use of "Americanizing the Vietnam War," Case Project, Kennedy School of Government, Harvard University.

7. *Public Papers of the Presidents of the United States: Lyndon B. Johnson, 1965*, vol. 2, 794–795.

8. "Top Secret: The Prophecy of the President Rejected" by George W. Ball, © 1972, as originally printed in *The Atlantic*, 230, July 1972, p. 37. Reprinted with permission.

9. *Weekly Compilation of Presidential Documents* 26 (August 10, 1990), 1255–1257.

10. Ibid., 27 (January 21, 1991), 50–52.

11. *Congressional Record*, vol. 137, no. 7, 102nd Cong., 1st sess. (January 11, 1991), S249–S254.

•10 COMPARISONS: SEEKING PATTERNS IN NUMBERS

Is America in Decline?

A strange thing happened during the early months of 1988. A historical work of almost 700 pages of small print, 83 pages of notes, 38 pages of bibliography, and 52 tables and charts climbed onto the bestseller list. Its author was featured in a cover article in the *New York Times Magazine,* was interviewed on network talk shows, and testified before congressional committees. The book provided the focal point for lead editorials in top newspapers and magazines throughout the country. The writer was Yale historian Paul Kennedy. The book was *The Rise and Fall of the Great Powers* (New York: Random House, 1987). The commotion was over Kennedy's thesis that America was in decline.

Forecasts of decline are nothing new in American history. They trace back at least as far as the late seventeenth century, when Puritan ministers in Massachusetts Bay Colony warned that the declining piety of the people would bring God's wrath down upon them. A century later, in the aftermath of the successful struggle for independence from Great Britain but faced with social unrest and immobilized by a weak central government, many American leaders feared that the nation would split apart before it even got going. During the last decade of the nineteenth century, numerous observers worried that the growing materialism of Americans, combined with the rising divisions between business and labor and the economic instability that had accompanied urbanization and industrialization, boded ill for the nation's future. The United States was supposedly on the verge of losing much of the dynamism and vitality that had distinguished it from the older, decaying countries of Europe. In the twentieth century, the 1970s were years of widespread pessimism, "a crisis of confidence" in the minds of many observers, including President Jimmy Carter. The U.S. experience in Vietnam, the energy crisis, the Watergate scandal, growing evidence of Soviet military superiority, and the Iran hostage crisis produced deep anxiety about America's future.

President Ronald Reagan openly challenged the idea of national decline. His upbeat rhetoric upon entering the White House in 1981, combined with an economic boom that prevailed during most of his eight years in office, produced a shift in national mood. Polling data showed that most U.S. citizens were more optimistic about their future than at any time in a quarter century. *Time* magazine declared "a rebirth of the American spirit."[1]

Still, the huge federal budget and trade deficits that characterized the Reagan years generated much concern, which Kennedy's book suggested was well founded. The greatest single source of the budget deficit was a massive increase in spending for defense, a course that Reagan insisted was essential to protect U.S. interests abroad and security at home. Although Kennedy devoted only a small portion of his treatise to the United States in the 1980s, his account of the decline of great powers throughout history indicated that Reagan was tragically mistaken, that by putting so much of the country's resources into military and foreign ventures, he — and his predecessors from Harry S Truman onward — had committed the error of "imperial overstretch." The overcommitment of national resources to ventures abroad, Kennedy argued, had contributed to the relative decline of other leading powers and was having the same impact on the United States.

Kennedy had his critics. Joseph Nye of Harvard University, for example, challenged Kennedy's use of the years immediately following World War II as the starting point for an analysis of America's present and future stature. World War II, Nye argued, left the United States in a unique position of dominance. The war rendered tremendous destruction to the industrial plants of Germany and Japan and temporarily eliminated them as independent actors in international politics. The Soviet Union emerged victorious from the war, but it lost 20 million people and suffered devastating blows to its productive capacity. Japan occupied and ravaged much of China, and in the war's aftermath civil conflict delayed China's development. The United States, in contrast, was never occupied or attacked, and its gross national product virtually doubled between 1940 and 1945.

The United States emerged from the war with an economic strength unprecedented in modern history, but it could hardly maintain that position indefinitely. As World War II's effects on the other great powers gradually diminished, Nye pointed out, so too did America's lead over them. Yet that lead had begun to shrink more and more slowly since the 1970s and, if we take into account a broad range of power sources — basic resources, military forces, economic strength, scientific and technological development, national cohesion, culture and ideology, international institutions — the United States seemed overall to be firmly entrenched at the top.[2]

Numbers over Time: Economic Indicators

Kennedy and his allies helped to fuel a debate that has continued to the present day. Some analysts follow in Kennedy's path, comparing data over time about all the great powers to reveal how the United States is doing compared with its prime competitors — Japan, Germany, China, and the Soviet Union (now Russia). Although these scholars argue over what data is accurate and pertinent to the issue, they agree that comparing the United States to other nations is the proper approach. Other analysts use an absolute rather than a relative standard to evaluate America's position. They examine data from different time periods but pertinent to the United States alone. Their emphasis centers on how the quality of life for Americans has changed over time and on what recent trends bode for the future.

Whatever the data addressed, there is little doubt that analysts need to approach the issue of America's decline through historical methods, especially quantitative ones: compiling data, putting it in numerical form, and comparing it across time and place. It is to this last step that we devote this chapter. Because analyzing quantitative data is ever more common in a world passing through an "information revolution," this skill will prove of considerable use to you outside the classroom.

The exercises presented in this chapter ask you to make comparisons with numbers as well as to consider the question of America's decline. We begin by looking at a common analogy: the United Kingdom's position in the late nineteenth century and the United States' position a century later. We move on to comparative statistics for nations in the 1980s alone to give you a sense of how the United States fared in recent years. These numbers should also provide a starting point for evaluating Joseph Nye's assertion that America's position relative to other great powers has been fairly steady since the mid-1970s. Then we provide comparative data on education, ranging from the 1960s, when sophisticated multinational testing efforts began, to the 1990s. Finally, by looking at life in the United States during recent decades, we address the question, Is America in decline?

EXERCISE 1: *The British-American Analogy*

One of the favorite exercises of forecasters of American decline is to compare the United States today with the United Kingdom in the late nineteenth century. These analysts see the recent trend of American development in relation to other great powers as similar to that of the United Kingdom a century ago, when it was the single most influential nation on earth but clearly was losing ground to others. Here we ask you to examine that analogy.

Unfortunately, it is not possible to provide comprehensive data on the relative positions of the two countries. Even if we could do so, the rapidly changing conditions over the last hundred years make comparisons inherently difficult and imprecise. Scholars are far from unanimous on the criteria for evaluating the positions of nations, so we begin by advising you to take care in drawing conclusions from the information presented here. Although these numbers may look precise, they represent approximations that, in some cases, are still open to dispute. Nonetheless, the information in Figures 10.1 and 10.2 and Tables 10.1, 10.2, and 10.3 provide some key comparisons. Study these tables and graphs carefully. Questions about each table and graph will help focus your thinking. Questions relating to the whole series of tables and graphs will help you reach some tentative conclusions. Finally, we ask you to write a paragraph on the pros and cons of the analogy based on the information at hand.

Figure 10.1 is a bar graph showing the average percentage of yearly growth of four leading countries over three different periods. An **average** is computed by adding together all the individual numbers in a series (in this case, individual years over a span of years) and then dividing the sum by the total number in the series (in the case of 1985 to 1994, 10). A bar graph displays quantities. The extent, amount, or number of each category (in this case an individual country) is represented by a rectangle whose base is the *x*-axis of a graph. The *y*-axis depicts the quantity (in this case, the average percentage of annual change).

Questions on Figure 10.1

1. What two countries' rates were highest in the late nineteenth century? _____

   Do the rates help explain events between 1914 and 1918? Explain. _____

   _____

2. How do the rates for the 1950–1984 and the 1985–1994 periods differ from those for

   the earlier period? _____

   _____

   _____

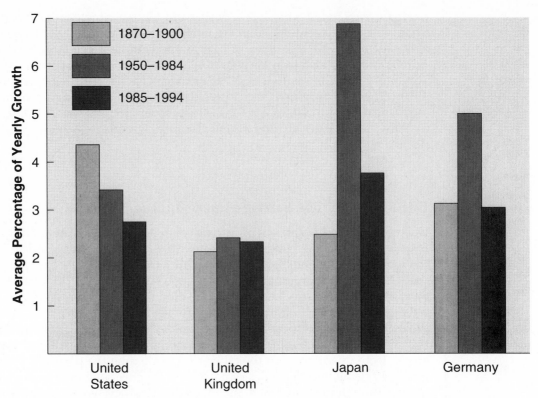

FIGURE 10.1 *Average Yearly Growth Rates in Gross Domestic Product* for Four Countries*[3]

* Gross domestic product is "the market value of all goods and services that have been bought for final use during a year. . . . GDP covers workers and capital employed within the nation's borders. GNP [in contrast] covers production by American residents, regardless of where it takes place."[4]

Can you see any long-term significance to these rates? _____

If so, what? _____

_____

Figure 10.2 shows three series of pie graphs. Frequently a pie graph is used to display the total evidence divided into its parts. Wedges represent the percentages that each group or category contributes to the whole. In Figure 10.2, each graph in an individual series, running horizontally, represents one aspect of a country's economy over a specific range of time. We could have presented the same information more concisely in a table, but instead we chose pie graphs to make the display more visually dramatic.

Questions on Figure 10.2

1. How are the rankings of the four countries for the first period different from the rankings for the last two periods? _____

_____

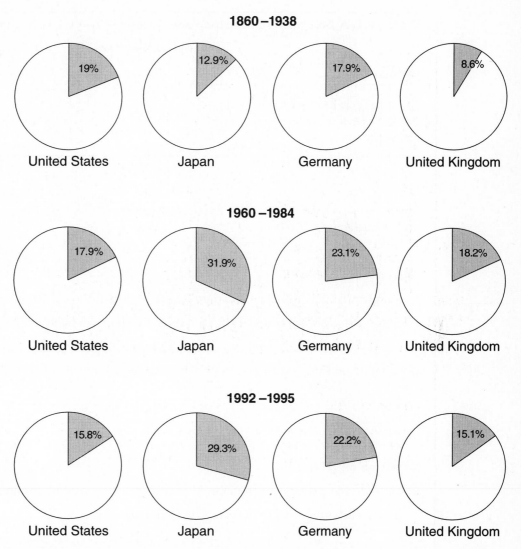

FIGURE 10.2 *Gross Fixed Capital Formation* as a Percentage of Gross National Product[5]*

*Capital formation is the acquisition of materials — such as machinery, ships, and airplanes — that may be used for future production or in the rendering of services.

2. Do you think there is any connection between levels of capital formation in a country and the overall growth of the economy? _____ Explain. _____

_____

_____

Tables summarize and tabulate the characteristics of variables. Tables are always comparative in nature — that is, they compare one variable with another or show how a single variable changes over time or place. Table 10.1 provides comparisons over time (five different years over a century and a half), place (the United Kingdom and the United

Table 10.1 A Comparison of British and American Global Rankings[6]

Category	United Kingdom			United States	
	1830	*1870*	*1913*	*1950*	*1992*
Gross national product	3rd	3rd	4th	1st	1st
Military spending	2nd	3rd	3rd	2nd	1st
Manufacturing	3rd	1st	3rd	1st	1st

States), and economic/financial categories (gross national product, military spending, and manufacturing).

Questions on Table 10.1

1. How do British rankings during the late nineteenth and early twentieth centuries compare to U.S. rankings during the second half of the twentieth century? _____

_____

2. What, if anything, does that comparison suggest about the British-American analogy?

_____

_____

Question on Table 10.2

1. How do the patterns of the United States and the United Kingdom compare in relation to each other and to the other two countries? _____

_____

Questions on Table 10.3

1. How did patterns change among the four nations between the late nineteenth and early twentieth centuries and the late twentieth century? _____

_____

Table 10.2 Population (in millions)[7]

Country	1880	1910	1950	1990	2000 (proj.)
United States	50.2	92.0	151.7	249.2	266.1
United Kingdom	35.1	45.0	50.6	57.2	58.4
Japan	37.0	49.6	82.9	123.5	128.5
Germany	45.2	64.9	69.0	77.7	82.4

Table 10.3 Defense Spending as Percentage of Gross National Product[8]

Year	U.K.	U.S.	Japan	Germany
1870	2.0	0.9	—	—
1890	2.2	0.5	2.1	3.3
1910	2.8	0.9	5.8	2.9
1950	6.4	3.5	0	4.5
1960	6.4	8.7	1.1	3.4
1978	4.5	4.9	0.9	3.3
1984	5.2	6.3	1.0	3.2
1988	4.3	6.3	1.0	2.9
1993	4.0	5.0	1.0	2.0

2. Are the patterns of the United Kingdom and the United States similar or different?

_____

_____

Questions on Figures 10.1 and 10.2 and Tables 10.1, 10.2, and 10.3

1. Look again at Figures 10.1 and 10.2 and Tables 10.1 and 10.2. What conclusions can you draw about the economy of the United Kingdom in the late nineteenth century and about the economy of the United States in the late twentieth century? _____

_____

_____

_____

_____

_____

_____

2. Does anything that happened in the world in general during the first fifty years of the twentieth century help to explain the rapidity of the United Kingdom's decline and the speed of America's rise? (*Hint:* You might find some of the material in the introduction to this chapter helpful.) Explain. _____

_____

_____

3. Do you see any connection between the population statistics in Table 10.2 and the relative rise or decline of the nations listed? (*Hint:* Consider rates of increase in population and size of population of the countries included.) Explain. _____

_____

4. Look again at the data in Table 10.3. What explanation does it suggest for the patterns you found in Figures 10.1 and 10.2? (*Hint:* Ask yourself whether the data supports Paul Kennedy's thesis outlined at the beginning of the chapter.) _____

_____

_____

5. Write a paragraph on a separate sheet of paper evaluating the pros and cons of the British analogy based on the information given above.

EXERCISE 2: *The 1980s — Comparing Real Gross National Products*

Following are three bar graphs on the real gross national products of several great powers. *Real gross national product* is the total monetary value of all the goods and services produced in a country over a specified period with inflation or deflation taken into account. For example, in 1923 Babe Ruth became the first baseball player with an annual salary of $50,000. In 1992 dollars, that salary would be worth $390,405. In comparing the salaries of major league baseball players in the 1920s to those of today, it would be important to take into account the declining value of the dollar between those two times. To

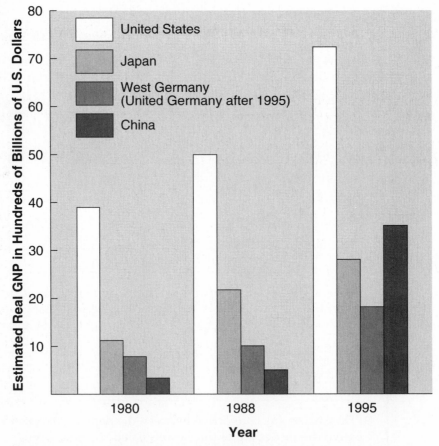

FIGURE 10.3 *Yearly Estimated Real Gross National Product (Gross Domestic Product in 1995) — in Hundreds of Billions of U.S. Dollars*[9]

do so, we would take the value of the dollar at one point in time, probably the present, and factor in its decline in value since the 1920s. Then we would adjust the earlier salaries accordingly. This method would give us a far more accurate idea of the magnitude of the change in salaries than if we used the raw numbers from both periods.

In Figures 10.3, 10.4, and 10.5, search for patterns in the numbers and think about what they suggest about nations' standing in relation to each other. Then answer the questions that follow.

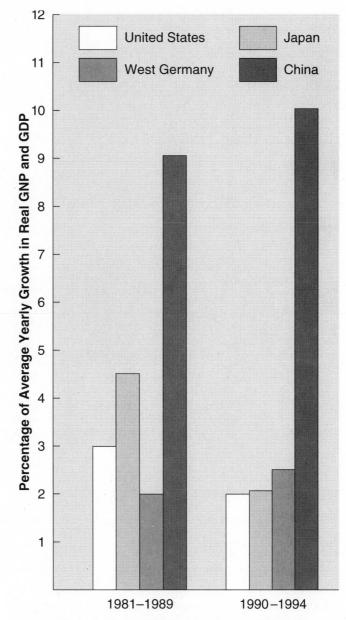

Figure 10.4 *Real Growth in Gross National Product, 1981–1989, and Gross Domestic Product, 1990–1994 (average yearly rate of growth in percentages)*

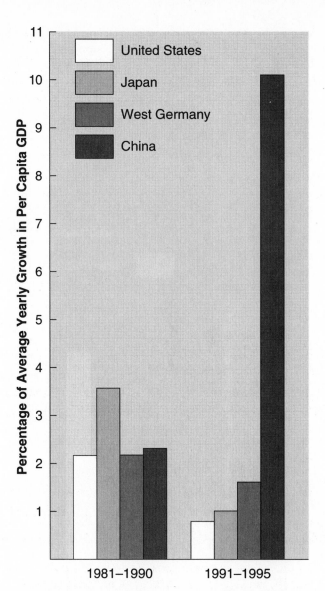

FIGURE 10.5 *Growth in Per Capita (Individual) Real Gross National Product, 1981–1990 and 1991–1995 (average yearly rate of growth in percentages)*

Questions on Figures 10.3, 10.4, and 10.5

1. Which of the three graphs (Figures 10.3, 10.4, or 10.5) puts the United States in the best light? _____ Explain. _____

_____

2. After reviewing Figures 10.3 through 10.5, explain why China's showing in Figures 10.4 and 10.5, if considered alone, could be misleading. (*Hint:* What are the starting points in 1981 for gross domestic product and per capita real gross domestic product?)

_____

_____

3. In determining the military potential of a nation, which of the three graphs would you consider the most important? _____ Explain. _____

_____

_____

_____

_____

4. China is the least advanced economically of the four countries listed in Figures 10.3, 10.4, and 10.5. Given that fact, if we had given figures on per capita gross domestic product rather than the growth of per capita gross domestic product, how do you think China would have fared in comparison with the other three countries? _____ Explain.

_____

_____

_____

_____

Which category, per capita gross domestic product or growth of per capita gross domestic product, would you regard as most important in determining countries' overall economic competitiveness in international markets? _____ Explain.

_____

_____

_____

_____

Your answers to those questions illustrate the fact that numbers reflecting different aspects of the same general topic — in this case, national productivity — can have very different implications. Thus we constantly must ask ourselves what the numbers before us mean. Numbers — like literary sources — need to be interpreted.

EXERCISE 3: *Education*

Education greatly concerned Americans during the 1980s. This concern gained concrete expression in 1984 in a presidential commission's report entitled *A Nation at Risk,* which argued that the country's long-term well-being was threatened by the inferior education its children were receiving. Following are two series of tables comparing American education with that of several other nations. Read Tables 10.4 through 10.7 in Series A and Tables 10.8 through 10.10 and Figure 10.6 in Series B, and answer the questions that follow each series. Keep in mind that testing students is exceedingly difficult and expensive and that these comparisons include only representative samples from participating nations. The comparative testing of students of several different nations goes back only to the mid-1960s and remains limited even today.

Series A

Table 10.4 Public Expenditures for Education as a Percentage of Gross National Product, 1987[10]	
United States	5.7
U.S.S.R.	7.3
Japan	5.0
West Germany	4.4
United Kingdom	5.0
Canada	7.2

Table 10.5 Number of Pupils per Teacher, Elementary Education, 1991[11]	
United States	15.5
France	22.7
Japan	20.3
West Germany	21.4
United Kingdom	22.2

Table 10.6 Average Length of School Year for Elementary and Secondary Education (in days)[12]	
United States	180
Japan	243
United Kingdom	196
Italy	210–215
West Germany	160–170

Table 10.7 Percentage of Population Aged 18 to 25 Engaged in Postsecondary Education, 1991[13]	
United States	53.1
Sweden	21.1
United Kingdom	23.8
Canada	41.9
West Germany	25.4

Questions on Series A Tables

1. Which two of the four Series A tables put the United States in the most favorable light? _____ Which one puts the United States in the least favorable light? _____ Explain.

   _____

   _____

   _____

   _____

2. Other than test results, what kind of information in addition to that provided in Tables 10.4 through 10.7 might help you evaluate American competitiveness in the area of education?

   a. _____

   _____

   b. _____

   _____

Series B

Table 10.8 Mathematics Achievement Test Scores for 13- and 17-Year-Olds, 1982
(numbers show the mean of questions answered correctly converted into percentages of total questions in the test)[14]

	13-Year-Olds	17-Year-Olds
United States	46.2	39.8
Japan	63.6	70.2
Sweden	43.4	57.5
United Kingdom	48.8	51.3
Canada	50.9	44.5

Table 10.9 Cognitive Achievement for Eighth-Grade Mathematics Students, 1989
(average percentage of items answered correctly)[15]

	All 157 Items on Test	30 Algebra Items
United States	45.3	42.1
Japan	62.1	60.3
England and Wales	47.3	40.1
Netherlands	57.1	51.3
France	52.5	55.0
Sweden	41.8	32.3

Table 10.10 Percentage of Undergraduate Degrees Awarded in Science in Selected Countries, 1991[16]

	All Science Degrees	Engineering Degrees
Austria	20.1	9.5
Canada	15.5	6.1
West Germany	31.5	20.2
Japan	23.5	21.1
United States	15.9	7.2

Questions on Series B Tables and Figure 10.6

1. Would you say that the test scores reflected in Tables 10.8 through 10.10 and Figure 10.6 put the U.S. educational system in (a) a consistently favorable light, (b) a mostly favorable light, (c) a consistently unfavorable light, or (d) a mostly unfavorable light? _____ Explain. _____

_____

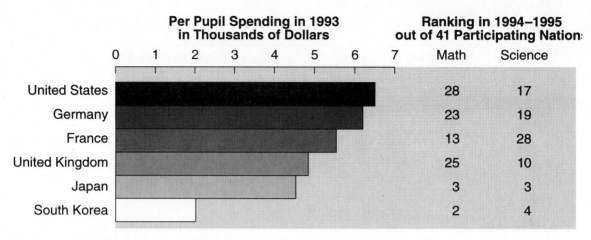

FIGURE 10.6 *Public Spending per Pupil (Bar Graph) and Ranking in Performance of 13-Year-Olds in Mathematics and Science Tests (Table)*[17]

2. The tests included in these tables and Figure 10.6 cover a chronological range from 1982 to 1995. Would you say the competitive position of the United States over that time (a) improved, (b) stayed the same, or (c) got worse? Circle one.

3. In the case in which tests were administered to more than one age group, did the mean scores of U.S. students get more or less competitive with increasing age? _____

4. What group of students that is *not* measured in Tables 10.8, 10.9, and 10.10 or in Figure 10.6 might put the United States in a better light? (*Hint:* Consider the information provided in Table 10.7.) Explain. _____

_____

_____

_____

How might the information in Table 10.10 qualify this hopeful perspective for the United States? _____

_____

_____

_____

5. Does the information provided in Figure 10.6 suggest a relationship between spending per pupil and performance in math and science? _____ Explain. _____

_____

_____

6. Does the information provided in the table portion of Figure 10.6 and in Table 10.6 suggest a relationship between the length of the school year in different countries and the performance of their students in math and science? _____ Explain. _____

_____

The United States and Absolute Decline

We move from comparative statistics to ones on the United States alone. The broad question we seek to address is, How has the quality of American life evolved during recent decades, and where is it likely to go in the near future? Has life become better for most people, stayed pretty much the same, or gotten worse — and is the recent trend likely to continue? Again, we make no attempt to provide data for a comprehensive assessment. Rather, we focus on life expectancy and income. As you examine the following data, think through the implications of the information presented and consider areas not represented that would assist you in grappling with this question.

EXERCISE 4: *Life Expectancy*

Tables 10.11 and 10.12 provide information on life expectancy. Read each table and answer the questions that follow.

Table 10.11 Expected Length of Life at Birth, 1970–1985, and Projections, 1990–2010[18]

Year	Total			White			Black		
	Total	*Male*	*Female*	*Total*	*Male*	*Female*	*Total*	*Male*	*Female*
1970	70.8	67.1	74.7	71.7	68.0	75.6	64.1	60.0	68.3
1990	75.6	72.1	79.0	76.2	72.7	79.6	71.4	67.7	75.0
2010	77.9	74.4	81.3	78.3	74.9	81.7	75.0	71.4	78.5

Table 10.12 Infant Deaths in Total Population, 1960–1988*[19]

Year	Total Number	Rate per 1,000 Population
1960	111,000	26.0
1970	75,000	20.0
1980	46,000	12.6
1988	39,000	9.9

*Infants are defined as babies less than 1 year old.

Questions on Tables 10.11 and 10.12

1. According to projections, will the change in life expectancy for those born between 1990 and 2010 be higher or lower than the change for those born between 1970 and 1990? _____

2. Is this true for both sexes and races? _____

3. Is the trend in Table 10.12 regarding the rate of change similar to the trend you detected in Table 10.11? _____ Is there a linkage between the *rate* of change in life expectancy and in infant mortality? Explain. _____

EXERCISE 5: *Income and Poverty*

Statistics on income provide one method to assess whether life is becoming better for Americans. When we break the numbers into specific income groups and by race and sex, however, we find that the picture is complex, a fact that Figures 10.7 and 10.8 and Tables 10.13 through 10.16 make clear.

Figure 10.7 is a line graph, which shows change in data over time or compares the change in quantities against each other. Figure 10.7 displays changes in median family

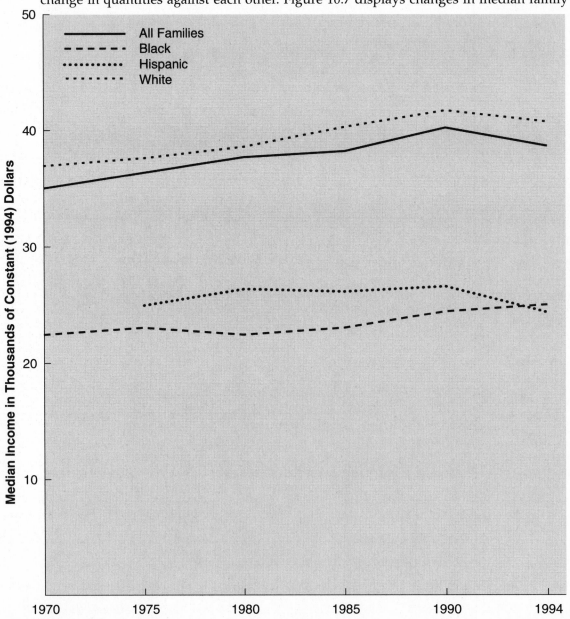

FIGURE 10.7 *Median Money Income of Families, 1970–1994 (by race and Hispanic origin of family in constant 1994 dollars)*[20]

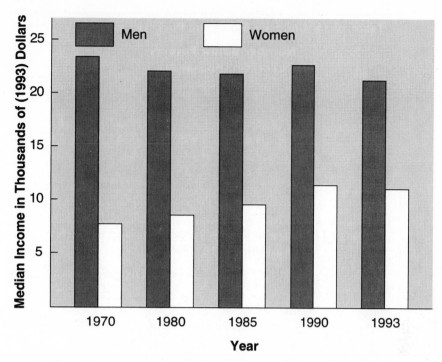

FIGURE 10.8 *Median Income of Men and Women, 1970–1993 (in constant 1993 dollars)*[21]

Table 10.13 Persons Below Poverty Level, 1960–1994 (by race and Hispanic origin)[22]

Year	Total Number in Millions				As Percentage of Entire Population			
	All Races	*White*	*Black*	*Hispanic*	*All Races*	*White*	*Black*	*Hispanic*
1960	39.9	28.3	na	na	22.2	17.8	na	na
1970	25.4	17.5	7.5	na	12.6	9.9	33.5	na
1975	25.9	17.8	7.5	3.0	12.3	9.7	31.3	26.9
1980	29.3	19.7	8.6	3.5	13.0	10.2	32.5	25.7
1985	33.1	22.9	8.9	5.2	14.0	11.4	31.3	29.0
1990	33.6	22.3	9.8	6.0	13.5	10.7	31.9	26.2
1994	38.1	25.4	10.2	8.4	14.5	11.7	30.6	30.7

Table 10.14 Persons 65 Years Old and over Below Poverty Level, 1970–1994
(by selected characteristics)[23]

Characteristic	Number Below Poverty Level (in thousands)			Percentage Below Poverty Level		
	1970	*1979*	*1994*	*1970*	*1979*	*1994*
Persons 65 and over	4,793	3,682	3,663	24.6	15.2	11.7
White	4,011	2,911	2,846	22.6	13.3	10.2
Black	735	740	700	47.7	36.3	27.4
Hispanic	na	154	323	na	26.8	22.6

Table 10.15 Children Below the Poverty Level, 1970–1994 (by race and Hispanic origin)[24]

Year	Number Below Poverty Level (in thousands)				Percentage Below Poverty Level			
	All Races	White	Black	Hispanic	All Races	White	Black	Hispanic
1970	10,235	6,138	3,922	na	14.9	10.5	41.5	na
1980	11,114	6,817	3,906	1,718	17.9	13.4	42.1	33.0
1987	12,435	7,550	4,297	2,631	20.0	15.0	45.1	39.3
1994	14,610	8,826	4,787	3,956	21.2	16.3	43.3	41.1

Table 10.16 Share of Total Income Received by Each Fifth and Top 5 Percent of Families, 1970–1994[25]

Year	Percent Distribution of Total Income					
	Lowest 5th	Second 5th	Third 5th	Fourth 5th	Highest 5th	Top 5%
1970	5.4	12.2	17.6	23.8	40.9	15.6
1980	5.1	11.6	17.5	24.3	41.6	15.3
1985	4.6	10.9	16.9	24.2	43.5	16.7
1990	4.6	10.8	16.6	23.8	44.3	17.4
1994	4.2	10.0	15.7	23.3	46.9	20.1

income from 1970 to 1994 by race and Hispanic origin. (The **median** is the point in a series of numbers that divides the series into two groups with equal numbers of entries. In the series 3, 4, 7, 9, 11, 14, and 16, for example, 9 is the median because there are 3 numbers on each side of it.) The *x*-axis represents years in five-year intervals beginning in 1970 (with the exception of 1994). The *y*-axis represents thousands of 1994 dollars. The lines on the graph show the income levels of four different kinds of family over the period from 1970 to 1994.

Questions on Figures 10.7 and 10.8 and Tables 10.13 through 10.16

1. In evaluating how Americans did financially from 1970 to the mid-1990s, which item, Figure 10.7 or Figure 10.8, is the more useful? (*Hint:* Read the headings of both graphs.) Explain. _____

   _____

2. *Overall*, how would you say Americans fared financially between 1970 and the mid-1990s? Explain. _____

   _____

3. Add Table 10.16 and the factors of race, class, and sex to your analysis. Now how would you say Americans did financially from 1970 to the mid-1990s? _____

   _____

4. Figure 10.8 shows that women still lag well behind men in income. Identify two reasons why you think this is so.

    a. _____

    _____

    b. _____

    _____

5. Do the figures in Figure 10.7 indicate that the 1970s or the 1980s were a better decade for Americans? _____

6. If you add Table 10.13 to your analysis, how does it affect your answer to question 5? Explain. _____

    _____

7. Do the trends revealed in Tables 10.14 and 10.15 show similar patterns regarding the elderly and children? _____ Explain. _____

    _____

8. Which of the trends revealed in Tables 10.14 and 10.15 would you consider most significant in influencing the direction of our country during the next generation or two? Explain. _____

    _____

    _____

9. In a single paragraph on a separate sheet of paper, analyze American life from 1970 to 1994 from the trends revealed in Figures 10.7 and 10.8 and Tables 10.13 through 10.16. Include in your paragraph an assessment of what these trends bode for the future. Organize your thoughts first by writing down on a piece of scrap paper all the age, gender, income, and ethnic or racial groups covered in these figures and tables. Also, write down the main point of your paragraph. Make sure the paragraph sticks to that point.

In completing this workbook and reaching the end of your American history survey course, you have learned much about your nation's past. But by studying and employing the methods used by historians, you have also gained skills that will help you to think and write effectively in the workplace. Researching primary and secondary sources, for example, demands familiarity with libraries and an ability to cast a critical eye on pieces of evidence. Disseminating your conclusions about that evidence in turn requires writing and organizational skills. Fully appreciating the significance of a sitcom or a movie requires the ability to place it in the context of the time within which it was created.

We hope that as you progress through your education and advance in your life you find all of these skills valuable.

NOTES

1. *Time*, September 24, 1984, p. 10.
2. Joseph S. Nye, Jr., *Bound to Lead: The Changing Nature of American Power* (New York: Basic Books, 1990).
3. The information in this figure is taken from Robert E. Lipsey and Irving B. Kravis,

Saving and Economic Growth: Is the United States Really Falling Behind? American Council of Life Insurance and The Conference Board, Report No. 901, p. 9; and U.S. Department of Commerce, *Statistical Abstract of the United States, 1993, 1994, and 1996* (Washington, D.C.: Government Printing Office, 1993, 1994, 1996 respectively), 853, 854–855, and 836 respectively.

4. *The World Almanac and Book of Facts 1997* (Mahwah, N.J.: World Almanac Books, 1996), 154.

5. Lipsey and Kravis, *Saving and Economic Growth*, 26; U.S. Department of Commerce, *Statistical Abstract of the United States, 1996*, 837.

6. Nye, *Bound to Lead*, 64.

7. W. S. Woytinsky and E. S. Woytinsky, *World Population and Production: Trends and Outlook* (New York: Twentieth Century Fund, 1953), p. 44; United Nations, Department of International Economic and Social Affairs, *World Population Prospects, 1990* (New York: United Nations, 1991).

8. Karen Rasler and William R. Thompson, "Defense Burdens, Capital Formation, and Economic Growth," *Journal of Conflict Resolution* 32 (March 1988): 71 (for figures before 1978); U.S. Arms Control and Disarmament Agency, *World Military Expenditures and Arms Transfers, 1989* (Washington, D.C.: Government Printing Office, 1990), 1978 onward; CIA, Directorate of Intelligence, *Handbook of International Economic Statistics, 1996* (Washington, D.C.: Government Printing Office, 1996), 26.

9. The data in the figures for Exercise 2 are taken from U.S. Central Intelligence Agency, *Handbook of Economic Statistics, 1990, 1995, 1996* (Washington, D.C.: Government Printing Office, 1990, 1995, 1996).

10. National Center for Education Statistics, *Digest of Education Statistics 1990* (Washington, D.C.: Government Printing Office, 1991), 375.

11. National Center for Education Statistics, *Digest of Education Statistics 1996* (Washington, D.C.: Government Printing Office, 1996), 437.

12. Kenneth Redd and Wayne Riddle, "Comparative Education: Statistics on Education in the United States and Selected Foreign Nations" (Washington, D.C.: Congressional Research Service, 1989), 31.

13. National Center for Education Statistics, *Digest of Education Statistics 1996*, 447.

14. Redd and Riddle, "Comparative Education," 27.

15. Tjeerd Plomp, "IEA: Its Role and Plans for International Comparative Research in Education" (paper presented at the annual meeting of the American Education Research Association, Boston, April 1990), 19.

16. National Center for Education Statistics, *Digest of Education Statistics 1996*, 447.

17. *The Economist*, March 29–April 4, 1997, 23.

18. U.S. Department of Commerce, *Statistical Abstract of the United States, 1996*, 88.

19. Ibid., 92.

20. Ibid., 467.

21. Ibid., 470.

22. Ibid., 472.

23. Ibid., 473.

24. Ibid., 472.

25. Ibid., 467.